The same principle is . . .

"A withering critique of federal spending programs, regulatory failures and social engineering schemes, containing a host of specific facts to match the author's solid grasp of basic principle."   —*M. Stanton Evans*

"An arsenal of timely arguments against collectivist practice, demonstrating the superior virtues of the private market system in a dozen different categories."
                                   —*National Review*

"An encouraging and exciting battlecall for freedom."   —*Private Practice Magazine*

"Phil Crane is one of the most articulate spokesmen of the conservative cause, and his book is an important contribution to the dialogue."   —*Congressman Abner Mikva,*
                           CHICAGO Magazine

"Crane, whom many consider to be one of the most brilliant, articulate and vigorous conservative spokesmen in the nation, reviews in vivid detail 40 years of liberal experimentation."   —*The Indianapolis Star*

"Not only tells us what has gone wrong with the republic but offers a whole series of practical reforms that could be effected without waiting for crisis to overwhelm us."
                   —*John Chamberlain, THE FREEMAN*

The Sum of Good Government

by
Philip M. Crane

Green Hill Publishers, Inc.
Ottawa, Illinois 61350

Dedication

To Arlene

who has patiently endured the absences and pressures a Congressional wife is subjected to with devotion, fortitude, and unfailing humor.

Acknowledgments

This volume has been a labor of love. There are those without whom this book would not have been possible to whom I am grateful and whose considerable help and cooperation I wish to acknowledge. I should like to thank Richard S. Williamson, Peter Brathwaite, Allan Brownfeld and Lynda Durfee.

Washington, D. C.   Philip M. Crane
July, 1976   Member of Congress

THE SUM OF GOOD GOVERNMENT

Copyright © 1976 by Philip M. Crane

All rights reserved, including the
right to reproduce this book, or
parts thereof, in any form,
except for inclusion of brief
quotations in a review.

Green Hill Publishers, Inc.
Post Office Box 738
Ottawa, Illinois 61350

Library of Congress Catalogue Card Number: 76-43560
Manufactured in the United States of America
ISBN: 0-916054-07-1

Second Printing, November, 1977

338.973
C 89/s

". . . a wise and frugal government which shall restrain men from injuring one another, shall leave them otherwise free to regulate their own pursuits of industry and improvement, and shall not take from the mouth of labor the bread it has earned. This is the sum of good government. . . ."

—THOMAS JEFFERSON
First Inaugural Address, 1801

Contents

1 THE NATURE OF THE AMERICAN
   POLITICAL PHILOSOPHY   1

2 ARE THE BLEEDING HEARTS
   FOR REAL?   25

3 AFFIRMATIVE ACTION—WELL
   INTENTIONED, BUT MISGUIDED   41

4 THE UNITED NATIONS—
   A REAPPRAISAL   62

5 IS THERE A HEALTH CARE
   CRISIS IN THE UNITED STATES?   74

6 THE FEDERAL BUDGET AND
   THE ECONOMY   96

7 IS BUSINESS AN ENDANGERED
   SPECIES?   105

8 REGULATORY AGENCIES OUT
   OF CONTROL   119

9 THE BLOATED BUREAUCRACY   141

10 PUBLIC EMPLOYEE UNIONS   161

11 A TIME FOR REFORM:
   SOME PROPOSALS   181

12 A LAST WORD   210
   RECOMMENDED READING   211

The Nature of the American Political Philosophy

There is a great danger that, as we celebrate the Bicentennial, we will overlook the most important thing Americans should be commemorating: the freedom that has existed in this country, under our republican form of government, for two hundred years.

We must not think such freedom is natural to societies of men. The places in which men have been free are rare. In today's world, with the exception of the United States and the countries with which we are allied in Western Europe, the rest of the English speaking world and Japan, free societies are difficult to locate on the world's map. How many members of the United Nations, for example, have governments that are elected by the people—and that must return to the people for their approval or disapproval during a stated interval? The numbers are few.

For the same reason freedom is found in so few places, in those few places there are always forces that continue to work against it. For a period of time in the ancient world, Greece and Rome had free societies. The power and authority of government in those countries was limited by law. The citizen had specific and enforceable rights, and a role to play in the determination of public policy. But freedom did not last very long in either Greece or Rome. For a variety of reasons, it died.

In the United States, freedom has been a reality for 200 years. If it is not to die as it did in those ancient states, we must think carefully about how it may be preserved and what its prerequisites may be. The real questions before us at this time should be: exactly what is the American philosophy, how has it maintained and protected a free society and how have we diverged from it in recent years?

Let us look briefly at the thoughts the Founding Fathers had about the nature of government in a free society. In

1

his first inaugural address in 1801, Thomas Jefferson said that " . . . a wise and frugal government which shall restrain men from injuring one another, shall leave them otherwise free to regulate their own pursuits of industry and improvement and shall not take from the mouth of labor the bread it has earned. This is the sum of good government."

At the beginning of his administration, Jefferson wrote to a friend that, "The path we have to pursue is so quiet that we have nothing scarcely to propose to our Legislature. A noiseless course not meddling with the affairs of others, unattractive of notice, is a mark that society is going on in happiness."

At the present time, as we all understand so well, there is almost no aspect of our lives that some agency of government does not consider within its jurisdiction. Government has told us when to buckle our seat belts, what medication we may take, which distant schools our children must be bused to, how many employees of each race and sex we must hire—the list is endless.

That government should be clearly limited and that power was a corrupting force were the essential perceptions held by the men who wrote the Constitution. In *The Federalist Papers* James Madison declared:

It may be a reflection on human nature that such devices should be necessary to control the abuses of government. But what is government itself but the greatest of all reflections on human nature? If men were angels, no government would be necessary. If angels were to govern men, neither external nor internal controls on government would be necessary. In framing a government which is to be administered by men over men, the great difficulty lies in this: you must first enable the government to control the governed and in the next place oblige it to control itself.

Unlike many of those who now speak in their name, the Founding Fathers were not utopians. They understood man's nature and attempted to form a government that was consistent with that nature. Alexander Hamilton, for example, noted:

Here we have already seen enough of the fallacy and extravagance of those idle theories which have amused us with promises of an exemption from the imperfections, weaknesses, and evils incident to society in every shape. Is it not time to awake from the deceitful dream of a golden age and to adopt as a practical maxim for the direction of our political conduct that we, as well as the other inhabitants of the globe, are yet remote from the happy empire of perfect wisdom and perfect virtue?

The framers of the Constitution did not view either man or government in the positive terms in which both are often viewed at the present time. John Adams expressed the view that, "Whoever would found a state and make proper laws for the government of it must presume that all men are bad by nature." As if addressing our twentieth-century believers in an egalitarian society that will eliminate war, racism, poverty, and disease and bring about a perfect—or nearly perfect—world, Adams went on:

> We may appeal to every page of history we have hitherto turned over, for proofs irrefragable, that the people, when they have been unchecked, have been as unjust, tyrannical, brutal, barbarous and cruel as any king or senate possessed of uncontrollable power. . . . All projects of government, formed upon a supposition of continual vigilance, sagacity, and virtue, firmness of the people, when possessed of the exercise of supreme power, are cheats and delusions. . . . The fundamental article of my political creed is that despotism, or unlimited sovereignty, or absolute power, is the same in a majority of a popular assembly, an aristocratic council, an oligarchical junto, and a single emperor. Equally arbitrary, cruel, bloody, and in every respect diabolical.

Of those whose writings had influence upon the Founding Fathers, the most important was the political philosopher, John Locke. Locke repeatedly emphasized his suspicion of government power and believed that if the authorities violate their trust, the regime should be dissolved. This philosophy expresses itself very clearly in the Declaration of Independence.

Locke also believed that the legislative branch of government, that branch closest to the people and most subject to their control, should be the most powerful governmental branch. In his *Second Treatise* Locke notes:

> Yet the legislative being only a fiduciary power to act for certain ends, there remains still in the people a supreme power to remove or alter the legislative, when they find the legislative act contrary to the trust reposed in them. . . . And thus the community perpetually retains a supreme power of saving themselves from the attempts and designs of any body, even of their legislators, whenever they shall be so foolish or so wicked as to lay

3

and carry on designs against the liberties and properties of the subject.

At the present time many Americans seem unaware that, in the Founding Fathers' view, one of the key roles for government was that of protecting private property. This was also one of the important priorities set forth by John Locke. In stressing this point, Locke declared:

The great and chief end, therefore, of man's uniting into commonwealths, and putting themselves under government, is the preservation of their property. . . . Every man has a property in his own person. This nobody has any right to but himself. The labor of his body and the work of his hands, we may say, are properly his. Whatsoever, then he removed out of the state that nature hath provided and left it in, he hath mixed his labor with it, and joined to it something that is his own, and thereby makes it his property.

Many now argue that property should be equally divided and claim that, in doing so, they are simply applying the philosophy of the Founding Fathers to matters of economic concern. Nothing could be farther from the truth.

In *The Federalist Papers,* for example, James Madison clearly dealt with this question when he wrote:

The diversity in the faculties of men, from which the rights of property originate, is not less an insuperable obstacle to a uniformity of interest. The protection of these faculties is the first object of government. From the protection of different and unequal faculties of acquiring property, the possession of different degrees and kinds of property immediately results.

It was believed at the time of the American Revolution that property was necessary because its protection ensured the survival of individual liberty and possibilities for achievement. Professor Donald Devine, in his volume, *The Political Culture of the United States,* notes that, "Property is a basic liberal value because its protection allows the individual to be free and secure."

From the very earliest days, the American colonists learned the important lesson that the entire idea of the "common ownership" of property was both impractical and unequitable. Discussing the experience at the Plymouth Colony in his book, *In Defense of Property,* Professor Gottfried Dietze writes:

Irrespective of what each one of the colonists produced, everything went into a common warehouse and the government doled out the proceeds of the warehouse as need seemed to require. However, this system soon proved to be unsatisfactory. The warehouse was constantly running out of provisions, and many of the colonists were starving. In view of this emergency, Governor Bradford and the remaining members of the colony agreed during the third winter to give up common ownership and to permit each colonist to keep the products of his work. This gave incentive to all. Came spring, reported Governor Bradford, "the women now wente willingly into ye field, and tooke their little-ones with them to set corne, which before would aledge weaknes and inabilitie; whom to have compelled would have bene thought great tiranie and oppression." The result of these efforts was a happy one.

Professor Dietze, reviewing the history of the entire American colonial period as well as the thinking of the framers of the Constitution, concludes ". . . the American Revolution became, to a great extent, a movement for the protection of property."

We can find a great deal of evidence that the value of private property was a central consideration to those who created the American government in its earliest day. James Otis' 1764 treatise, *The Rights of the British Colonies Asserted and Proved*, requests the right to participate in Parliament as a means for the protection of the colonists' liberty and property. The resolutions of the Stamp Act Congress of 1765, as well as John Dickinson's *Farmers Letters*, show that the colonists considered property rights an essential part of freedom. A Massachusetts circular letter of 1768, drafted by Samuel Adams, stated that:

It is an essential unalterable right in nature, ungrafted into the British Constitution, as a fundamental law, and ever held sacred and irrevocable by the Subjects within the Realm, that what a man has honestly acquired is absolutely his own, which he may freely give, but cannot be taken from him without his consent.

In the first concerted action before Independence, the Continental Congress of 1774 expressed a general sentiment when it declared that the American colonists are entitled to their property "by the immutable laws of nature" and that no sovereign has the right to infringe upon it without their consent. The same sentiment is evident in the Second Continental Congress, which declared independence.

The Declaration of Independence is to a large extent a

5

document in defense of property. Some have asked why Jefferson spoke of the inalienable rights of "life, liberty and the pursuit of happiness" rather than "life, liberty and property" as enunciated by John Locke. Professor Dietze responds:

> . . . this substitution does not imply that Jefferson cared less about property than Locke. The strong influence of *The Second Treatise of Government* on the Declaration is undisputed. There is no reason why Jefferson, who admired Locke so greatly that the Declaration, in its form, in its phraseology, follows closely certain sentences in Locke's *Second Treatise*, should not have believed in the truth of the treatise's major idea, namely that property is sacrosanct and that government is instituted mainly for its protection. It may be argued that the substitution of "pursuit of happiness" for "property," in view of the close resemblance of the Declaration to the *Second Treatise*, must have been made for urgent reasons and that it demonstrates a deviation from Locke's emphasis on property. However, this argument is scarcely convincing. If Jefferson had wanted to omit an emphasis on property, then he would have refrained from denouncing the king's infringements upon the colonists' property so emphatically.

John Adams, in his *Defence of the Constitution of Government of the United States,* also urged his countrymen to recognize the need for protection of private property. Shortly after the end of the American Revolution those in the colonies who disagreed with this idea with regard to property rights and sought an equal distribution of property, much as those who advocate egalitarianism do today, rebelled. The movement came to a head in Massachusetts with Shays' Rebellion when the debtors, unable to capture the legislature of the state, revolted. The Federal Constitutional Convention was convened, many historians argue, largely because of a belief in the ethics of property and the necessity to protect such property from the kinds of rebellions that had occurred in Massachusetts.

In this connection, John Adams declared that "property is surely a right of mankind as really as liberty. . . . The moment the idea is admitted into society that property is not as sacred as the laws of God, and that there is not a force of law and public justice to protect it, anarchy and tyranny commence."

If belief in the sanctity of private property is one essen-

6

tial element of the American political philosophy, another key element is suspicion and fear of arbitrary governmental power and authority. During the colonial period, Americans became all too familiar with such dangers. The Revolution was fought largely to prevent such governmental abuses and to make certain that individual citizens might be secure in their lives and property.

When the Articles of Confederation were being considered, fears of excessive concentration of authority were often expressed. The town of West Springfield, Massachusetts, to cite one example, reminded its representatives of the weakness of human nature and growing thirst for power.

    . . . It is *freedom*, Gentlemen, it is freedom, and not a choice of the forms of servitude for which we contend, and we rely on your fidelity, that you will not consent to the present plan of Union, til after the most calm and dispassionate examination you are fully convinced that it is well calculated to secure so great and desirable an object.

One of the early textbooks of the American patriots was *Cato's Letters*, the joint product of Thomas Gordon and John Trenchard. Written during 1720-1723, it was widely read in the colonies together with James Burgh's *Political Disquisitions*. The basic concept stressed in both works is the evil effect of power. "The love of power is natural," wrote Burgh, "it is insatiable; it is whetted, not cloyed by possession."

Gordon and Trenchard, as "Cato," observed, "Power renders man wanton, insolent to others, and fond of themselves. . . . All history affords but few instances of men trusted with great power without abusing it, when with security they could." The people must retain power in their own hands, grant it sparingly, and then only under the strictest supervision. "The people can never be too jealous of their liberties," Burgh warned. "Power is of an elastic nature, ever extending itself and encroaching on the liberties of the subjects." "Cato" also believed that "Political jealousy . . . in the people is a necessary and laudable passion." Therefore, people must select their rulers with care, and these must be "narrowly watched and checked with Restraints stronger than their Temptation to break them."

Anyone who reads the words of the men who led the Revolution will find many examples of their fear and suspicion of power and the men who hold it. Samuel Adams, one of those considered "radical" at the time of the Revolution, asserted:

There is a degree of watchfulness over all men possessed of power or influence upon which the liberties of mankind much depend. It is necessary to guard against the infirmities of the best as well as the wickedness of the worst of men . . . . Jealousy is the best security of public liberty.

Those who would understand American political philosophy must remember that corruption of power and the oppression of strong government, together with the need to protect life and property, are and have been its essential elements.

In 1800 Jefferson wrote of his belief that "a single consolidated government would become the most corrupt government on earth." Twenty-one years later he remarked, "Our government is now taking so steady a course as to show by what road it will pass to destruction, to wit: by consolidation first, and then corruption, its necessary consequence."

For many years we have been pursuing precisely the kinds of policies against which Jefferson and the other founders of the nation warned us. We have not viewed government as something to be feared but, instead, have turned to it repeatedly as the "answer" to whatever problems the society, and individuals within the society, faced. Finally, at least some Americans are coming to the conclusion that such an approach has failed; that it has made the problems worse not better.

Discussing the programs of the New Frontier and the Great Society—programs which, unfortunately, have been continued to a greater or lesser extent under succeeding Republican administrations—Daniel P. Moynihan, a long-time supporter of these programs, noted, ". . . so many things of which so much was expected were more or less tried out in the 1960s and more or less didn't work."

The American people are well aware that those programs did not work and are equally aware of the extraordinary cost involved in funding their failure. Every recent poll indicates public disenchantment with government. One of the most interesting of these polls was conducted in New York City in 1973 by the Daniel Yankelovich organization under commission from *The New York Times*. That poll, which was released by *The Times* on January 15, 1974, indicated that in New York, allegedly the nation's most "liberal" city, more city residents view themselves as conservatives rather than either moderates or liberals.

The Times noted:

This ideological swing to the right is reflected in strong attitudes among New Yorkers in favor of the restoration of the death penalty, in giving life sentences without parole to drug pushers, in support of crackdowns on pornography and in opposition to the busing of children to achieve racial balance in the city's schools.

In a city that has traditionally elected liberals to public office, one-third of those polled described themselves as conservatives, 31 percent as moderates, and only 25 percent as liberals. Three years earlier a similar survey produced the reverse results. At that time, liberals were the largest bloc, with 33 percent, followed by moderates at 31 percent and conservatives at 27 percent.

The poll indicated that a high percentage of blacks—31 percent, compared with 35 percent among whites—characterized themselves as conservatives. On at least one issue, whether those on welfare get "too much of a break" from the city, moderates were even more emphatic than the conservatives in believing that welfare recipients are pampered. Sixty-nine percent of moderates and 61 percent of conservatives said that the city was overly kind to welfare recipients. Fifty-five percent of liberals agreed, for an overall finding of 61 percent.

Every indication points to the conclusion that the majority of the American people are opposed to recent trends in government, particularly the centralization of power in Washington. In this sense, the political philosophy that motivated the Founding Fathers in 1776 and 1789 appears still to be the dominant political philosophy of the majority of Americans. One of the most significant recent changes has been the rediscovery of the traditional American philosophy of limited government and strict checks and balances by men and women who had abandoned it and had adopted the view that government should solve—and could solve—all problems facing society. One socialist professor, for example, grudgingly admitted that "On the whole, those systems that have put liberty ahead of equality have done better by equality than those that have put equality above liberty."

Concerning the "revolution of equality" of the 1960s Professor Nathan Glazer now calls into question the liberal dogma that all men should have the same status and re-

9

wards. He now agrees with the older American idea that, since men are inherently individual and different, some will progress farther than others. A free society, he believes, gives each man the opportunity to go as far as his ability will take him.

The shift in rhetoric against faith and reliance in unlimited government that characterized so many once-liberal academicians can be seen in the political arena as well. Governors Edmund Brown, Jr. of California and Michael Dukakis of Massachusetts have sensed that the public is increasingly suspicious of big government and excessive spending, and both have characterized their own administrations as being opposed to such trends. Moreover, former Governor Jimmy Carter has campaigned for the presidency in 1976 on an anti-Washington theme.

In the U.S. Senate, Edmund Muskie (D-Maine), long a proponent of big spending programs and of virtually unlimited governmental power and authority, is shifting, at least in rhetoric. Speaking to the Liberal Party of New York in October, 1975, Senator Muskie asked:

Why can't liberals start raising hell about a government so big, so complex, so expensive and unresponsive that it's dragging down every good program we've worked for? Why can't liberals talk about fiscal responsibility and productivity without feeling uncomfortable? We're in a rut. Our emotional stake in government is so great that we regard common-sense criticism of government almost as a personal attack.

All who have been concerned with the growth of government power and the accompanying diminution of individual freedom can only be pleased that those who have been largely responsible for that growth in government seem now to recognize the futility of such a position. Nevertheless, since individuals must bear responsibility for the policies they have supported and enacted, a simple shift in rhetoric should not suffice to exonerate them for the roles they have played.

The Washington Star, in an October 18, 1975, editorial, in response to Senator Muskie, made two points that are worthy of consideration:

First, if liberal thinking is so out of the mainstream, why do Mr. Muskie and his colleagues continue to look to the liberals for answers to these questions? There are plenty of others around who are "raising hell" about big, complex, expensive, unresponsive government. Second,

Mr. Muskie's "basic question" is misdirected. It isn't the Liberal Party of New York, or even liberals in general, that tolerates the governmental sprawl. It's Mr. Muskie's colleagues in the Congress.

Despite the all-too-human tendency to say, "I told you so," to those who, at this late date, have finally decided that total government power is a negative, not a positive, force in society, the fact remains that their arrival at this viewpoint, whether it is sincere or opportunistic, marks what may be a turning point in our political life. If liberals themselves believe that government has become too large, too expensive, too cumbersome, and too much involved in the lives of individual citizens, there may be some real hope of reversing the trends toward centralization which have been at work since Ratification of the Constitution in 1789.

It is essential, however, that Americans analyze the basic principles of political life—not simply rebel at large and bureaucratic government without considering what the criteria for proper and virtuous government should be. In this connection it is essential to understand the connection between the economic system of free enterprise and the larger concept of a free society. The two go hand in hand. Capitalism is, after all, freedom applied to the marketplace.

One of the first questions that must be confronted by those who advance the view that free enterprise and freedom go hand in hand is the assertion that a dichotomy somehow exists between "human" rights and "property" rights. Such a dichotomy is, in fact, illusory. The right to the fruit of one's labor—to private property—is an essential human right, in fact the one upon which all others depend.

Discussing the concept of a dichotomy between "human" and "property" rights, Professor Murray Rothbard, in his book, *For a New Liberty*, notes:

> . . . the two are inextricably intertwined; they stand or fall together. . . . Take, for example, the liberal socialist who advocates government ownership of all the "means of production" while upholding the "human" right of freedom of speech or press. How is this "human" right to be exercised if the individuals constituting the public are denied their right to ownership of property? If, for example, the government owns all the newsprint and all the printing shops, how is the right to a free press to be exercised? If the government owns all the newsprint, it then necessarily has the right and the power

11

to allocate that newsprint, and someone's "right to a free press" becomes a mockery if the government decides not to allocate newsprint in his direction. . . .

In the same vein, Professor Rothbard adds:

The same is true for the "right to free speech" if the government owns all the assembly halls, and therefore allocates those halls as it sees fit. Or, for example, if the government of Soviet Russia, being atheistic, decides not to allocate many scarce resources to the production of matzohs for Orthodox Jews, the "freedom of religion" becomes a mockery; but again, the Soviet government can always rebut that Orthodox Jews are a small minority and that capital equipment should not be diverted to matzoh production . . . to sustain his "human right"— or his property rights in his own person—he must also have the property right in the material world, in the objects which he produces. Property rights are human rights, and are essential to the human rights which liberals attempt to maintain.

The goal of the American society, from its very earliest days, was the enhancement of individual freedom. This could best be done, the framers of the Constitution believed, by instituting a system of representative government, with clear limits upon what government could and could not do. The system of federalism and of checks and balances constituted their effort to make certain that government would not have enough power to deprive individual men and women of rights they believed to be "inalienable."

The American political philosophy, at once suspicious of centralized power and engaged in the constitutional effort to clearly delineate legitimate government power, did not overlook the question of economics.

As in their consideration of the form of government that would best maintain a free and open society, the Founding Fathers also asked themselves which form of economic organization would best maintain the free society they were creating. Clearly, the answer was free enterprise. For men suspicious of government power this was an obvious choice. They could hardly have decided any other way.

In his important volume, *Capitalism and Freedom*, Professor Milton Friedman points out, "The kind of economic organization that provides economic freedom directly, namely, competitive capitalism, also promotes political freedom because it separates economic power from political

power and in this way enables the one to offset the other."
Professor Friedman continues:

Political freedom means the absence of coercion of a
man by his fellow men. The fundamental threat to freedom is power to coerce, be it in the hands of a monarch,
a dictator, an oligarchy or a momentary majority. The
preservation of freedom requires the elimination of such
concentration of power to the fullest possible extent and
the dispersal and distribution of whatever power cannot
be eliminated—a system of checks and balances. By removing the organization of economic activity from the
control of political authority, the market eliminates this
source of coercive power. It enables economic strength
to be a check to political power rather than a reinforcement.

Unfortunately, many Americans, regardless of which
party they belong to or which political philosophy they
appear to espouse, seem ready to eliminate such checks and
balances for some presumed short-term economic or political good. This was the case, for example, when President
Richard Nixon, an apparent advocate of free enterprise,
imposed wage and price controls upon the American economy. At that time *The Wall Street Journal* commented,
"Without wanting to sound apocalyptic, we find rather dismaying the ease with which the business community and a
Republican Administration have accepted—and often welcomed—the prospect of a controlled economy."

The Journal reminded its readers of the larger questions
that are often forgotten:

Beyond all that is a question of politico-economic
philosophy. We see a free economy (and we would have
assumed most businessmen and supposedly conservative
government officials do likewise) not only as something
good and marvelously productive in itself. It is also part
and parcel of the whole broader concept of individual
freedom. This is what has made the U.S. pre-eminent,
both economically and as a political model. But at the
root individual freedom is a moral issue.

The Nixon Administration's experiment with wage and
price controls was, of course, a failure. This should come as
no surprise to any who have carefully considered the history
of governmental intervention in economic matters. The
classic example of the attempt by government to improve
the life of the people by restricting their choice is that of
Roman Emperor Diocletian about the year A.D. 300. Diocle-

tian was faced with the familiar problem of rising prices in the wake of an increase in the quantity of money and a debasement of its value.

The historian Duray writes:

Under the impression that to give to a piece of metal whatever value they liked, it sufficed to engrave the Emperor's name upon it, the Roman Government had ended by putting in circulation pieces of "silver" and "gold" which contained neither silver nor gold. . . . Very high prices resulted therefore from the depreciation of the currency.

In his effort to bring prices down to what he considered a normal level, Diocletian did not content himself with such half measures as we in the United States have attempted. Instead, he fixed the maximum prices at which beef, grain, eggs, clothing, and other articles should be sold, and prescribed the penalty of death for anyone who disposed of his goods at a higher price.

A contemporary historian, Lactantius, writing within a decade or so of the event, presented the considered verdict on Diocletian's actions:

After many oppressions which he put in practice had brought a general dearth upon the empire, he set himself to regulate the prices of all vendible things. There was also much blood shed upon very slight and trifling accounts; and the people brought provisions no more to markets, since they could not get a reasonable price for them; and this increased the dearth so much, that at last after many had died by it, the law was laid aside.

It was left to the Emperor Constantine to restore confidence and stability by reintroducing a reliable currency based on gold, which the people knew could not be debased for the convenience of politicians, as could paper or other substitute currencies.

Another method used by government to reduce choice is to "nationalize" a particular activity and to inhibit competition from private companies. In his book, *Must History Repeat Itself?*, Antony Fisher writes:

An interesting and little known test of public enterprise was provided by the British Labour Government in 1930. Two large airships were built, one by the state and one by a private firm. One was finished long before the other and crossed the Atlantic and back; while the other on its maiden flight crashed in flames, killing all but six

14

on board. There are no prizes for guessing which of the two was built by the state.

State control of the economy has failed so often that it is difficult to understand why so many in public life continue to tell us that the answer to various economic problems is additional state intervention. Another example cited by Fisher is that of two Canadian railroads, the privately-run Canadian Pacific and the nationalized Canadian National. He writes:

> The comparison of financial returns over 18 years, from 1941 to 1958, revealed that where one company earned a profit of $669 million the other suffered a loss of $663 million. Again, there is no prize for guessing which was the result of nationalization. But it might surprise some readers to hear that in addition to paying its share-holders almost $370 million, the private enterprise company also paid a similar sum in taxation, in contrast to the nationalized company's charge of over $600 million against taxation.

Many Americans criticize particular aspects of governmental intervention in the economy without placing their criticism in a larger perspective. Thus, the problem with the policy of wage and price controls is not that they are inequitably administered, which they may be, but that they are wrong in principle.

The reason economic controls do not work, states economist Murray Rothbard, is:

> . . . they don't tackle the cause of inflation, but only lash out at its symptoms. . . . Every price is simply the terms of an exchange on the market. . . . When I buy a newspaper for a dime, ten cents in money is being exchanged for one newspaper. . . . And so the key to what makes prices high or low is the relationship between the supply of goods available and the supply of money. . . . Suppose that by some magic process, the quantity of money in the country doubles overnight. The supply of goods remains the same, for nothing has really happened to lower or raise them. But then we will all enter the market with twice as many dollars burning a hole in our pocket as compared to yesterday . . . we will all have to pay twenty cents for the same newspaper.

Professor Rothbard elaborates:

> . . . the supply of dollars has continued to go up, and even to accelerate, especially under the Johnson and Nixon Administrations. And, as the supply of dollars has risen and

15

risen ever faster, prices have gone up as well. . . . In 1971, for example, the supply of money increased at a rate of 12-16%. . . . The culprit is none other than the federal government itself. It is the federal government . . . that has absolute control of the supply of money, and regulates it to its own content. It has been the federal government that has been merrily increasing the supply of money, to "stimulate" the economy, to finance its own enormous budget deficits, to help out favored borrowers, to lower interest rates, or for any other reason.

The root of many of our modern difficulties may rest with the manner in which American political leaders and the people they represent have abandoned the Founding Fathers' suspicion of governmental power and have instead looked to government for a solution to all economic and societal ills.

Thus, while the framers of the Constitution attempted in that document to limit clearly the power of government, those limits can work only if public opinion is concerned about keeping a proper check upon governmental power. Professor Aaron Wildavsky, writing in *The Public Interest*, expresses this view:

> . . . institutions are not everything. They function in a climate of opinion that both limits and shapes what they can do. Those who operate them respond to the rewards and punishments of the environment in which they are situated. A people who punish truthfulness will get lies; a people who reward symbolic actions will get rhetoric instead of realism. So long as the people appear to make contradictory demands for domestic policies, they will be supplied by contrary politicians. . . . Long before the current disenchantment, Henry Fairlie, in his book *The Kennedy Promise*, had questioned whether Americans did not have too exalted an opinion of what politics could do. . . . Fairlie discerned in the Kennedys an excessive conception of what government could do, a sense of politics over society that would come to no good.

Mr. Fairlie, a British correspondent in Washington, put it this way: "The people are encouraged to expect too much of their political institutions and of their political leaders. They cease to inquire what politics may accomplish for them, and what they must do for themselves. Instead, they expect politics to take the place religion once held in their lives. . . ."

The manner in which our two-party system has operated in recent years has produced a situation in which voters have little choice. No matter who they elect, it seems, the same expanding government programs tend to continue and the areas of life in which government extends its authority continue to grow.

In 1974, for example, the rhetoric of the political campaigns was much the same as in past years—with representatives of each party promising disaster were the opposition to be elected. But the American people seemed increasingly less willing to play this traditional game.

The evidence of a refusal to identify with party labels that seem to have lost all substance and meaning is overwhelming. A Gallup Poll late in 1974 showed independents increasing from 20 percent of the electorate in 1940 to 25 percent in 1966, to 33 percent in 1974, with almost the entire increase coming from Republicans, who fell from 38 percent to 23 percent.

In their book, *The Ticket Splitter*, Walter Devries and Lance Tarrance show that there has been a corresponding rise in districts where a Presidential nominee of one party and a House nominee of the other won in the same election. There were 11 such districts in 1920, 53 in 1940, 114 in 1960, and 139 in 1968. "The ticket splitter," according to Devries and Tarrance, "is somewhat younger, somewhat more educated, somewhat more white-collar and more suburban than the typical middle-class voter. In addition, the ticket splitter tends to consume more media output about politics."

The results of the 1974 election showed the influence of such ticket splitters. In Maryland Marvin Mandel, a Democrat, won the Governorship while Charles Mathias, a Republican, was elected Senator. In Iowa Robert Ray, a Republican, was elected Governor, while John Culver, a Democrat, was elected to the Senate. In New York Republican Jacob Javits was elected to the Senate while Democrat Hugh Carey was elected Governor. The list is long.

Equally interesting is the rise of Independent candidates who are challenging both major parties. Two successful candidates are now in the U.S. Senate: Harry F. Byrd, Jr., of Virginia, and James L. Buckley of New York. Now, an independent, non party candidate has been elected Governor of Maine. After his election Governor James Longley declared, "Maybe what happened in Maine can be a bellwether of what can happen around the country. My elec-

17

tion says the voters are no longer going to tolerate partisan politics."

Americans seem slowly to be coming to the conclusion that the parties are only vehicles for power, and the only thing most candidates really disagree about is who should be elected. Regardless of which party has been in power in recent years, the traditional American political philosophy of limited government, check and balances, federalism, respect for private property, and individual freedom, has been almost forgotten.

The current two-party system is, in large measure, one of the major causes of present disenchantment with politics. The system, according to Abraham Maslow in his book, *Eupsychian Management,* is dangerous because

> . . . it tends to leave the selection of candidates to just exactly those self-seekers, those people who neurotically need power in the sense of power over other people, rather than getting into office the person who is best suited to the job and who may be modest and humble about the matter and would not like to push himself forward . . . the person who seeks for power is the one who is just exactly likely to be the one who shouldn't have it, because he neurotically and compulsively needs power. Such people are apt to use power badly. . . .

The recent experience of Watergate is ample proof of this analysis. On the one hand, government has expanded its areas of authority far beyond anything envisioned by the Constitution. On the other, political leadership has declined dramatically from that which the nation had at a time when the role of government was severely limited.

In his book, *The Bewildered Society,* George Roche writes,

> American democratic politics has operated according to Gresham's Law. The worst political type generally drives out the best. In America our politicians tend to choose themselves. Some individual decides that he wants to hold political office, and sets about the task of winning office for himself.

Unfortunately, both our political parties have tended to reject their role of providing meaningful choices of policy direction to the American people. They have, instead, followed the predictions of political philosophers from the time of Plato, of expanding the jurisdiction of government as they gained power, opposing the expansion when they were out of power, and reversing their position upon assum-

18

ing office. The growth of government, as a result, seems never ending.

In 1800, for example, the Anti-Federalists took power as the party of strict construction. Once in office, however, they turned that philosophy around on behalf of the special interests they represented. The Federalists, on the other hand, were nominally for loose construction, yet they fought bitterly every one of the opposing party's loose constructionist measures—the embargo, the protective tariff, and the national bank. They were constitutional nationalists in New England, but threatened secession during the War of 1812. Political "principles" meant as little to the Federalists and the Anti-Federalists in 1800 as they do to many in today's American political arena.

Observing the American two-party system in 1893, Lord Bryce, in his important book, *The American Commonwealth*, noted:

> Neither party has any clear cut principles, any distinctive tenets. Both have traditions. Both claim to have tendencies. Both certainly have war cries, organizations, interests listed in their support. But these interests are in the main interest of getting or keeping the patronage of the government. The American parties now continue to exist because they have existed. The mill has been constructed, and its machinery goes on turning even where there is no grist to grind.

A similar view was expressed by author Richard Whalen in a collection of essays entitled *Taking Sides*. In his discussion of the atmosphere of the White House that produced Watergate, Whalen expresses the opinion that those who thought of the Watergate conspirators as "ruthless, brilliant men scheming for the highest prizes" were mistaken. Instead, he notes that:

> . . . stupid men also scheme. Conspirators may be motived by nothing more than fear of losing what they have. The fictionalized ambition to seize power by a bold stroke becomes in real life the petty desire to hold on to the trappings and satisfactions of power—the luxurious jets, the fleet of limousines, the protected villas and retreats, the warm feeling of total security. To most of those who possess it, power is not desired as a means to a great end. It is a perfectly satisfying end in itself.

Whalen was not only discussing the Nixon White House. He found much the same to be true in the White House of John F. Kennedy. He refers to President Kennedy as "a man without a goal beyond personal victory" and declares that he won election "by projecting an image of 'freshness' and 'vigor' in a time of national self-doubt. He practiced a media-oriented politics of illusion, which only a few skeptics challenged. . . ."

"In my family," John F. Kennedy once told an interviewer, "we were interested not so much in the ideas of politics as in the mechanics of the whole thing." In 1957 Joseph Kennedy told *The New York Times* columnist Arthur Krock, "We're going to sell Jack like soapflakes."

The negative effect of the mass media upon the American political process cannot be overstated. Richard Whalen observes:

> Abraham Lincoln could be physically unattractive yet popular at the same time. The images on the screen are contrived to satisfy the values not of traditional politics but of mass entertainment; and the politicians who entered the realm of the entertainers were judged by their standards.

The traditional American political concerns—the defense of private property, of individual rights, of limited and carefully circumscribed government—evaporate in an era of mass-media politics in which candidates for public office are judged not on the basis of their philosophy or position on the issues but on the basis of a manufactured media image.

In *The Selling of the President 1968* author Joe McGinniss, then a 26-year-old former sportswriter and columnist for the *Philadelphia Inquirer*, tells the story of this new politics of public relations in some detail. Initially, he learned that the Doyle Dane Bernbach advertising agency intended to "turn Hubert Humphrey into Abraham Lincoln" by election time and thought he would like to document this feat in a book. When that agency would not cooperate the author called Harry Treleaven, a former vice-president of the J. Walter Thompson firm which was at that time in charge of promotion for the Nixon campaign. McGinniss was invited to cover the Nixon side of the campaign and his book was the result.

The person responsible for almost all of Nixon's commercial television appearances was Roger Ailes, who had been executive producer of "The Mike Douglas Show." Ailes' biggest problem was in putting together panels to question Nixon. Nixon's advisers felt that it was essential to have a "balanced" group. McGinniss reports:

First, this meant a Negro. One Negro, not two. Two would be offensive to whites, perhaps to Negroes as well. Two would be trying too hard. . . . Texas would be tricky though. Do you have a Negro and a Mexican-American. . . ? Besides the Negro, the panel for the first show included a Jewish attorney, the president of a Polish-Hungarian group, a suburban housewife, a businessman, a representative of the white lower middle class, and, for authenticity, two newsmen. . . . But then someone called from New York and insisted that he add a farmer. A farmer for Christ's sake. Roger Ailes had been born in Ohio, but even so he knew you did not want a farmer on a television show. All they did was ask complicated questions about things like parities, which nobody else understood or cared about, including Richard Nixon. . . .

This volume shows the candidate being directed through the entire campaign by public relations men. An example of this occurs when Nixon, standing in front of the camera at the end of a taping session, spontaneously decides to do one more commercial on his own. He makes an extemporaneous, hard-line, law-and-order statement about the New York City teachers' strike then in progress. But the message is sharply out of keeping with the soft, friendly Nixon image and an adviser, Leonard Garment, is upset. Treleaven, however, reassures him. "That's all right, Len," he says, "it'll never get on the air."

This book was important, not as an expose of the Nixon campaign, but as an indication of the current state of American politics. A similar book might be written about John F. Kennedy or Lyndon Johnson. The low state of our political discourse cuts across party and sectional lines. It is a dilemma that all Americans share and together must face.

The fact is that the American society is in serious trouble. The very political ideals that motivated the Founding Fathers, a fear of centralized governmental power and a desire for the maximum amount of individual freedom consistent with order, are now under attack. Instead of fearing government power, we look to government as the answer to our problems. Instead of being jealous of our liberties, we seem all too eager to barter them for security or for whatever else those who seek our support promise in return.

Writing in 1922, the Englishman G.K. Chesterton observed, "At the present moment the matter which America has very seriously to consider is not how near it is to its birth and beginning, but how near it may be to its end. It is only a verbal question whether the American civilization is young; it may become a very urgent and practical question whether it is dying."

Chesterton continues:

When once we cast aside . . . the fanciful metaphor involved in the word "youth," what serious evidence have we that America is a fresh force and not a stale one? It has a great many people, like China; it has a great deal of money, like defeated Carthage or dying Venice. It is full of bustle and excitability, like Athens after its ruin, and all the Greek cities in their decline. It is fond of new things; but the old are always fond of new things. . . . It admires strength and good looks; it admires a big and barbaric beauty in its women, for instance; but so did Rome when the Goth was at the gates. . . .

All these are things quite compatible with fundamental tedium and decay. There are three main shapes or symbols in which a nation can show itself essentially glad and great; by the heroic in government, by the heroic in arms, and by the heroic in art. . . . Subjected to these eternal tests, America does not appear by any means as particularly fresh or untouched. She appears with all the weaknesses of modern England, or of any other Western power. In her politics, she has broken up . . . into a bewildering opportunism and insincerity.

If such a sophisticated observer as G.K. Chesterton believed that the American political process had succumbed to "opportunism" and "insincerity" in 1922, what would he say today? It required 163 years, from 1789 to 1952, for governmental expenditures for domestic programs to reach $34 billion; in the succeeding 20 years they virtually exploded from $34 to $257 billion. Government has become the predominant force in the American society. If the current rate of growth were to continue, domestic public expenditures would, within less than 40 years, account for all of the gross national product.

The unfortunate fact is that the entire basis of the traditional American political philosophy—federalism and a system of checks and balances—no longer really exists. As Dr. Roger Freeman states:

By its massive entry over the past two decades into the field of domestic public services, the national government has decisively altered the nature of the American federal system. In establishing a federal structure with an intri-

22

cate system of checks and balances, the founding fathers had aimed to disperse authority so widely that no one branch or level of government—and no one man—could prevail over the others. They concluded from history that concentration of power corrupts and sooner or later leads to abuse and tyranny. Whenever the wisdom of the age-old lesson is disregarded, its truth is brought home to the nation sooner or later with a brutal shock.

The number of federal grants multiplied from a few dozen in the immediate post-World War II period to well over 500 (according to some the figure is close to 1,000) in recent years. Their amount jumped from $2.6 billion in 1952, to $36 billion in 1972, to an estimated $52 billion in fiscal 1975. The accompanying shift of power to the national government diminishes the entire notion of states' rights and divided governmental authority.

Concerning the long-run effects of this transformation, Dr. Freeman observes:

Extension of federal grants into every nook and cranny of local services smoothed the road and conditioned public attitudes toward increasing federal regulation and interference by new laws, administrative rules, practices of dedicated and power-hungry bureaucrats, and orders of ambitious judges who shifted from interpreting the law to policy making and amending the meaning of the Constitution. There are few if any activities or practices left to local governments, business firms, associations or individuals that are not governed and often drastically changed by federal authorities under the sanction of law.

American society has strayed far from its beginnings. Instead of desiring freedom from governmental interference; instead of looking to the government primarily as a source of protection from foreign or domestic enemies and not as the provider of services and benefits, Americans have embraced the very centralized government the Founding Fathers urged them to fear and hold in check.

Samuel P. Huntington points out that:

By the early 1970s Americans were progressively demanding and receiving more benefits from their government and yet having less confidence in their government than they had a decade earlier. . . . The key question is: To what extent will this expansion be limited in scope and time . . . or to what extent will it be an open-ended

23

continuing phenomenon? These are not easy questions to answer. . . . The activities—and expenditures—of government expand, and yet the success of government in achieving its goals seems dubious.

If a free society is to be preserved, and not to be lost or abandoned, it is essential that we rediscover the political philosophy that motivated the Founding Fathers—the philosophy that for its first 200 years has made the United States the most free country in the history of the world. We stand in serious danger of forgetting that philosophy and losing that freedom. What the future holds is up to us.

Are the Bleeding Hearts for Real?

During the past thirty years liberals have been telling the American people that they are on the side of "humanity, justice, peace and freedom." They have assumed for themselves all of the "positive" terms—"kindness, sympathy, compassion, pity." They have charged that conservatives are adequately described only by the "negative" terms which are available—"champions of privilege, vested interest, selfishness, unconcern for the little man."

Any man or group who sets the ground rules and the definitions of the language which is to be used in the political arena will, of course, choose to portray himself in a positive manner, and portray those in the opposition in a negative manner. Words, used under such circumstances, lose their real meaning.

What has been happening in American politics in the recent past is very much akin to the distortion of language described by Lewis Carroll in *Alice in Wonderland*:

"When I use a word," Humpty Dumpty said, in rather a scornful tone, "it means just what I choose it to mean—neither more nor less."

"The question is," said Alice, "whether you *can* make words mean so many different things."

"The question is," said Humpty Dumpty, "which is to be master—that's all."

Thus, liberals are "kind, sympathetic, and compassionate" on their own terms, not necessarily according to the meaning of those words. For such words traditionally have meant a real care and concern for those at whom such kindness, sympathy and compassion was aimed. The record of liberalism in America since the years of the New Deal indicates not that liberalism has in any sense helped the so-called "little man" who is the stated subject of its concern, but almost precisely the opposite.

25

Those who seek truly to understand American politics as it is should look carefully at the record of those who proclaim themselves to be liberals. It is on the basis of real evidence, not fanciful rhetoric, that conclusions should be drawn.

Modern liberalism has set forth the thesis that all of our social problems—poverty, discrimination, unemployment, housing, agriculture, inflation—can best be solved by government intervention and control. It is clear that after approximately four decades this philosophy has produced not solutions to such problems but, instead, more racial tension, more unemployment, more inflation, and more problems in almost every area entered by government.

The literature of liberal disillusionment with traditional liberal answers has now become voluminous. Professor Hans Morganthau says:

The general crisis of democracy is the result of three factors: the shift of effective material power from the people to the government, and the ability of government to destroy its own citizens in the process of defending them. . . . The great national decisions of life and death are rendered by technological elites and both the Congress and the people at large retain little more than the illusion of making the decisions which the theory of democracy supposes them to make.

The measures advocated for some time in the field of housing are an important example of the failure of an approach that tends to believe that the creation of a welfare state will solve all of our problems. Political conservatives have always opposed this approach, so their opposition is to be expected. But today even the former advocates of that approach recognize its own futility and failure.

Jason R. Nathan, New York City Housing and Development Administrator told former Senator Paul Douglas' National Commission on Urban Problems: "The entire concept of Federal aid as we know it may be completely wrong." Nathan continued, "Even if the Federal Government spent ten times the money they do now—which they won't—it would not be enough. After ten or fifteen years of traditional programs, for example, we have not even begun to approach the problem in Bedford-Stuyvesant in Brooklyn."

Urban renewal programs, as a case in point, were meant to ease the problem of low-cost housing scarcity. Exactly the opposite has resulted. The United States Commission on Civil Rights found that federal projects in Cleveland had drastically reduced the amount of low-rent housing in the city and contributed to the creation of a new ghetto. Out of the resentments that were produced a new bitterness grew, culminating ultimately in riots. Commenting on the Cleveland developments, Father Theodore Hesburgh, President of the University of Notre Dame and a member of the Civil Rights Commission, said:

These enormous federal programs . . . are coming in, supposedly to help the community. They want to rebuild our society. What has happened in many cases is that people who are presently in the worst situation have their houses swept out from under them by bulldozers, they are given very little help in finding houses and they generally do worse then where they came from. This is immoral.

John P. Roche, past chairman of Americans for Democratic Action, described President Kennedy's urban renewal programs as a policy of replacing Blacks with trees. Professor Martin Anderson, in his book *The Federal Bulldozer,* notes that in the decade of the Fifties approximately 125,000 low income units were destroyed while only 20 percent of them were replaced; most of these with rentals affordable only to upper income families.

Richard Cloward of the Columbia University School of Social Work, in a publication issued by the Center for the Study of Democratic Institutions, offers this statistical summary:

Since the public housing program was legislated in 1933 some 600,000 low-income housing units have been built, but in the last 15 years urban renewal and highway construction alone have demolished 700,000 low-rental units. . . . In this same period, urban renewal has built at the most 100,000 new units. So . . . the net loss in low-income housing is probably about 250,000 units.

Many former advocates of such liberal programs have come to the conclusion that they have not, in fact, solved any of the problems at which they were aimed, but rather have aggravated them.

In the mid-1950s two agricultural sociologists, Charles P. Loomis and I. Allen Beegle, made a survey of depressed farming areas. They were, they found, exactly as they had been in the Thirties. The New Deal and subsequent programs had passed over these areas without touching them.

Michael Harrington has noted that the liberal approach

27

to government has produced "socialism for the rich" and "free enterprise for the poor." In his volume, *The Other America*, he writes that "The welfare state is upside down. The protection, the guarantees, the help all tend to go to the strong and to the organized. The weakest in society are those who are always disposed of in some congressional log-rolling session."

The welfare-state philosophy, which is the cornerstone of modern liberal thinking, has not given people a stake in their communities or hope for a better future. Bayard Rustin, director of the A. Philip Randolph Institute in New York, and a prominent black spokesman, said that the welfare-state philosophy inherent in the war on poverty is an "immoral bag of tricks" amounting to a new form of slavery. He stated that "The problem for Negroes, Puerto Ricans, and poor whites . . . is that America has no commitment to turn muscle power into skills."

In his *Autobiography*, Malcolm X said to white liberals, those he found most guilty of supporting the idea of a dole for the ghetto:

If . . . they wanted more to do, they could work on the roots of such ghetto evils as the little children out in the streets at midnight with apartment keys on strings around their necks to let themselves in, and their mothers and fathers drunk, drug addicts, thieves, and prostitutes. Or . . . they could light some fires under Northern city halls, unions, and major industries to give more jobs to Negroes to remove so many of them from the relief and welfare rolls, which created laziness, and which deteriorated the ghettoes into steadily worse places for humans to live . . . one thing the white man never can give the black man is self-respect. The black man never can become independent and recognized as a human being who is truly equal with other human beings until he has what they have, and until he is doing for himself what others are doing for themselves.

More and more black leaders have come to the realization that government is not going to solve any of their real problems. They are rapidly turning away from the standard liberal responses of a previous generation.

Thomas B. Jones, a black economist in New York, has stated, "The economic problems of the Negro have not been solved by government programs or a changing attitude on the part of the power structure. The Negro, therefore, decided that self-development is a practical, realizable approach to the solution of his problem."

Dr. Thomas Matthew, leader of the National Economic and Growth Reconstruction Organization (NEGRO) received a franchise to operate a bus line in California, but not in New York. His response:

We got the fullest cooperation from Governor Reagan and Mayor Yorty. You see, those with a less liberal viewpoint are really happy with our efforts. Many of them never believed we would help ourselves. They're willing to give us a chance, though, and we are making the most of it. Many liberals like Mayor Lindsay want to do it for the Negro and not let him do it for himself. That's why, at this point, it's easier to work with conservatives.

The fact is that government has been a failure in most areas of society it has entered. While it has attempted to create a welfare state, it has instead created a society with more poverty, more unemployment, and more social tensions than the kind of society it replaced.

In his important book, *Crisis In Black and White,* Charles Silberman points out that, "The rate of expenditure for public assistance has been rising rapidly in every large city, without making a dent in any of the problems they are supposed to solve. Indeed, a good many of these expenditures seem to have been a waste of money at best, and at worst a positive disservice to the people they are supposed to help. . . ." Professor S. M. Miller of Syracuse University has declared that, "Welfare assistance in its present form tends to encourage dependence, withdrawal, diffused hostility, indifference, ennui."

Although liberals spend a good deal of time expressing concern for the poor and needy, the fact is that the programs they have implemented have made things worse, not better, and have hurt the very people they were meant to help—and at great cost. The welfare system they have brought forth is self-perpetuating and, far from relieving dependency, it encourages dependency.

As far back as 1963 a study by the management consulting firm of Greenliegh Associates for the Moreland Commission reported that existing policies and procedures lead to *increased* dependency. In addition, a national study at that time of the Federal Aid To Dependent Children program, made by M. Elaine Burgess and Daniel O. Price of the University of North Carolina for the American Public Welfare Association, called for major changes to reduce long-term dependency and prevent the continued development of second-generation dependents. Charles Silberman noted that ". . . one sometimes has the feeling that welfare agencies almost welcome failure, for failure, if repeated frequently enough, only demonstrates the need to expand their services more."

Blacks have been the most vocal opponents of a system designed not to help them to achieve independence and meaningful and constructive positions in society, but to make them almost permanent wards of the state. The Congress of Racial Equality, to cite another example, called for the black community to develop its own commerce and industry. "We seek to harness the creative energy of private enterprise to achieve a solution to America's crisis. Handouts are demeaning. They do violence to a man, strip him of dignity, and breed in him a hatred of the total system." CORE's answer has been a community development program "to draw funds from many sources and promote self-generating growth with the aim in time of ending reliance on the taxpayer."

What do liberals say in response to the clear failure of their programs and to the hostility so vocally expressed by those in the black community who really do seek to make a real contribution to the American society. Their response is not a program to end dependence but, instead, one of a guaranteed annual income that fosters such dependence and brings even more people under its domination. Do such liberals really care about the people they say they want to help? The evidence leads to a contrary conclusion.

Another example of a stated liberal concern for the "working man" or "little man" or whatever phrase is current in describing those in whose name the proponents of government control and domination advance their ever more costly and damaging programs, is that of the minimum wage. Liberals, it must be remembered, are forever urging an increase in the minimum wage, and say they are doing it because of their compassion for those at the bottom of the economic scale. Conservatives have traditionally opposed such legislation, thereby incurring the wrath of liberals for their alleged insensitivity to the "little man" and support for "vested interests." Let us look briefly at the facts in this case.

The legal minimum wage has been pushed up 207 percent between early 1956 and 1976, though average hourly earnings in manufacturing rose only 163 percent. In addition, the federal minimum wage has been expanded to cover many new job categories during this period.

The net result of this, according to economist Henry Hazlitt, "has been to force up the wage rates of unskilled labor much more than those of skilled labor. A result of this, in turn, has been that though an increasing shortage has developed in skilled labor, the proportion of unemployed among the unskilled, among teen-agers, females and non-whites has been growing."

Mr. Hazlitt continues: "The outstanding victim has been the Negro, and particularly the Negro teenager. In 1952, the unemployment rate among white teenagers and non-white teenagers was the same—9 percent. But year by year, as the minimum wage has been jacked higher and higher, a disparity has grown and increased." It should be noted, in this context, that the unemployment rate among white teenagers in June, 1976, was 16.1 percent, while among non-white teenagers it has reached a level of 40.3 percent.

By a minimum wage of, for example, $2.30 an hour we have forbidden anyone to work forty hours a week for less than $92.00. If we offer the same amount, or something somewhat less, in welfare payments we are saying, in effect, that we have forbidden a man to be usefully employed at $85.00 a week, in order that we may support him at either the same amount or something less in idleness. Such an approach deprives society of the value of his services and deprives the individual involved of the independence and self respect that comes from self-support, even at a low level, and from performing wanted work, that might lead to his being trained for a future job at a rate far higher than the minimum wage.

All of us agree that we would like to see American workers earning as much as possible. The way to raise the real earnings of our citizens, however, is not through the legislative process. We cannot, after all, distribute more wealth than is created and labor cannot be paid more than it produces.

Economist Hazlitt expresses this view:
The best way to raise wages . . . is to raise labor productivity. This can be done by many methods: by an increase in capital accumulation, i.e., by an increase in the machines with which the workers are aided; by new inventions and improvements; by more efficient management on the part of employers; by more industriousness

31

and efficiency on the part of the workers; by better education and training. The more the individual worker produces, the more he increases the wealth of the whole community. The more he produces, the more his services are worth to consumers, and hence to employers. And the more he is worth to employers, the more he will be paid. Real wages come out of production, not out of government decrees.

Shortly before Christmas, 1929, Harvard University fired, without notice, Mrs. Katherine Donahue, Mrs. Hannah Hogan, and 18 other scrubwomen in the Widener Library rather than raise their pay from 35 cents to 37 cents an hour as demanded by the Massachusetts Minimum Wage Commission. To avoid paying the extra 2 cents, Harvard replaced the women with men, who were not covered by the state's minimum wage law.

A few years ago, economist Paul Samuelson asked: "What good does it do a black youth to know that an employer must pay him $1.60 per hour if the fact that he must be paid that amount is what keeps him from getting a job?" Economist Milton Friedman refers to the Fair Labor Standards Act of 1938, the base of the minimum wage, as "the most anti-Negro law on our statute books—in its effect, not its intent."

Economists Gene L. Chapin and Douglas K. Adie of Ohio University, in a paper presented before the twenty-third annual meeting of the Industrial Relations Research Association, declare that, "Increases in federal minimum wage cause unemployment among teenagers. The effects tend to persist for considerable periods of time. And the effects seem to be strengthening as coverage is increased and enforcement of the laws become more rigorous."

Although liberals proclaim their concern for the poor, the black, and the downtrodden, the programs they have advocated and legislated into law, such as the minimum wage, have had an opposite effect. Increased unemployment, not a better life, has been the result for the very men and women the liberals so often tell us they seek to provide with better conditions and a more meaningful existence.

Another example of a similar approach by liberals is that of compulsory Social Security which was again put into law to help the poor, the black, and the "underprivileged" members of society.

Slowly, however, those who understand something about the reality of Social Security are coming to the conclusion that its critics have not only been right, but have, in fact, been understating the case against the system. One indication that informed Americans are beginning to understand the dangers of the Social Security system is the fact that 138 cities, counties and local government agencies—including the Metropolitan Washington Council of Governments—have abandoned the Social Security system in the past two years. Another 207 government bodies, most prominently the state of Alaska and the city of New York, have notified the Social Security Administration that they, too, intend to withdraw.

The fact is that Social Security is, and always has been, a fraudulent system. This fact has never been better highlighted than in the book, *Social Security: The Fraud In Your Future* by Warren Shore, former consumer affairs editor of *Chicago Today*.

In its sky-blue booklet, the Social Security system states that, "Nine out of ten working people in the U.S. are now building protection for themselves and their families under the Social Security program." Mr. Shore declares "The great majority of Americans believe that sentence to be true. . . . Believing that sentence is the most expensive single decision most of us will make during our lives. The average American is betting more than $100,000 of his earnings that the booklet is right and he is counting on his children to bet twice that much. But the sentence is not true. . . . The fact is that the American Social Security system is neither insurance nor a contribution."

The Social Security system tells those whom it taxes that their funds go into "special trust funds" from which benefits will be paid. By generally accepted legal definition, a trust is "a legal title to property held by one party (the trustee) for the benefit of another (the beneficiary)."

Mr. Shore writes that: "The truth is there is no trust fund and hasn't been for years. . . . In 1960 the total assets of the Social Security trust funds stood at $22.6 billion which were to insure the benefits of some 67.5 million American workers. By 1966 the working population 'covered' had swelled to 76 million . . . a rise of 12.6 per cent . . . total assets in the funds dropped by more than $300 million during the six year period to $22.3 billion."

Rather than a trust fund existing, the fact is that in 1973, the Social Security system paid out more than the alleged trust fund contained—a negative benefit to reserve ratio of 114 per cent, which would have put any private insurance company out of business long ago. Private insurance companies are regulated by government and are not permitted to conduct business in such an irresponsible manner. At the end of 1973, the total life insurance in force in the U.S. was $1.8 trillion. This was backed by reserves of $208 billion, slightly more than 10 percent. Social Security, on the other hand, has liabilities estimated at $1 trillion but, as of June 30, 1976, has only $48.1 billion in its trust funds. To meet its future obligations, the system is dependent on "contributions" coming in from the current work force.

In order to pay those who have retired even a portion of what they thought they were entitled to, current workers will see their Social Security taxes skyrocket. As it is, payroll taxes have gone up from one percent per worker in 1944 to 5.85 percent per worker today—an increase of 485 percent. In addition, the President has requested another increase of 0.3 percent to go into effect in 1977 and projects still another one percent increase by the year 2011 when the full impact of the post-World War II baby boom will hit the system. However, if the predictions of those who figure the Social Security Trust Fund will be out of money by 1980 or shortly thereafter come true, payroll taxes will have to increase 50-100 percent by the year 2000 just to keep Social Security afloat. Ironically, those most hurt by such an increase are those that can afford it the least—lower and middle income folks.

The question then arises, what do they get for their investment which, for a person earning $15,000 in 1975 came to $1,649.70 (including the employer's contribution)? The Social Security Administration claims that the worker is buying $213,762.20 worth of protection for himself and his family. The trouble, as Mr. Shore points out, is that the value of that protection (the amount of money that would have to be invested now to provide the same level of coverage) is only $107,143 and it could have been achieved by purchasing life insurance in that amount at a cost of only $544.50. Moreover, the survivors of that worker would have far more flexibility in deciding how that life insurance money was to be spent to meet their needs than with Social Security benefits. Furthermore, if the worker does not live until he or she becomes eligible for Social Security benefits and does not have a spouse or children who qualify for benefits, the only return he or his heirs may ever see for

34

all the money invested in the Social Security system is a $255 burial benefit.

Discussing the subterfuge inherent in government statements about Social Security, economist Milton Friedman notes that, "What nine out of ten working people are now doing is paying taxes to finance benefits to persons who are not working. An individual working person is in no sense building his own protection—as a person who contributes to a private pension system is doing. Persons now receiving benefits are receiving much more than the actuarial value of the taxes that were paid on their behalf. Young persons are now being promised much less than the actuarial value of the taxes that were paid on their behalf."

A spokesman for the Illinois Department of Insurance notes that, "If a private insurance company attempted to sell a plan in Illinois which cost so much and paid so little, we would drum them out of the state as frauds."

The authoritarian nature of the system is described this way by Warren Shore: "Perhaps the most single incredible element of Social Security is the Administration's insistence that the program is insurance, while at the same time, basing the entire benefits structure on a handbook of regulations the use of which would land most insurance company officials in jail. The regulations . . . contain more than 500 circumstances under which the government will not pay. . . . A private insurance plan which costs as much as Social Security and contained as many grounds for not paying benefits . . . would not be allowed to stay in business."

The American worker does not "own" the money that has been withheld from him in ever increasing amounts. He may never see a penny of it and his widowed spouse may only get a fraction of it. Because of the built-in inequities, he or she may receive far less than the surviving spouse of someone who has contributed half of what he did.

The Social Security system is not only unfair, but has been misrepresented. Milton Friedman declares that, "People who would not lie to their children . . . have propagated a false view of Social Security." Now is the time to set the record straight—and begin to correct it.

Yet another example of the elitist determination to fasten unwanted and irresponsible programs upon both the "little man" and the vast majority of tax-paying Americans can be found in the efforts of some liberal politicians to secure passage of a nationalized health care package as

35

proposed by Senator Edward M. Kennedy (D-Mass.) and others.

Not only is the analysis of our health care situation in America a sloppily researched misrepresentation of the problems we do have (for example, charges of inferior medical care, high infant mortality rates, general doctor shortages, and so forth), but it does not meet the stated objectives of the sponsors to provide better quality health care at lower cost.

Both objective and subjective studies of government health care (in this country as well as abroad) belie the claim of better quality care, and the cost of health care to the average American under Senator Kennedy's proposal would be more than double the annual health care costs to the average American today.

Finally, the sponsors of this legislation have failed to poll the "little man" to discover his feelings on the subject. But Opinion Research Corp., a highly respected independent polling organization, did just that with 500 adults representing a cross-section of poverty level families in California in May, 1972. The results would startle the champions of national health schemes. Among other findings the study revealed that "little people" from the barrios and ghettoes of southern California with incomes of $0-$350 per month preferred private physicians by a resounding eight-to-one vote. They indicated that private practitioners provided better medical care than public practitioners by a vote of five to one. More than three-fourths of the people who expressed a choice said they would rather use a private hospital.

Welfare, urban renewal, agricultural subsidies, minimum wage laws, compulsory Social Security—these are important elements in the liberal plan to help the downtrodden, to ease poverty, to eliminate racial tensions, and to create a better and more decent society. The only problem is that such programs do not work, are based on a philosophy of government coercion, and make problems worse, not better. Liberal rhetoric may exhibit concern for the "have nots." Liberal programs, however, ensure that they will remain "have nots."

Liberals have long advocated a policy in which government spent more money than it had available, and in which government, through its control of the money supply, issued dollars for which no backing existed. The principal objectives of such policies were to stimulate economic growth and reduce unemployment. But again, we should

36

examine the validity of the premise and analyze the consequences.

In order to pay for expensive and futile liberal programs, government has had to spend far more money than it has received in taxes. The result has been an artificial rise in the cost of everything in society, which is inflation. This has hit hardest those very citizens the liberal theoreticians claim they want to help—the old, the poor, those on fixed incomes, on pensions, those receiving public assistance, and those wage earners on the bottom rung of the economic ladder.

Economist Henry Hazlitt points out:

The poor are usually more heavily taxed by inflation, in percentage terms, than the rich, for they do not have the same means of protecting themselves by speculative purchases of real equities. Inflation is a kind of tax that is out of control of the tax authorities. It strikes wantonly in all directions. The rate of tax imposed by inflation is not a fixed one: it cannot be determined in advance. . . . It discourages prudence and thrift. It encourages squandering, gambling, reckless wastes of all kinds.

Just as liberals hurt the very people they say they want to help with their programs of deficit spending and mounting inflation, the same is true with regard to the allegedly "new" programs they are now advocating—also in the name of the proverbial "little man" or "average American."

In 1972, for example, the Congress passed a bill that, its sponsors told us, will produce clean lakes and rivers all across America. The bill provided a clear-cut timetable: by June 30, 1974, municipal sewage pollution facilities to provide for the equivalent of secondary treatment; by July 1, 1974, construction grants for treatment facilities on a regional, or areawide basis, rather than on a city or town basis as in the past; by January 1, 1976, the best practicable control technology for industrial sources of pollution; by January 1, 1981, the end of water pollution discharges; and by 1985 the elimination of all polluting discharges from all sources into navigable water.

Despite the fact that Administration and industry representatives argued that the setting of these goals and deadlines was unrealistic and could lead to a new undermining of the confidence of the citizens in their government when the expectations were not fulfilled, liberals in the Congress saw to it that this legislation was passed.

Former Environmental Protection Agency Administrator William Ruckelshaus stated that the provision for elimination of all discharges into waterways by 1985 was not technically feasible. The demands made upon American industry may be not only unreasonable, but technologically and economically impossible. Expert testimony indicated the cost of 100 percent clean water by 1985 would be $2.3 trillion, more than the GNP of the entire world!

It is worthy of note that liberals in Congress who are concerned with unemployment and the fact that American industry is becoming less and less competitive in the world market would place such new restrictions and limitations, as well as expenses, upon business, consumers and taxpayers. Economist Paul McCracken warned that the impact of this water legislation could "turn out to be proportionately heavy on industries and products that are important to our foreign trade" and could lead to enlarged structural unemployment, the most difficult to control because it is caused by disappearing markets. The AFL-CIO indicated that the bill could possibly put "millions" of Americans out of work. And even sponsors of the legislation were unsure what impact it would have on other aspects of our environment.

Despite the fact that it is clear that the imposition of government controls and regulations cannot help but feed our inflation, increase our unemployment, and make it certain that we can no longer compete in world markets, liberals tell us that they are supporting such programs because of their concern for the "average American."

Invariably, the "average American" is the one who suffers most from the programs enacted on his behalf and in his name.

There are many liberals in America who now speak repeatedly of an impending crisis in growth and call for a slowing down of the growth rate. They argue, to cite one example, that the burning of fuels by industry is using up the earth's oxygen and that eventually there will not be enough left to sustain human life. But the National Science Foundation recently collected air samples at 78 sites around the world and compared them with samples taken 61 years ago. Result? There is precisely the same amount of oxygen in the air as there was in 1910—2.95 percent.

To the argument set forth by many liberals that our society is becoming overpopulated and that, as a result, some form of compulsory birth control instituted by government to divert a "disaster" is needed, the facts respond. The birth rate in the United States has been dropping continuously since 1955 and is now at the lowest point in history. If the trend continues, it is remotely possible that by the year 4000 there won't be anyone left in the country. But I would not fret about underpopulation either. Populations have a way of adjusting to conditions, and I have no doubt that our birth rate will pick up in due course.

Those liberals who urge a slower growth rate do not make it clear that it is those in whose name they claim to speak —the poor, the residents of the inner city, those receiving public assistance—who will be denied the fruits of an affluent and growing society were such a policy instituted. It is the height of cynicism to tell society to freeze itself at its present level and say that this policy is being advanced in the name of those who would be frozen at the very bottom, those who, under a growing economy, can look forward to a higher standard of living, and a better life.

Commenting upon this specious liberal call for a slowdown in our growth rate, Professor Henry C. Wallich of the Department of Economics at Yale University noted, "The ecologists do not seem to be aware of what it would mean to freeze total income anywhere near today's level. Do they mean that the present income distribution is to be preserved, with the poor frozen into their inadequacies? Would that go for underdeveloped countries too? Or do they have in mind equalization of incomes?"

Professor Wallich declares:

It will take pretty drastic cuts in upper-income bracket standards to bring them down to the average American family income of about $10,000, to say nothing of a cut to average world income. . . . The ecologists also do not seem to be aware of what their prescriptions, contrary to their wishes, might do to the environment. If growth came to a halt, it is obvious that every last penny of public and private income would be drawn upon to provide minimal consumer satisfactions. There would be very little left for the cleaning-up job that needs to be done. Growth is the main source from which that job must be financed.

Liberals have been accused of a blatant double standard with regard to the race question, a question upon which they have been very vocal for some time. Liberals advocate a policy that compels a man to join a labor union, even if he does not wish to join it, before he may hold a job. The labor union, which liberals support and by which they are supported, has in turn discriminated against blacks in hiring.

Discussing this question Charles Silberman observes:

39

The trade union movement . . . is the worst offender . . . the railroad and building trades unions have been guilty of discrimination; Walter Reuther's United Auto Workers . . . didn't abolish separate seniority systems for Negro and white workers in southern factories until a few years ago. And none of the liberal unions have made any real effort to develop Negro leadership; trade union leaders are no more willing than businessmen or politicians to share any of the power they now enjoy.

The fact is that while liberals speak of their compassion, concern, and solicitude for black Americans, for the poor, and the underprivileged, they are pursuing policies that are detrimental to each of these groups. The real crisis our country faces is not of the things so often discussed by the liberal intellectual establishment. The real crisis may be the loss of freedom that is brought upon us by those whose answer to every problem in society is higher taxes, new regulations, and additional government control of and involvement in our lives.

It is ironical, indeed, that those who demand freedom in other areas of their lives care little about economic freedom, a freedom that has made available to the average American luxuries that a short time ago were beyond the reach of the wealthiest of men.

Conservatives, if you examine the facts, are not really associated with the negative terms such as "champions of privilege, vested interest, selfishness, and unconcern for the little man." Instead, conservatives have learned from history that there is no way to increase our standard of living, improve our competitive standing in world markets, ease the problems of unemployment, defeat inflation, help the average American, and give consumers the choice they desire except by taking government out of the economy, not giving it control over the totality of our lives.

The liberal programs have been tried ever since the New Deal. As you can see, they have failed. Liberal theoreticians have admitted their failures. The liberal's heart may bleed, but his programs do not heal. Whatever the intentions of their advocates, such programs have harmed the average American, not helped him.

It is time to rethink the real meaning of what is a liberal and what is a conservative. I am confident that any real examination of the question will lead to conclusions far different from those we have witnessed in the recent past.

40

Affirmative Action—Well Intentioned but Misguided

In many different areas of American life our traditional idea of individualism—of each man going as far as his ability and hard work will take him—is under attack. Instead of urging that past inequities be eliminated by providing all Americans, regardless of race, ethnic origin, or economic status, through equal opportunity to fulfill their own unique destinies, we are now confronting a far different challenge.

We are confronting a call for special privileges for some, such as blacks and women, who are members of groups that, in the past, have suffered special discrimination. Those who urge such special treatment, often called "affirmative action," are undoubtedly well-intentioned. They desire to provide equality of opportunity in the long run by giving special privileges to some in the short run. What they fail to understand is that the policies they are advancing may do so much damage in the short run that the long run will never be reached.

In no area of our society is the call for special and unequal treament more damaging than in our schools, colleges, and universities. As a former college teacher and headmaster of a private school, I have a particular interest and concern for what is happening to American education. It is my belief that current trends, if not reversed, will not only do irreparable harm to American education but will, in addition, do serious damage to the very groups in whose name such policies are being implemented.

Education is only one target of what may be called the quota-system mentality that has emerged in many intellectual and political circles. Our society seems to be rushing with all of its energy toward an institutional quota system that judges individuals not on the basis of their unique worth and merit but, instead, on the basis of which group they belong to. Such groups may be racial, religious, ethnic,

41

or sexual depending upon the prejudices the particular quota system is meant either to foster or combat. It is especially ironic that one finds it increasingly difficult to tell the difference between a quota meant to fight discrimination and one meant to do the opposite. Likewise, it is also ironic to note that the Nixon Administration, under whose auspices the quota-system mentality was institutionalized as a result of pressure from various bureaucrats, stated repeatedly that it was against quotas.

Speaking to the nation on Labor Day, 1972, President Nixon declared that, "In employment and in politics, we are confronted with the rise of the fixed quota system—as artificial and unfair a yardstick as has ever been used to deny opportunity to anyone." While President Nixon made a clear and unequivocal statement against quotas, his own appointees were eagerly pursuing precisely the opposite policies. The Department of Health, Education and Welfare (HEW), for example, set forth guidelines for eligibility for federal funds which virtually oblige colleges to set up quota systems for the hiring of women and "minority group members." Universities have now hired special staff members to enforce the quota system. The University of California calls its officer the "Affirmative Action Coordinator."

The policy President Nixon said he did not support, and which Congress has certainly never written into the law (Congress has written the opposite into the Civil Rights Act of 1964, forbidding discrimination on the basis of race, sex, or creed), has been implemented with a ferocity rarely seen in Washington by bureaucrats who are intent upon proving that conservatives knew what they were talking about when they said that government money is always accompanied by government controls.

The whole concept of quotas is a rejection of our traditional commitment to individualism and individual freedom. Furthermore, the system raises more barriers than it eliminates. It is patronizing and degrading. Discussing this question, Milton Himmelfarb, writing in *Commentary*, voiced this opinion: "Equality and justice used to mean No Discrimination (against individuals). Now they tend to mean Fair Shares (for groups). How does one assure Fair Shares? By legislating proportionality or quotas."

Even nongovernmental organizations have begun to follow the growing trend of imposing quotas. One of these is the National Education Association (NEA), which hopes eventually to control American schools and teachers. It is difficult to believe that this organization and its members can teach such concepts as equality of opportunity to students if it does not practice equality of opportunity itself. In the summer of 1973, the NEA adopted a Constitution and By-Laws that held, "There shall be a minimum of twenty per cent ethnic-minority representation on each committee." Their constitution also stipulates, "If after eleven years no member of an ethnic-minority group has served as President, nominations at the subsequent Representative Assembly shall be restricted to members of such groups."

Who is a member of a "minority?" Lest anything be left to the imagination, or to individual judgment, the NEA constitution specifies that the term "minorities" shall include "Black, Mexican-American (Chicano) and other Spanish-speaking groups, Oriental and Indian." The director of the NEA's teacher rights program, Samuel Ethridge, declares that more than 210,000 more minority group educators must be hired by the nation's public schools in order to "bring about equity and parity" for minorities.

The NEA, seeking to represent teachers in undemocratic closed-shop arrangements, has itself become an organization that has turned its back upon traditional American ideas of judging each individual upon his or her own merits—regardless of race, creed, or ethnic origin. This should be some indication of the deep trouble we are in, for when teachers don't know the difference between judging individual merit and insisting upon group indentification and membership, we know that collectivism, and not individualism, has taken over.

Speaking to the 1972 Republican convention in Miami Beach, President Nixon declared, "The way to end discrimination against some is not to begin discrimination against others." George McGovern was defeated in 1972 at least in part because Americans were repelled by the kind of society he promised, including racial and sexual quota systems. Unfortunately, this kind of society seems nevertheless to be emerging. Clearly, something has gone wrong.

Few understand how the program of "affirmative action" in faculty hiring really began. The Office of Civil Rights derives its claim to authority in affirmative action matters via the Department of HEW from the Department of Labor which, in turn, bases its authority on Executive Order 11246, signed by President Lyndon Johnson in 1965 pursuant to the Civil Rights Act of 1964.

Discussing the unusual origins of this program, Dr. George

Roche III, President of Hillsdale College, stated, "There are good reasons for doubting that President Johnson or anyone else concerned with the original civil rights legislation and its implementation anticipated the extent to which middle-echelon bureaucrats could pervert antidiscrimination legislation into discriminatory programs. Yet this is exactly what has occurred."

Though the final draft of the 1964 Civil Rights Act did not mention the phrase, "affirmative action," it continued to find its way into discussions of tactics to enforce the legislation. "It was suggested," as Dr. Roche points out in his important book, *The Balancing Act*, "that overall racial proportions should be used as evidence measuring intent and performance by institutions covered by the Civil Rights Act. Presumably such 'evidence' would allow the enforcing federal officials to bypass the slow process of individual court cases. . . ."

When President Johnson issued his 1967 executive order calling for affirmative action to eliminate employment discrimination among federal contractors the order's original nondiscriminatory intent was changed into a weapon to enforce discriminatory hiring. Percentage hiring goals, first imposed upon the construction industry in the "Philadelphia Plan" and the "Long Island Plan," spread quickly to racial and sexual quotas for other industrial hiring. This has rapidly spread to all universities that receive or apply for any form of federal assistance.

Recently, Dr. Roche has written, "Complicated surveys examining the ethnic backgrounds of faculty members are being undertaken. Announcements of job openings appearing in professional circles openly mention specific racial, sexual or ethnic 'qualifications' for employment. De facto discrimination is now commonplace."

Consider several examples. A letter sent from Claremont Men's College in California, declaring that it "has a vacancy in [a] Department as a result of retirement," stipulates, "We desire to appoint a black or Chicano, preferably female." Or another letter from the Department of Philosophy at the University of Washington stating that it "is seeking qualified women and minority candidates for faculty positions at all levels." Instead of ending discrimination based on race, sex, or ethnic background, Dr. Roche charges that, "Affirmative action now began enforcement on the basis of race and sex which had been expressly forbidden by the Civil Rights Act."

44

In fact, HEW was asking universities to keep the very racial and sexual statistics that were in many instances forbidden by state antidiscrimination laws. As a result, the Office of Civil Rights has forced a number of schools into such bizarre antics as judging racial or ethnic origin by analyzing the name or physical appearance of a professor. For this reason, there has been great emphasis on "candidates with Spanish and Indian surnames," "visual surveys" of faculty, and similar unusual and unorthodox means of analyzing a collegiate teaching staff.

When federal aid to education was first instituted, critics charged that it would inevitably lead to governmental control of the schools. This has now occurred. Elie Abel, Dean of the Columbia Graduate School of Journalism, states that, "We can't, in essence, hire, promote, or give a raise to anyone without clearing it over there (HEW). Are they really trying to tell us we cannot promote our own assistant professors without setting up a nationwide search?"

In *The Balancing Act*, George Roche charges that the philosophy inherent in the affirmative action approach is one that challenges our traditional concept of judging each individual on his or her own merits. "At the heart of this matter," he writes, "lies a fundamental question concerning group rights vs. individual rights. The HEW directives which now attempt enforcement of group proportional rights are pushing toward a major change in this nation's traditional conception of equality and opportunity."

What will be the effect upon higher education of the affirmative action program? There is little evidence that it will be good. Quality and quotas do not go together. For example, in the assault upon academic quality that necessarily accompanies the imposition of minority quotas, the Jewish community has a great deal to lose because of its high concentration of students and professors in higher education. Jews make up some 3 percent of the general population, but a far higher percentage of the academy, including many of its most highly qualified members.

Discussing the affirmative action program, one Jewish organization produced this tongue-in-cheek comment: "Jews come from athletically deprived backgrounds. Irving is kept off the sandlot by too much homework and too many music lessons. He is now 25 and still can't play ball, but he 'has the desire to learn.' Therefore, we are demanding that New York City which has a 24 per cent Jewish population, fill the city's ball teams with 24 per cent Jews."

45

The fact is that a racial quota system is highly detrimental to those among the "protected classes." What quotas and special privileges are saying, in effect, is that the minority group member does not have what it takes to be successful and that, therefore, he must be given what he is unqualified to earn. Under such a situation, even the minority group member who earns his competence will be undermined. The suspicion will be ever present in his mind, and the minds of others, that his success may be due to special privilege rather than talent and hard work. No one should resent this aspect of affirmative action more than the qualified minority member himself.

Discussing the harm done to minority group students and faculty members, black economist Thomas Sowell, a member of the faculty at UCLA, states:

Despite all the brave talk in academia about "affirmative action" without lowering quality standards, you and I both know that it takes many years to create a qualified faculty member of any color, and no increased demand is going to increase the supply unless you lower quality. Now what good is going to come from lower standards that will make "black" equivalent to substandard in the eyes of black and white students alike?"

Dr. Sowell then asks:

Can you imagine that this is going to *reduce* racism? On the contrary, more and more thoughtful people are beginning to worry that the next generation will see an increasing amount of bigotry among those whites educated at some of the most liberal institutions, where this is the picture that is presented to them, however noble the rhetoric that accompanies it.

Faculty members throughout the country have been vocal in expressing their opposition to the affirmative action program. In December 1974 several dozen prominent university profesors signed a letter to President Ford opposing affirmative action. "The evidence of the ineffectiveness and injustice of the quota programs is by now overwhelming," the letter states. "We call on you to end the numbers games played by Government administrators."

Among the 74 signers of the letter are three Nobel laureates —Sir John Eccles, Distinguished Professor of Physiology at the State University of New York at Buffalo; Robert S. Mulliken, Distinguished Service Professor of Physics and Chemistry at the University of Chicago; and Eugene P. Wigner, professor of physics at Rockefeller University—plus

Sidney Hook, professor emeritus of philosophy at New York University and a leading critic of affirmative action. Their letter declares that, "We are deeply concerned at the relentless continuation of unjust and discriminatory quota programs which are imposed on every college and university in America with federal contracts. That these programs, imposed in gross defiance of the Civil Rights Act of 1964 and Executive Order 11246, not to mention the explicit campaign promises of both parties in 1972, have been established in the name of 'affirmative action' in no way mitigates the evil they accomplish."

Among the other signers of the letter are the distinguished historian and Librarian of Congress, Daniel Boorstin; Cleanth Brooks of Yale, Loren Eiseley of the University of Pennsylvania, Milton Friedman of the University of Chicago, Oscar Handlin of Harvard, Gertrude Himmelfarb of Brooklyn College, Fritze Machlup of New York University, Paul Seabury of the University of California at Berkeley, and Thomas Sowell of the University of California at Los Angeles.

During August and September 1974 the Special Subcommittee on Education of the House Education and Labor Committee held hearings that probed into the entire area of anti-bias regulation of postsecondary education. The hearings opened on August 8 with a statement by Congressman James G. O'Hara (D-Mich.), Chairman of the Subcommittee, who declared that there was no such thing as "reverse" discrimination, but only discrimination—whoever the victim and whatever the cause.

Peter Holmes, Director of the Office for Civil Rights (OCR) of the Department of HEW and Dr. Mary Lepper, Director of the Higher Education Division within OCR, outlined and defended the existing programs. According to Holmes, preferential hiring is illegal, and goals are merely targets at which good faith efforts are meant to arrive. However, when testimony by university officials was presented, differing views previously aired only in private, began to emerge.

Robert Stith, a lawyer who has represented Columbia University, sharply criticized the HEW policy whereby any regional official can terminate federal funding for a university merely by putting through a telephone call. He asked for hearings at which the university could defend itself before any withholding of funds. He also pointed out the folly of requiring arbitration and adjudication of grievances by a university when there was no corresponding requirement for plaintiffs to use the mechanisms provided. President Robben Fleming of the University of Michigan testified as to the "astonishingly" great cost in time and money of compiling vast statistical data to determine "availability" figures in the service of essentially fictional goals. He said: "When the whole procedure is a form of punishment which is disguised to produce better conduct in the future, it is hard to see what really useful purpose it is serving. Meanwhile, it is imposing an enormous burden on universities. Surely a far simpler system could be devised which could be at least as effective, and I am confident that the academic associations would join in a cooperative effort to devise such a system."

Such a streamlined set of regulations would, in his opinion, do away with the existing "multiple jurisdiction monstrosity." Dr. Fleming concluded, "To impose a statistical measure of success or failure [on affirmative action programs] is, I think, both unworkable and counterproductive."

As the hearings continued, President James Hester of New York University questioned the procedural practices of various federal agencies: "Periodically investigators from the Department of Labor will appear, as they have for more than a year now, to ask far-ranging questions in wages and hours pertaining to possible sex discrimination without indicating whether specific charges have been made against us."

Dr. Hester also pointed out that of the 43 complaints of discrimination brought in the last six years against New York University, nine were still pending and 34 had been either dismissed or withdrawn. With regard to goals and timetables, Dr. Hester argued that if they were actually going to be enforced, "it would be disastrous." President Fleming contributed the information that affirmative action plans often hang in limbo. To his knowledge, no one "in the Chicago area has ever heard" whether or not proposed plans were approved.

After reviewing the testimony heard before his committee, Congressman O'Hara presented his own thoughtful assessment in a speech given to the American Council on Education on October 9, 1974:

I think the university, not for itself alone, but for all of the society in which it lives, must gently but firmly reassert the proposition that sex, race, color, national origin, and creed are completely irrelevant to job qualifications, and that the way to end the practice of taking them into account is to end it—not simply to look for a new set of victims.

To those who ask how results are to be measured without something approximating quotas, Congressman O'Hara replies:

The law does not mandate that 51 percent of the faculty or administrative staff shall be women, or that 14 percent shall be black, or 5 percent of Spanish-speaking ancestry, any more than it mandates that 49 percent must be men, or 86 percent shall not be black. The law does not, in short, mandate results. It mandates that discriminatory practices be avoided. It does not mandate "proportionate representation," but it does mandate an end to giving preference to one sex or one race over another without regard for motives. And more than incidentally, the law does not specify which race or which sex may not be given preference, it says unequivocally that none can be.

The fact is that discrimination on the basis of race, religion, sex, and age has occurred in the past, both in the university and in other areas of our national life. That discrimination has always been immoral and has flown in the face of our philosphy of judging each man and woman on the basis of individual talents and merits. It represents a collectivistic categorization of individuals, something a free society enters into only at great peril.

Whereas such discrimination has always been immoral, through enactment of the 1964 Civil Rights Act, it is now illegal as well. The law mandates that each individual must be judged on the basis of individual merits and demerits, not on the arbitrary basis of race, sex, age, religion, or national origin. Those empowered to enforce this law, however, have interpreted it to mean its opposite. What they have been doing is not enforcing the law passed by the elected representatives of the people in the Congress but, quite to the contrary, have been making a new law of their own.

The moral basis of legislating through bureaucratic fiat is highly questionable. It is unquestionably a perversion of the concept of self-government. What is the real remedy for the discrimination of the past? Surely it cannot be new discrimination in the present. Discussing this question, Professor Sidney Hook, writing in *The New York Times* of November 12, 1974, states:

No one would argue that because many years ago blacks were deprived of their right to vote and women denied

49

the franchise that today blacks and women should be compensated for past discrimination by being given the right to cast an extra vote or two at the expense of their fellow citizens or that some white men should be barred from voting.

Discussing what he believed to be a more relevant case, Dr. Hook made the following important point:

For years, blacks were disgracefully barred from professional sports. Would it not be absurd to argue that today in compensation for the past there should be discrimination against whites? All that black players want is to be judged as players, not blacks. Would any fair and sensible person try to fix the ratio of whites and blacks on our ball teams in relation to their racial availability? . . . Why should it be any different when we are seeking the best qualified mathematician to teach topology or the best medieval philosophy scholar? Why not drop all color, sex and religious bars in honest quest for the best qualified for any post—no matter what the distribution turns out to be?

What Dr. Hook believes to be sensible is precisely what the Congress wrote into the 1964 law, simply an end to all discrimination based on race, age, sex, national origin, or creed. It is an unfortunate example of the manner in which nonelected bureaucrats have assumed the law-making function by "interpreting" the clear word of the law to mean its opposite while in the process of allegedly "implementing" the Congressional statute.

This new racial discrimination has been imposed upon universities not only with regard to faculty hiring but also in the area of student admission.

In 1973 the U.S. Supreme Court agreed to consider one of the many challenges to the reverse racism being imposed by so many university admissions departments. The challenge came from a white graduate of the University of Washington, Marco DeFunis, Jr. In 1969, when he was a senior at the university with a near-A average and on his way to a B.A. degree magna cum laude, he applied to the law school. He was rejected. He discovered that 39 other applicants, all members of racial minorities with Law School Aptitude Test Scores lower than his, had been admitted under the school's program to expanded minority enrollment.

DeFunis charged discrimination, contending that the law school had two sets of admission standards and that he thus was deprived of equal protection of the laws guaranteed by the 14th Amendment.

The university conceded that it applied the quota system to achieve a "more balanced" student body. It claimed that the law school had the right to decide whether its overall quality would be improved by a larger percentage of minority students. It admitted that it had one admission standard for whites and another for minorities.

The Washington Superior Court ruled for DeFunis and he was admitted to the law school. The university appealed to the State Supreme Court, which reversed the decision, ruling that the law school had a right to consider race as a special factor in admitting minority students. Since DeFunis was permitted to remain in law school while his case was appealed to the Supreme Court, by 1973, when the Supreme Court agreed to hear it, DeFunis had already graduated. On the narrow legalistic ground that the particular case of Marco DeFunis was now resolved, the Court did not make any substantive decision. Thus, reverse racism in university admissions continues, and the constitutionality of this practice remains unresolved.

What we do know at this time is that the dropout rate and other failures among minority students admitted under "special circumstances" has been much higher than normal. Professor Millard H. Ruud, executive director of the Association of American Law Schools, notes that such students, admitted despite their lack of qualification, know they have been admitted under special dispensations, and this hurts their egos and sometimes leads to an expectation of failure.

An attorney for the Anti-Defamation League of B'nai B'rith has argued that discrimination in favor of minorities clearly remains discrimination. He calls it "the reverse of the classic discrimination and unlike the victims of the old type of discrimination, the victims of reverse discrimination do not have access to redress from the regular civil rights groups."

The practice of reverse racism, as many of its supporters forget, is also patronizing to black students, implying that they are unable to meet normal entrance standards. While white liberals enjoy basking in this paternalism, black scholars resent it.

In his book, *Black Education: Myths and Tragedies*, Dr. Thomas Sowell argues against all policies of open admission. He writes: "A different kind of black student is now

51

attending white colleges, selected by different kinds of criteria and expected to play different kinds of roles on campus."

According to the new criteria, moderate and qualified black students are rejected as "middle class" while recruiters comb the inner cities in search of students with "native ability" and the ability to present the "black viewpoint" on campus. Dr. Sowell argues, "It is this philosophy which leads to the educational failures which are either covered up or attributed to cultural deprivation."

The serious attack upon the integrity of the university that is inherent in the "open admissions" program may be observed in the case of the experience of the City University of New York. When the policy of open admission—which would guarantee a place for any New York City high school graduate at the City University of New York regardless of grades, test scores, or other traditional criteria —was first instituted, many expressed the view that it was doomed to failure.

At a time when New York high schools graduate many young men and women who are unable to read and write at college level, it seemed highly unlikely that those who could not meet the traditional entrance requirements for the City University would succeed in that institution. Now, some results are in. Those who doubted the success of open admission have clearly been proven correct. As a whole, the University now has a retention rate of 52.4 percent, a figure that university officials believe is substantially lower than existed under the former selective-admission policy, when perhaps 70 percent of the entering students completed college. Furthermore, a study entitled "Student Retention and Graduation at City University of New York: September 1970 Enrollees Through Seven Semesters," by Professor David E. Lavin of Lehman College, shows that only 36.3 percent of the 5,940 students who entered the university with high school averages under 70 were still enrolled three and one-half years later. In addition, a greater percentage of City College students got low marks in 1972, after open admissions, than in 1967. The report also confirmed the finding of an earlier study by the university, based on the first two years of open admissions. That study found that the higher a student's high school average the more likely he was to remain in college. Among students with a high school average of 80 or more, 68.3 percent were enrolled in the seventh semester or had received a two-year degree. The figure was 52.4 percent for students with high school averages of 75 to 79.9 and 43.4 percent for those with averages below 70.

Of the constituent colleges in the New York City University system, John Jay College had the worst senior-college retention rate after seven semesters: 39.3 percent. It also received the largest group of underprepared students of any of the four-year colleges.

The lesson emanating out of these figures seems obvious. Young people who failed to master their subjects in high school can hardly be fit for a real university. New York's "open admission" plan provides ample evidence of this fact.

Finally, after much discussion, debate, and outrage on the part of college professors and administrators, the bureaucrats at the Department of HEW appear to be reconsidering the affirmative action program which was, of course, their own creation—in no way established or sanctioned by law. On December 13, 1974, a memorandum was sent to 2,800 college presidents by Peter E. Holmes, director of the HEW Office of Civil Rights. It stated that in all cases the most qualified applicant for any job is the one that should be hired and it warned colleges and universities that it is illegal to give preferential hiring treatment to women and minorities in trying to implement affirmative action programs.

At a press conference Holmes said that there had been "widespread misinterpretation" of the guidelines issued to implement the executive order requiring colleges to take affirmative action to hire and promote women and minorities. "The impression has been that the federal government requires the lowering of standards to meet certain goals," Holmes said, adding that "there have been examples of misinterpretation of the goals on the part of our own people."

The latest HEW memorandum makes clear that in no case should a less-qualified woman or member of a minority group be hired over a more fully qualified white male. Mr. Holmes said, however, that the executive order does require universities to make good faith efforts to see to it that women and minorities are included in their recruitment pools in proportion to their availability in any particular field. The memorandum also makes clear that, "colleges and universities, not the federal government, determine what constitutes qualification for any particular position."

It is unusual that, at the very moment when HEW has seen fit to make clear that it does not support racial and sexual quotas, Mr. Holmes also noted that there is nothing in the December 1974 memorandum which contradicts the guidelines issued in October 1972. He said only that because of "misinterpretations" and after complaints that the government was forcing promotion and hiring of women and minority members over better qualified white males that it was necessary to clarify that policy.

It is difficult to tell what all of this means. Obviously the criticism of distinguished academicians and others has had an effect, but the fact remains that nonelected government administrators did seek to enforce racial and sexual quotas in faculty hiring in violation of the law, and this policy continues. Whether the December 1974 memorandum will change that policy remains to be seen.

Certainly the effect of the "affirmative action" mandate is not restricted to education as the labor-management field clearly demonstrates. Contrary to the time-tested legal maxim, "innocent until proven guilty," a 158-page booklet published by the Equal Employment Opportunity Commission (EEOC), *Affirmative Action and Equal Employment*, warns businessmen that: "If a statistical survey shows that minorities and females are not participating in your work force at all levels in reasonable relations to their presence in the population, the burden of proof is on you to show that this is not the result of discrimination, however inadvertent."

Despite a variety of statements to the effect that goals do not mean quotas and that affirmative action does not mean hiring a less competent or an incompetent person when a competent one is available, the practical effect of such a warning has become obvious. Business firms, just like the universities, have been bending over backwards to avoid being dragged into court, or worse yet, losing a court case.

And who can blame them after looking at what has happened to AT&T, the steel industry, and many smaller firms. In the last three years AT&T has had to pay out some $75 million as a result of disagreements with the EEOC and just last year nine steel companies, along with the United Steelworkers Union, agreed to a settlement with the government that will cost them upwards of $60 million.

As a consequence of these settlements, AT&T now gives its equal employment officer a budget of $0.5 million a year and reportedly spends an additional $3 million a year to collect the data necessary to file the required progress reports with the EEOC. Moreover, AT&T is not alone;

Pfizer Inc. spends over $1 million annually just to fill out the required forms, a figure many other firms reportedly match.

Another aspect of the problem is the cost of contesting a job discrimination case. Celanese Corp. for example had two suits filed against it by employees and its legal fees were estimated to be anywhere from $100,000 to $300,000. Moreover, if a company loses, the costs can be astronomical, with back pay awards running into the millions of dollars. It is little wonder that equal employment consulting firms have sprung up and are getting fees from $10,000 to $100,000 just to keep their clients out of trouble.

Who is hurt most by these suits? Ironically, those who collect in these cases are likely to be hurt by them in the long run. Fear of future suits is tying up large amounts of capital that business might otherwise use for plant expansion, which could, in turn, produce badly needed jobs in these difficult economic times. But in view of the situation company managers cannot afford to take any chances, so hiring and promotion programs are being altered to fit the existing circumstances.

For instance, one firm, according to the August 2, 1974, issue of *The Wall Street Journal*, has begun tying a manager's annual bonus to his success in implementing equal employment programs. In one instance, a manager was docked $15,000 as a result of "poor performance in the EEO area" and "an incredible change took place in that company." No doubt it did, but one has to wonder how many white males were hired afterwards, regardless of how well qualified they were.

This is the problem. Companies, or their employees, faced with financial threats to either themselves or their firms are not going to take chances, given the virtually unlimited resources of the federal government. They are likely to discriminate in reverse rather than hire on merit and be charged with outright discrimination.

Evidence that reverse discrimination is becoming increasingly prevalent can be seen as some of the victims begin to fight back. In January 1975, for instance, the New York State Division of Human Rights overturned the appointment of a female high school principal from Puerto Rico and ordered her replaced by a white New Yorker on the grounds that the latter was far better qualified.

Likewise, the New York Supreme Court recently ruled in favor of seven white men who claimed they were better qualified than three Latinos previously hired by the Suffolk County (N.Y.) police department.

Along the same lines, the Virginia State Legislature, in response to a controversial Fairfax County (Va.) policy of hiring minority group members for their police force in order to reach a certain quota, nearly passed a bill outlawing the use of quota hiring systems. What made this situation particularly interesting is the fact that the Fairfax County quota for minorities on its police force was set at 28.2 percent, equal to the percentage of blacks, American Indians, and Spanish Americans in the Washington Metropolitan Area, even though those same minorities represent only 6 percent of the population of Fairfax County.

Yet another example took place in San Francisco several years ago. In this instance, the Civil Service Commission became disturbed by the San Francisco Fire Department's policy of hiring one black for every four whites, regardless of qualifications. The result was an effort to clarify the definition of affirmative action so as to differentiate it more successfully from quotas. However, the futility and failure of that effort can clearly be seen in the decision of the San Francisco school board to award preference points on the basis of race. Not surprisingly, when a layoff became necessary, the twenty teachers to lose their jobs were all white.

The problem therefore becomes one of recognizing and applying to all situations involving discrimination the old proverb that two wrongs do not make a right. Make no mistake about it. Discrimination is wrong, and using it to remedy its previous use does not make things any better. As columnist Jenkins Lloyd Jones has pointed out, there is no reason for whites to like being discriminated against any more than blacks did.

But many in our society are not willing to accept this point of view. Nowhere is this more evident than in our political party structure where the battle over quotas is being fought as intensely as it is in the fields of education and employment.

The Democratic Party is now seriously divided over the question of racial, sexual, and ethnic quotas. In August 1974, at a Kansas City meeting of the Democratic Charter Commission that was established to write the party's first constitution outlining rules and procedures, far-left elements walked out of the meeting, accusing their opponents of attempting to eliminate hard-won "reforms" designed to "broaden participation."

The confrontation, which was not fully resolved at the Democrats' Mini-Convention held in December 1974, is between two basic groups: 1) The "regulars," consisting mainly of office-holders, labor political strategists, and, in most cases, Party Chairman Robert Strauss. Many in this group believe that the followers of Senator George McGovern "stole" their party from them in 1972 by changing the party's ground rules, and they remain determined to regain control; and 2) The "reformers" and advocates of a "new politics," consisting of former McGovern supporters, including many minorities, women, and leftist labor unions such as the United Auto Workers and the Communications Workers. Many in this group charge that the "old guard" wants to turn the party back to a "closed clique."

The real battle centered on delegate selection to the conventions that selected the 1976 presidential candidates. Democrats in 1972 required quotas—euphemistically called "affirmative action"—by state and local party organizations in seeking to ensure that minorities, women, and youth were adequately represented at conventions.

One reason the Democrats lost in a landslide in 1972 seems to be that the party was not representative of the wishes of the majority of Americans and was not even representative of the wishes of the majority of Democrats. According to a study of the 1972 presidential nominating conventions by Professor Jeane Kirkpatrick of Georgetown University, political parties can be highly unrepresentative of their own rank and file in ideas and values. By matching delegates' views on a series of key political issues against the views of party members in general, as measured by national opinion surveys, written questionnaires, and interviews, Dr. Kirkpatrick found, further, that while 1972 Democratic convention delegates were unrepresentative of Democrats in general, McGovern delegates were more so. Republican delegates unaffected by quotas for age, sex, and race were closer to the attitudes of Democratic voters than Democratic delegates.

The first opinion survey, made in December 1971 by International Research Associates, took place before the nominating conventions and comprised personal interviews with 2,014 probable voters. A second study of voters, also by face-to-face interview, was made in 1972 after the conventions under the auspices of the University of Michigan's

Center for Political Studies. To complete her study, Dr. Kirkpatrick compared the attitudes of party convention delegates and party members at large in five issue areas: welfare, busing, crime, foreign policy, and the economy. In all five, Democratic convention delegates differed more from rank-and-file opinion than Republican delegates did, and McGovern delegates differed most of all from party mainstream thinking.

On school busing, 82 percent of all Democrats said no. But among all convention delegates, 66 percent said yes and among McGovern delegates, 87 percent said yes. Half of all Democrats took positions favoring law and order over protection of the accused. Yet 78 percent of convention delegates and 95 percent of the McGovern delegates took the opposite position. Moreover, Republican delegates and rank-and-file Democrats had similar scores—with 56 percent of the GOP delegates on the law and order side.

The whole idea of racial, ethnic, and sexual quotas is inimical to a free society in which individuals are to be judged on their own merits. By pursuing the path of quotas, the Democratic Party made itself representative of a small, far-left fringe, not of the majority of Americans of either party.

At its December 1974 meeting in Kansas City, the Democratic Party expressed rhetorical opposition to the concept of quotas, but they made few substantive changes. Discussing the results of this meeting, columnists Rowland Evans and Robert Novak, writing in the *Washington Post* of December 11, 1974, noted that "Reassurances and claims by party leaders cannot erase the reality of the midterm convention: the retreat of the Democratic governors under threat of a black walkout raises the specter of racial quotas at the 1976 convention."

Prior to the Kansas City meeting, the Democrats, at a meeting at Hilton Head, South Carolina, reached a compromise that eliminated the system of racial quotas. In Kansas City the advocates of racial quotas rejected that compromise. While rejecting "mandatory quotas," the meeting endorsed "affirmative action." If a state party is accused of discrimination in forming its convention delegation, the state party's performance under the "affirmative action" program will be considered "relevant" evidence.

The compromise language adopted in South Carolina held that the composition of a state delegation "shall not constitute *prima facie* evidence of discrimination, nor shall it shift the burden of proof to the challenged party." This section was deleted at Kansas City.

Discussing the meaning of this deletion, columnist George Will, writing in the *Washington Post* of December 13, 1974, states:

By deleting that language the Democrats demonstrated that today, as in 1972, they think an "unreasonable" racial, sexual or age composition of a state delegation should be considered prima facie evidence that the state party is guilty of discrimination. And the burden should be on the state party to prove that it is not guilty. If, in 1972, the Democrats had a quota system, then they have not gotten rid of it. The distinction between what they had then and what they have now is another distinction without a difference.

Unfortunately, the quota-system mentality is far advanced in the American society. If Democrats see fit to inflict it upon the internal organization of their own party, now that they have an overwhelming majority in both houses of the Congress there is great danger that they will seek to inflict it upon many other areas of the American society. Beyond this, Republican officials, under the Nixon Administration, spoke vocally against racial, sexual and ethnic quotas but imposed them nevertheless. Both Democrats and Republicans alike proclaim their opposition to quotas. Yet quotas are being imposed upon universities, construction sites, political party delegate selections, and a host of other aspects of our national life. We persist in speaking in euphemisms rather than in clearly defined terms. We say we are against quotas, yet quotas are aggressively advancing in our society under different labels.

Today men and women advance political arguments not in a substantive way, but by using the terms which have become the "god words" of our age. (According to Professor Richard Weaver these are "expressions about which all other expressions are ranked as subordinate and serving dominations and powers.") One of these "god words" is "progressive." How many times have we heard a program supported not because it was good or bad, right or wrong, productive or unproductive, but because it was "progressive?"

Still another term used to support programs which have little reason to command public enthusiasm—such as arbitrarily imposed quotas—is that such programs are "modern." Professor Weaver states that:

Where progress is real, there is a natural presumption that

59

the latest will be the best. Hence, it is generally thought that to describe anything as "modern" is to credit it with all the improvements which have been made up to now. Then by a transference the term is applied to realms where valuation is, or ought to be, of a different nature. In consequence, we have "modern living" urged upon us as an ideal; the "modern mind" is mentioned as something superior to previous minds. . . .

It is high time we spoke of the real world in real terms. The concept of judging men and women upon anything but their individual abilities and merits is contrary to all of our traditional values. Simply because we violated those same values in the past by imposing arbitrary and unfair racial or sexual tests for employment, for university admission, or for participation in a political party is no reason for violating them in a contrary direction at the present time. In either instance, such action is wrong.

Many in today's America argue that "society," and not the individual, is responsible for all actions; that the goal of the body politic is the achievement of "equality"—not the traditional idea of equal opportunity, but the opposite notion of equality of condition. The appeal of such a philosophy, Eric Hoffer tells us in his important volume, *The True Believer*, is the same appeal held by Nazism, Fascism, and Communism. He writes, "The passion for equality is partly a passion for anonymity, to be one thread of the many which make up a tunic, one thread not distinguishable from the others. . . . They want to eliminate free competition and the ruthless testing to which the individual is continually subjected in a free society."

As Eric Hoffer sees the American past, it was personal liberty—and the heavy burden of work that goes with it—that gave the ordinary American the scope he needed to excel. The freedom to be left alone, to be free of coercion by state or society, has always been crucial. When Hoffer traveled from New York to California as a young man and saw the country for the first time, he "looked around," as he puts it, "and I liked what I saw. This was a country in which you could be left alone. . . . This country was made largely by people who wanted to be left alone. Those who couldn't thrive when left to themselves never felt at ease in America."

The American dream remains the creation of a society in which each man and woman, regardless of race, religion, or ethnic origin, can go as far as his or her ability will provide.

The entire notion of quotas, whether the old-fashioned quotas that excluded minority group members or the current variety that provide them with special privileges, is in opposition to that tradition and to that dream. The Congress has never seen fit to impose such quotas, and it is essential that legislators refuse to continue to permit non-elected officials to turn them into law.

America must remember the principles of individuality and freedom that have brought it to its current greatness. We must not turn our backs upon them in an effort to create a society in which groups have rights but individuals do not. If we were to do so, the entire dream of a free and open society would have been defeated.

The United Nations—A Reappraisal

When the United Nations was formally initiated in 1945, many Americans held out great hope that this organization would help to usher an era of peace, brotherhood, and tranquility into the affairs of men and nations.

Unfortunately, as many critics of the United Nations pointed out from the very beginning, this could hardly be the case when the very nations that most threatened the peace of the world were to become leading members.

The lessons the world should have learned from the experience it had with the League of Nations were ignored, as so many historical lessons have been ignored at such great cost to mankind. Utopian dreams of a peaceful future offered more hope to a war-weary world than did the hard realism of those who understood all too well the pitfalls into which such a world organization would inevitably fall. Unfortunately, utopian dreams die hard, and usually only after much has been sacrificed in their pursuit.

The United States was so determined to create a United Nations that it gave in almost immediately to the demands of the Soviet Union. This capitulation made it clear at the beginning that such an organization would inevitably fail.

Former Governor James H. Byrnes of South Carolina, who later served as Secretary of State under President Truman, accompanied President Franklin Roosevelt to the Yalta Conference where the matter of the creation of the United Nations was discussed. Governor Byrnes found that President Roosevelt "was more interested in the establishment of the United Nations than in any other item on the agenda." Soviet leader Josef Stalin wanted full membership status for the Ukraine and Byelorussia. Both are Republics of the Soviet Union, meaning that Stalin was clearly asking for three votes for the Soviet Union in the General Assembly of the planned organization. Governor Byrnes believed strongly that it was a mistake to give in to the Soviet Union on this demand. However, according to Byrnes, the President told him that his objection to the Soviet demand might endanger the adoption of the resolution—concerning the organization of the United Nations—by the Soviets.

Thus, the Soviet Union received three votes to one for every other member state, including the United States. From the very beginning the United Nations was flawed by the unreasonable demands of totalitarians and the acquiescence in those demands by the U.S. government and by the free world.

Within the past several years it has become clear that the United Nations is a force not for peace but for international discord and turmoil. This is obvious even to many of its longtime friends, to men and women who overlooked so much in the past but cannot in good faith overlook the overwhelming negative reality of today. Consider several of the steps the United Nations has taken in violation of its own charter and in opposition to the best interests of world peace.

According to Article Four of the Charter of the United Nations, "Membership in the UN is open to all peace-loving states which accept the obligations contained in the present Charter. . . ." Many now seem willing to forget that communist China was condemned by the United Nations for its aggressive role in Korea. In fact, the UN went to war to protect South Korea against Communist aggression. Now, by stretching the definition found in Article Four to include Communist China, the UN has shown that its own Charter is irrelevant to its real operating procedures. It has now embraced the philosophy of "universality," a phrase not found in the Charter, rather than the concept of "peace-loving," which is specifically set forth. Yet "universality" does not cover Taiwan, which has been expelled; Rhodesia, against whom an embargo has been declared; or the Republic of South Africa.

Once seated in the United Nations, the Communist Chinese quickly revealed their complete disregard for the so-called international civil service status of UN employees of Chinese nationality. Of the approximately 160 Chinese working for the UN Secretariat in early 1972, about 85 percent held passports from the Republic of China on Taiwan.

To set an example, the Communist Chinese warned the Chinese translators on the UN staff "to straighten up and fly left," as *The New York Daily News* put it, and "to improve their political accents." To prove their loyalty to Communist China, they were instructed to study such publications as the *Peking Review* and the Communist Chinese *People's Daily*. The obvious choice for the Chinese UN staff members was to bow to such political coercion or face unemployment. In addition, at the demand of the Chinese Communists, press representatives from the Republic of China have been stripped of their UN credentials. The remainder of the UN membership, while vocally supporting the new concept of "universality," has silently acquiesced in such actions.

The Chinese situation is but an example of a United Nations' record that has clearly been negative from the outset. Whatever peace the world has had since 1945 has been in spite of the United Nations, not as a result of it.

During the first 25 years of the United Nations' existence, 75 armed conflicts were fought between nations. Additional conflicts have been added to this record during the 1970s. Aggression in Korea was stopped, supposedly under UN auspices but actually it was the achievement of American arms with minimal support from other UN members. Further, the war was one in which the aggressor was temporarily stopped, but not finally defeated.

Discussing this circumstance, General Mark Clark, UN Supreme Commander in Korea, recalled, "In carrying out the instructions of my government I gained the unenviable distinction of being the first United States Army commander in history to sign an armistice without a victory." As one consequence, the United States today still maintains substantial Army contingents along the Korean armistice line to discourage Communist aggression.

When the people of Hungary rose up in 1956 against Soviet oppression the United Nations did nothing. When the Communists built the Berlin Wall in violation of international law and of the United Nations Charter itself, the UN did nothing. When the people of Czechoslovakia rose up against their Communist government, the UN remained silent.

In June 1963 the United Nations accepted the credentials of the government the Soviet Union had forcibly imposed upon the people of Hungary. Discussing this action, the Assembly of Captive European Nations declared that, "the approval of the credentials of the Kadar regime by the United Nations Credentials Committee will come as a great shock to the people of Hungary and other captive nations. The absence of any attempt to challenge the legitimacy of the representatives appointed by a regime the UN has branded as one established by Soviet military intervention will, we feel, be viewed as proof that to all practical purposes the question of Hungary has been dropped, as proof that sheer expediency and not principle determines the policies."

The hypocrisy of the United Nations was discussed in these terms by John C. Wetzel in his study, *The United Nations: Myth Versus Reality:*

The sheer hypocrisy and inconsistency of UN policies has by no means been limited to Communist aggression. In December, 1961, India, whose late leader Nehru had always been an ardent advocate of the United Nations, invaded the small Portugese enclaves of Goa, Damao, and Diu. Using superior force, at the ratio of ten to one in favor of the aggressors, the Indians struck viciously against the small territories which had been under Portugese rule for more than 450 years. Preaching non-violence, neutrality and non-aggression to the rest of the world, the Indians—in complete violation of the UN Charter—resorted to military force to advance their imperialist designs. What happened in the halls of the United Nations? . . . The Security Council's resolution calling for a cease-fire and condemning the Indian aggression was vetoed by the Soviet Union, which later received Nehru's thanks. . . . Whatever else the UN was supposed to accomplish, its advocates always defended it on the grounds that at least it served as a sort of world conscience, a place where civilized mankind could condemn and act against the barbarians amongst us. . . . Americans will have to get used to the fact that the UN is *not* the answer to the world's problems and crises.

It is interesting to note that in December, 1963, two years after the Indian invasion of Goa, a delegation of Goans chosen by representatives of Goan communities all over the world came to the UN with a plea for self-determination for their more than 700,000 fellow Goans. The UN refused to hear the Goan plea. How different was the UN reaction in 1974 to the plea of the Palestine Liberation Organization (PLO). But the Goans had murdered no one, had hijacked no airplanes, and threatened the destruction of no sovereign state. Their only sin was that the country that had invaded their territory was India, rather than a nation in less favor with the current UN majority.

Even the firmest supporters of the United Nations in our own country have been forced to express their opposition to the UN decision with regard to the PLO. One example is provided by the UN Association of New York. The Association's *Newsletter* for January 1975 reports that the Board of Directors expressed "support and admiration" for U.S. Ambassador John Scali who, in his December 6, 1974, address, scored the Assembly for violating basic UN principles and warned that the organization's effectiveness would be injured by the "tyranny of the majority."

The members of the UN Association also voiced "deep concern regarding votes of the General Assembly which purport to bring about a recognition of . . . an organization which has openly espoused the use of guerrillas and terrorists, operated contrary to past Resolutions of the UN and disturbed the peace of the world by mounting attacks against a member nation of the UN."

While condemning recent UN actions, the UN Association of New York remains a supporter of the world body. This is not true, however, in the case of many other one-time supporters.

The reaction of Professor John Roche of Brandeis University, former chairman of the Americans for Democratic Action, is one example. Speaking to his fellow liberals in an article in *New America* of November 30, 1974, Professor Roche writes that:

> One of the reasons so few top government officials are ever fired is that the act of dismissal constitutes an admission of incompetent judgment by the President. In other words, he has a vested interest in his mistakes. So do we all—as evidenced by the liberal community's refusal to face up to the baleful reality of the United Nations.

Dr. Roche also observed that:

> Gradually over the past decade I have been getting more and more infuriated, and Algerian Foreign Minister Bouteflike lit the fuse with his inaugural speech as President of the current UN General Assembly. In the name of the progressive third world he declared war on the United States, the Western Alliance, Israel and wicked imperialists everywhere. Then the Palestinian guerrillas were accorded 'observer status' at the UN (next the Mafia?). . . . The ousting of Taiwan was outrageous. . . . I favored the ad-

mission of Peking, but saw absolutely no justification for expelling a real country. South Africa is a real country dominated by a regime I despise. But the very last time I did a count I discovered sadly that about 80 percent of the member nations of the UN are run by regimes I despise—the democratic countries could caucus in my living room.

Assessing recent trends, Dr. Roche added, "To put it bluntly, the United Nations has been taken over by a coalition of anti-democratic nations. . . . The last time I looked the United States was putting in about a quarter of the money, to say nothing of the choice of location and other perks. Now I don't like anti-democratic organizations, but I am prepared to accept their existence—so long as I don't pay for their fun and games."

So outrageous has been the highhandedness of current majorities in the United Nations that such longtime friends of the world body as *The New York Times* are urging a reconsideration of our relationship to it. *The Times* commented, for example:

The suspension of South Africa from the current U.N. General Assembly is illegal and dangerous. It is a disastrous precedent for an organization that cannot be effective unless its membership is universal. It is a grim irony that virtually the same Assembly majority that suspended a founding member of the UN one day could on the next enthusiastically welcome the leader of a terrorist organization whose goal is destruction of another member state.

The attitude of the United Nations toward international terrorism was confirmed in January 1975 when Secretary General Kurt Waldheim permitted the Vietcong to open an office in Geneva. The Vietcong's Provisional Revolutionary Government was authorized by the Swiss government, at Mr. Waldheim's request, to establish an office at United Nations' Geneva headquarters for contacts with the world organization's aid agencies there.

This step was taken despite the strongest protests from Secretary of State Henry Kissinger. It came at the very moment when the United States was charging that the North Vietnamese were violating the 1973 cease-fire agreements signed in Paris and were carrying out a military build-up in Communist controlled areas in the South. The U.S. raised the proper legal objections, insisting that the Vietcong authorities did not represent a government and should not be given any form of international recognition. Mr.

Waldheim, however, was unresponsive to such protestations. Once again, as in the case of the PLO, the United Nations showed its willingness to recognize international terrorism and, while seeing fit to remove such existing governments as those of Taiwan and South Africa, has provided terrorists with international legitimacy.

Discussing the current UN majorities and their recent actions, *The Chicago Tribune* noted editorially that, "The Third World flouted rules and custom and a common respect for decency by insisting that Yasir Arafat of the PLO be invited to address the assembly, even tho he represents no nation, and thus in effect rewarding the PLO for the dastardly acts of terrorism that have been committed in its name. . . . The spreading miasma of bias and hatred permeating the UN can produce only revulsion and mistrust on the part of the more developed democracies upon which the UN depends primarily for its support."

The actions of the United Nations in violation of its own Charter continue unabated. When the United Nations Educational, Scientific and Cultural Organization (UNESCO) barred Israel from its European region and failed to place it in membership in any other region, it once again violated that Charter. Stephen Hess, a senior fellow at the Brookings Institution and formerly a member of the U.S. delegation to UNESCO, declared, "The withdrawal of all UNESCO funds from Israel . . . and denying Israel a place in the organization's regional structure are entirely alien to the purpose of the Organization."

A letter to the U.S. delegation from longtime UNESCO supporters Leo Rudloff and Mrs. Reinhold Niebuhr stated, "It is tragic that at this moment in history that UNESCO should become an organ of propaganda." Intellectuals and scholars from throughout the world, men and women such as Jean Paul Sartre, Simone de Beauvoir, Francoise Giroud, Isaac Stern, and Leonard Bernstein have signed a letter stating that they will no longer participate in UNESCO activities. In addition, the UNESCO action has already produced one sign of financial retribution. Switzerland, incensed over the UN's action, is now considering a 10 percent reduction in her contribution to the organization.

The current UN majority is intent upon imposing its will on the world body—a body most of whose bills are paid by the United States. The President of the General Assembly, Abdelaziz Bouteflike of Algeria, for example, invoked his Afro-Asian majority to sharply limit the voice of Israel during the assembly debate on Palestine. He used his presidential powers to order a chief of state welcome for PLO chief Yasir Arafat in the Assembly and also made the extraordinary ruling that South Africa could no longer participate in the work of the current session. Many diplomats viewed that action as the first step toward the total exclusion of Israel as well. One UN official lamented, "We are in the hands of the revolution." An American diplomat commented that the current majority had "driven another nail" into the coffin of the UN.

The UN has refused to condemn violence and terrorism. It has, quite to the contrary, encouraged it—not only on the part of the Palestinians but also on the part of a variety of radical guerrilla organizations in Africa and elsewhere.

The casualty tolls resulting from acts of political terrorism in the six years ending December 31, 1973, was 268 dead and 576 wounded. Two U.S. Ambassadors, Cleo A. Noel, and his chief deputy, S. Curtis Morris, as well as a Belgian chargé d'affaires, Guy Eid, were killed. The eight members of the Black September Movement responsible for the assassinations were arrested in the Sudan. They were brought to court and convicted, then sent to Cairo to be turned over to the PLO. They have now been released.

The United Nations has refused to take any action against terrorism. As long ago as the opening of the 1972 session of the General Assembly, the United States requested such action. The UN finally established an ad hoc committee of 35 appointed by the Secretary General to arrive at a definition of terrorism. It met beginning July 16, 1973 and failed to come to any conclusion.

The reason the UN does not condemn terrorism is that the majority of its current membership supports such activity. The UN has refused to condemn slave labor camps in the Soviet Union, mass murders in Communist China, a denial of religious and political freedom throughout Eastern Europe, and terror in Uganda and Tanzania. It has, however, been frequent and vehement in its condemnation of several "easy targets": South Africa, Portugal, and Israel.

William F. Buckley, Jr., in his book, *United Nations Journal: A Delegate's Odyssey*, discusses his experiences as a member of the U.S. delegation to the General Assembly and as U.S. Representative on the Human Rights Committee. Although all UN members gave lip service to such human rights as freedom of speech, press, religion, assembly, and travel, the fact is, as Buckley points out, "Of the 135 members of the United Nations, 20 are governed by parliamentary representation."

The Soviet Union, for example, ratified the Declaration of Human Rights Convention. Yet, Buckley writes:

Within four months Soviet State police (a) having publicly reviled Solzhenitsyn, (b) denied him a legal residence in Moscow, (c) censored his work and denied him royalties, (d) forced their way into his apartment, (c) dragged him away without serving him with a warrant, (f) stripped him of his clothing and possessions, (g) charged him with a crime, (h) divested him of citizenship, (i) put him in an airplane, and (j) dumped him, an exile, in West Germany. In doing so, the Soviet Union violated at least 15 articles of the Declaration.

Yet the United Nations, Buckley found, would consider only the infractions of Israel, South Africa, and the Western nations. It was totally uninterested in any violation of human rights perpetrated by Communist states or by nations in the Third World—clearly the ones in most serious violation.

Buckley writes:

One learns almost instantly at the United Nations that the convention is very simply to ignore Soviet infractions against the stated ideals of the organization. . . . This becomes something in which everyone is automatically trained; even as, say, altogether spontaneous conversations deploring drunkenness will take place in households in which a principal is an alcoholic; after a while nobody notices.

United Nations Secretary General Kurt Waldheim recently stated, "We must not lose sight of the ideal." Former delegate Buckley responds, "What he does not realize is that they have abandoned their own ideal. . . . How an organization which cannot muster the courage to pronounce the word 'Soviet Union' in a discussion of human rights, could enforce human rights . . . is the kind of thing that produces the distinctive mistiness of United Nations rhetoric."

Another longtime supporter of the United Nations, and one who has served as U.S. delegate to the General Assembly, who has become disillusioned with the world organization is Colgate W. Darden, Jr., formerly Governor of Virginia.

In a speech delivered at the Virginia Military Institute, he stated:

The UN has shown with its greatly enlarged membership a marked disposition to impose unreasonable burdens upon the more advanced industrial nations. It appears bogged down in petty bickering and self-serving ventures. . . . The structure of the present organization should be re-examined, and if it cannot be revamped so as to bring about a reasonable balance between the members it should be abandoned and some other plan devised.

It is the belief of this writer, and has been for many years, that an organization that includes within its ranks those nations having aggressive designs toward others can never be a force for peace. What is needed, and has long been needed, is an organization that unites the freedom-loving nations so they might work together to make it clear aggression will not be permitted to succeed.

If we decide not to leave the United Nations, we should at the very least see to it that the UN does not actively work for the destruction of the principles it was established to promote. With regard to the Middle East, for example, we should make our position abundantly clear.

A proposal worthy of consideration was made by Clare Boothe Luce, who declared, "President Ford should forcefully remind the UN that the UN created Israel, and that if that august body does not, and damn soon overwhelmingly pass a Resolution upholding the right of Israel to exist as an independent and sovereign nation within the borders set by the UN itself in the Security Council's Resolution 242 of 1967, the United States will forthwith quit the UN and exercise its sovereign right to expel the UN from our shores, leaving it to find its home, and its finances, elsewhere."

Mrs. Luce further suggests, "We should also tell the UN that we intend to offer a firm military treaty to Israel, guaranteeing those borders against Arab—or Palestinian—aggression, and invite Israel's Arab neighbors, if they are so inclined, to seek similar guarantees from their friendly neighbors."

To those of us who have long been aware of the shortcomings inherent in the organization of the United Nations, it is pleasing to see many liberals who placed such great faith in the United Nations for so many years—even though such faith was never rewarded by accomplishments, finally learning that this organization has not only been a failure but, with the use of U.S. funds, made the world less rather than more safe.

It is unfortunate that they did not come to this realiza-

71

tion much earlier. They would have done well, for example, to consider the analysis presented by William Henry Chamberlin in a 1964 article in *The Freeman*: "The very expression, United Nations, is a misnomer, because of the deep divisions of ideology and national interest by which the world is divided. To expect the United Nations, given these differences and given its archaic and unrealistic Charter, to point a clear united lead in time of crisis is to expect swift action from a Tower of Babel."

Despite previous reluctance to recognize the reality of the UN's inherent futility, we must now welcome those who have finally come to this realization to the effort many of us have long pursued with regard to cutting U.S. funding to the UN.

Since its creation the United Nations has spent more than $5.5 billion of the U.S. taxpayers' dollars. In 1972, Congress limited annual U.S. payments to 25 percent of the United Nations' budget. Previously the U.S. payment had been more than 30 percent. That 25 percent is still the highest paid by any nation. The Soviet Union's payment is 12.9 per cent—when it pays. In 1964, when the Soviet Union had been in default for more than two years and under the Charter was threatened with losing its voting rights, the Soviet leaders promised to pay. The voting challenge was dropped, but to this day the payments have not been made.

Of the 144 UN members, 98 were in arrears $182 million, as of January 1, 1975. More than one half of this indebtedness—$110 million—is owed by the Soviet Union and its client states. In September 1974, while submitting a $540.4 million two-year budget, UN Secretary General Kurt Waldheim warned that only $447.8 million income could be expected. Thus, he proposed a budget with a $92.6 million deficit.

That same month, the UN was so strapped for funds that Waldheim asked the United States to pay its final 1974 installment of $10 million in advance, which we did. The debtors—the Soviet Union, black African countries, India—continued in arrears, but saw fit to expel South Africa, limit Israel, and invite the PLO.

It is certainly time for the United States to consider carefully the possibility of ending its relationship with the United Nations. The results of such an action would be far less dramatic than many supporters of the United Nations suppose. Discussing this possibility, columnist James J. Kilpatrick wrote as follows:

What would happen if the United States formally withdrew from the United Nations? Nothing very much. The United Nations would sputter along for a few years, passing windy resolutions and making impotent gestures, but the structure of world power would not be altered. Questions of war and peace would be resolved as they always have been resolved, by arms or negotiation. The International service agencies, even now headquartered in Geneva, Berne, Montreal, Rome and Vienna, would function as before. It would be charged, of course, that the United States had killed the UN, but the charge would be untrue. A dream dies of its own accord when the dreamer awakes.

If we have not yet awakened from that dream, if we are not yet prepared to take this important step, we must at the very least limit our financial support to this organization.

For the second time in five years I have introduced into the House a bill that would reduce the amount of money the United States spends to support the United Nations. I have been joined by 44 of my colleagues in both parties. Under this proposal, the U.S. contribution to the United Nations would be reduced from approximately 25 percent of the overall UN budget to 5.6 percent. This reduction would be accomplished simply by basing our contribution on our population taken as a percentage of the total population of UN member nations.

The reduction, in addition to saving the American taxpayer approximately $338 million a year, might have a salutory effect on the irresponsible majority which heretofore has been able to direct policy without having to face the financial consequences. It is essential that we recognize the changed reality of the United Nations. Writing in the *Swiss Review of World Affairs*, Alfred Cattani notes:

Back in a comparatively idyllic time, a certain potentate once banged his shoe on the table to gain the General Assembly's attention. Today the younger generation of political leaders who now set the tone send their representatives into the plenary chamber armed with a pistol. The United Nations is in danger of becoming a political grand guignol the cost of which, ironically enough, continues to be borne primarily by those states most continuously subjected to calumny and derision in its halls.

One way or another, our exercise in masochism with regard to the United Nations must come to a halt. No more appropriate time exists for such an ending than now.

Is There a Health Care Crisis in the United States?

An article I recently read dealing with the imminent sixty-second birthday of the federal income tax contained excerpts from discussions that went on in Congress at the time that tax was adopted. These comments can show us interesting parallels government has already taken with respect to the health care field. They may even open the eyes of some who view with equanimity the piecemeal efforts government is making toward moving us still nearer to a national health care system.

The article voices the fears of those who were unsure of the wisdom of using a tax on income to raise federal revenue. One speaker voiced the fear that once a tax on income was enacted, rates would tend to rise perhaps even as high as 20 percent. "Not so," Senator William Borah of Idaho angrily retorted. "No one could impose such a socialistic confiscatory rate. How could Congress, the Representatives of the American people, be so lacking in fairness, justice, and patriotism as to do such a dreadful thing?"

We have seen the accuracy of that well-meant prediction. That unheard-of 20 percent bite has become a 50 percent chunk and more of personal incomes in the professions. What lessons do these developments hold for us today?

Advocates of a nationalized system of health care are found in both the Democratic and Republican parties. Too often, the only disagreement to be heard is with regard to what *kind* of nationalized system of health care we should have, not *whether* such a system is needed or would be an improvement over our present private practice approach to medicine.

The advocates of this form of governmental intervention tell us that the United States is in the midst of a "health care crisis," and that only intervention by Washington can adequately deal with the problem. The only major disagreement between one proposed plan and another is over administrative details. The point of agreement, however—the existence of a health care crisis—must be carefully examined. If that crisis does not in fact exist, the programs advocated as a means of dealing with the "crisis" will be, by definition, superfluous and unnecessary.

The fact is that under our current medical system, the health of the American people has been improving steadily and often dramatically. In 1900 the life expectancy of the average American at birth was 49.2 years; today life expectancy is more than 70 years. One-fourth of the babies born in 1850 died before the age of five; one-fourth of the babies born as late as 1900 died before the age of 25; three-fourths of the babies born today can expect to live to at least age 62. Of every 1,000 infants born alive in 1900, approximately 125 would not survive one year. Today, the annual infant mortality rate is 18.5 per thousand—an improvement of more than 350 percent. Moreover, this rate is superior to that of the Common Market countries where the ratio is over 20 per thousand.

Tuberculosis and polio have been virtually wiped out. Open-heart surgery is almost commonplace. The death rate from cancer of the uterus has been reduced by half in the last thirty years. Medicine has been progressing steadily, sometimes spectacularly. Men and women throughout the world—many in countries with long-standing socialized medical systems—look to our private researchers and doctors to find a cure for cancer as they found a cure for polio and other fatal diseases. This is a sign of success. It is a sign those who would scuttle private practice totally fail to recognize or acknowledge.

Another commonly cited element of the "crisis" in health care is the alleged "maldistribution" of doctors in the United States. Many Americans, we are told, find themselves far away from any qualified medical care. This, however, is far from the truth.

If the "doctorless" counties in the United States were examined by those who make this charge, they would discover that of the 3,084 counties in the country, only 132 actually lack doctors. A recently conducted study by Hillsdale College in Michigan produced some interesting explanations for this situation.

The "doctorless" counties, it was discovered, ranged from Hinsdale County, Colorado, which has a population of 202 people, to Stafford County, Virginia, just south of

Prince William County and north of Fredericksburg, which has a population of 25,000 people. Thirty-six of the "doctorless" counties are adjacent to a standard metropolitan statistical area (SMSA). It is a fifteen-minute drive from the heart of Stafford County to Fredericksburg, where there are 48 physicians, or into Prince William County, where there are 50 physicians; thus no real shortage of doctors exists. The fact is that only 0.2 percent of the population of the United States lives in the 132 doctorless counties. These counties, it seems, lack doctors for the same reasons they lack supermarkets and motion picture theaters: the population base simply does not warrant it. It would be a misallocation of a valuable resource to compel a physician or a dentist to relocate there.

It is quite obvious that those who argue that nationalized medical care would create a more "equitable" distribution of doctors than we have today cannot have studied the figures, either in our own country or in countries that do have socialized systems.

Another charge has been made concerning the distribution of doctors in our country. Too few doctors, it is said, are to be found in the inner cities. But a 1968 study of this subject revealed contradictory evidence. In Boston the study found the same ratio of physician to patients in the inner city as in the suburbs. In Chicago, however, there were 62 physicians per 100,000 patients, as opposed to twice that number of physicians to 100,000 patients in the suburbs.

This is hardly a basis for indicting our health care system. It may be a much harsher indictment of the administration of our cities. Chicago has many other inner city difficulties, including a flight of business and a breakdown of order. For the same reasons that businessmen leave the inner city, so do physicians and other professionals. The inner city is an unsafe place to be. While this is admittedly a distressing problem, it should not be blamed on our system of health care. That system did not create these difficulties, but is only responding to them.

The success of nongovernmental health care is often ignored, as can be seen in a recent attempt to manipulate the number and type of first-year residencies available to medical students in the United States. This effort was based on the assumption that residencies in the primary care specialties were diminishing and must be encouraged by government. The legislation involved certain provisions of the Health Manpower Act, also known as H.R. 5546. Fortunately, Rep. James T. Broyhill (R-NC) pointed out the fallacy of the assumption and was able to get the offending provisions deleted.

In his statement on the subject, Rep. Broyhill declared: In the last five years the number of first-year residencies in these primary care fields has increased from one percent to 10 percent of the total. There is every reason to believe that this increase will continue at this rate and it is estimated by 1980, 50 percent of the first-year residents will be in the primary care field. . . . I see no reason to set up this bureaucracy to make these decisions. I see no reason to arbitrarily stop the trend that is already going on.

Those who advance the idea of crisis in American health care not only discuss an alleged maldistribution of doctors but also discuss an absolute doctor shortage. Somehow, they say, government control of medicine will ease this "shortage." Unfortunately, most of the participants in the debate accept as a given the notion that a doctor shortage exists, and then argue only about the best way to deal with it. Their conclusion, however, is based on a false assessment of the situation.

Since 1965 the number of doctors has increased by more than 50,000, or approximately 17 percent. The rise has been roughly three times as great as the growth of population, and projections for the next decade indicate the same ratio of production of physicians over population growth. Yet much of the discussion about the alleged shortage of doctors has proceeded as if there had been no change in the situation. In fact, rather than a doctor shortage such as the one critics of American medicine have manufactured, we are likely to have more physicians than we can properly employ.

It is also forgotten that the equivalent ratio of doctors to patients in a country such as Great Britain, which has had nationalized medicine for a generation, is one doctor for every 750 patients. That ratio is threatened by the large emigration of doctors from England, primarily because of serious political interference with the private practice of medicine. The same is true with regard to Sweden, and the doctor-patient ratio in the Soviet Union is far worse than in the United States. In the Common Market countries the ratio of patients to physicians was 670 to 1 in a study conducted two years ago. At that time the

U.S. ratio was 600 to 1 and today is down to 590 to 1—the best of any large, industrial society.

The arguments presented by those who charge that a medical crisis exists—a crisis for which their own proposals are the proper remedy—usually conclude by citing high medical costs. With regard to this question, Marvin Edwards, in his book, *Hazardous to Your Health,* notes that, "the plainest of all the misrepresentations advanced by foes of private medicine is the argument that something inherent in free enterprise keeps driving medical costs continually higher. The rise in costs is directly traceable not to free enterprise, but to the interventions of government. The most obvious culprit is government-spawned inflation."

Beyond inflation, another major explanation of the rise in hospital costs is the unionization of hospital staffs and the accompanying increase in salaries. In hospital management, approximately 65 percent of costs are related to salaried employees. When these costs increase, all hospital costs increased with them. Moreover, construction workers are among the highest paid in the nation—adding to the cost of building. Nurses, too, are demanding better pay and better working conditions.

Still other factors increasing the costs of hospital operation include the added cost involved in the introduction of sophisticated new life-saving equipment, the escalation in the cost of malpractice insurance, and the fact that Medicare has increased the cost of hospital care for private patients, since the government does not reimburse fully for the costs of these patients.

Many who decry escalation of health care costs argue that doctors' fees were a major factor contributing to the increase, but this contention is not borne out by the facts. According to the Department of Labor, doctors' fees increased at an annual average rate of 3.7 percent during the period from 1956 to 1968. For workers as a whole, wages were rising at an average annual rate of 4.2 percent. The average physician's income in 1972 was approximately $40,500 for an average workweek of 63 hours. If this hourly rate were applied to a 40-hour workweek the figure would be approximately $26,000 a year, which is less than New York City's garbage collectors are making when one factors in their fringe benefits. Considering the years of commitment, expense, and dedication on the part of doctors to develop their skills, such an income hardly seems excessive.

Would the socialization of American medicine, or one of

the lesser steps in that direction, in any way lower the *real* cost of health care in the United States? The advocates of such programs imply that it would. Their *real* meaning seems to be that, since all individuals will pay for medical care *indirectly through taxes* rather than directly to the doctors and hospitals involved, it will *seem* like less. The result would, of course, be politically advantageous.

For one indication of foreseeable costs, we use here the figures produced by the Committee for National Health Insurance, the group responsible for drafting the legislation now being advanced by Senator Edward M. Kennedy. The plan's sponsors figure that for fiscal 1969 the federal government spent over $9 billion for all personal health programs. If their program had been in effect then, they say, it would have disbursed most of that amount and would have required an additional $6 billion from the general tax revenues.

But as we know the costs of all government programs tend to rise significantly above initial estimates. Thus, an article in *The New Republic* by Washington health writer Mel Schechter states that Medicare alone, without any changes, needs more payroll taxes to meet a 25-year projected deficit of $236 billion in hospital-related benefits. This is a shocking overrun of nearly 100 percent.

Involving the federal government in direct control of medical care in our own country would, according to Ralph R. Rooke of the National Association of Retail Druggists, "produce an administrative nightmare, with federal officials . . . working out contracts with 6,000 hospitals, 25,000 nursing homes, 700 visiting nurse groups, and, later, with 208,000 doctors and 55,000 retail pharmacists." The paperwork involved in processing the millions of resulting claims "staggers the imagination. An extremely large force of government workers would undoubtedly be required to do the job."

In the end, would American health services be better served by government than they are under our current system? A report on the National Health Service (NHS) by Professor John Jewkes, who served on Britain's Royal Commission on Renumeration of Doctors and Dentists, concluded that "the average American now has more medical services than the average Briton and the gap between the two has been widening" since the inception of the National Health Service.

More and more Britons, according to the evidence presented by Jewkes, are seeking medical care outside of the National Health Service. These people are "ready to make sacrifices in other directions in order to enjoy prompt hospital and specialist treatment, free choice of consultant and private accommodation." To make things even more difficult, there is a massive exodus of doctors from Great Britain—their reaction against the regimentation of the National Health Service.

It seems clear that medical care would be far more costly under a nationalized system than it is today. If the experience in England, France, and Sweden is indicative, people would tend to overcrowd the existing facilities. Writing in *Private Practice*, Dr. Klaus Rentzsch of Hamburg, West Germany, notes that while U.S. patients stay in the hospital from six to eight days on the average, "in Germany we have a twenty-four day average hospital stay. The situation is comparable in every country with a total medical-care program such as ours."

In its issue of August 15, 1973, the West German newspaper *Bremer Nachrichten* discusses the long waiting lists for surgery in the semi-socialist medical system of that country. The paper notes: "Patients needing complex surgery are often forced to wait a matter of months or years. Many large hospitals have drawn up waiting lists. Heart operations involving the use of heart and lung machines, transplants, tonsillectomies and fitting of false joints are often subject to long delays." Waiting lists of up to six months are looked at as "almost-normal" at large hospitals in Baden-Wurtemberg, the paper reported. In Hamburg, for example, there is a waiting list of about 1,000 for operations involving use of the city's only heart and lung machine. One hospital in Stuttgart has a two-and-a-half-year waiting list for patients requiring an artificial limb and in Dortmund the delay can be as long as three years.

The unfortunate fact is that, although advocates of government involvement in medicine tell us that it will decrease costs and improve quality, the evidence of our own Medicare and Medicaid programs shows precisely the opposite—it will increase costs and decrease quality, not unlike our experience with a government-run postal system.

Further investigation of the British experience with socialized medicine suggests all too clearly the deterioration of medical care and increase in medical costs that would befall the United States were such a program to be adopted. In December 1950, less than three years after Britain's National

Health Service went into effect, the Ministry of Health announced that 533,557 people were on the waiting list for hospital beds—100,000 of them in London. Shortly after NHS went into effect a group of health administrators informed the London Institute of Public Administration: "The public is adopting the attitude that because of the Welfare State they have no responsibility for their aged parents." As a result many of the aged who were mentally deficient or helpless were left without care and had to shift for themselves, since there was no room in the overcrowded hospitals.

Harold Gurden, a Member of Parliament from Birmingham, has called for a public investigation into waiting lists for children to have ear operations. In 1969, Gurden said, 50 Birmingham children were going permanently deaf each year because they were unable to receive hospital treatment in time. The situation has not improved.

Sir Keith Joseph, a leading Conservative Member of Parliament, states that the socialized system from the very beginning fostered a "something for nothing" attitude among its potential users. "The idea," he declared, "was that the so-called bottomless purse of the taxpayer is there to maintain standards, to meet all requirements, to eliminate all inconveniences, to provide utopia. . . ." Even the radical Aneurin Bevan came to doubt this aspect of NHS, complaining about "the ceaseless cascade of medicine being poured down British throats." When people think the medical care is "free," however, this is the inevitable result.

How "free" has the British system been? The NHS is not a "health insurance plan," although each family must pay $230 a year in mandatory contributions, which is similar to the premium rate for high-option private group health insurance in the United States. Approximately 85 percent of the total cost of NHS comes from general revenues, and this has skyrocketed since the plan began. Initially, the annual cost was about $600 million. By 1951 it passed the $1 billion point and it increased to $5 billion in 1969. At the present time, the estimate is $6.2 billion (out of a total national budget of nearly $90 billion).

Much of the money in question goes not for sick people or new facilities, which are virtually nonexistent, but for administrative costs. In an article concerning the British experience with socialized medicine, Rep. Robert Bauman (R-Md) wrote in *Human Events* that, "A recent 'reorganization' of the entire system has produced no fewer than

81

five separate levels of bureaucracy topped off by the Department of Health and Social Services, under which fall 14 Regional Health Authorities, 90 Area Health Authorities, numerous District Management Teams, and lastly, the Sectors, which is the euphemism for the local hospital. . . . Things have gotten so bad . . . that it takes 14 separate administrative steps to obtain approval for one new registrar (resident) to practice at a London area hospital."

The manner in which patients are treated by the system makes it less likely than ever that adequate health care will be received. At any one time England has from 500,000 to 700,000 people waiting for operations or treatment in hospitals. Fully one quarter have been waiting for two years or more, according to government estimates. Rep. Bauman reported about a typical case: ". . . that of a woman who had a lump in her breast and had to wait eight weeks for its removal. She then waited weeks to learn that the growth was malignant but was not given a date for further surgery which was needed." Perhaps the classic case of the now traditional waiting list and its application is that of a 54-year old patient, the late Mrs. Alice Higgs of Cardiff, Wales. Sir Alan Marre, the Health Service Commissioner, revealed in his 1975 report to Parliament that during more than a year of waiting for recommended open heart surgery, Mrs. Higgs had been admitted and fully prepared for the surgery three different times.

The first admission came six months after the initial diagnosis, but after five days at the hospital she was sent home. Her anxiety increased and in June, 1973, after another six months, she was again admitted and prepared for surgery, only to be sent home again because of other scheduled operations. Two weeks later, she returned and was again cancelled. Her husband reported that after this she could not eat or sleep, and within a few days she died. The government's reason for this death: "administrative failures, regrettable if unintentional." Unfortunately, this case is not atypical.

Many advocates of socialized medicine in England admit its failures, but argue that with additional funds the system would work smoothly. This approach totally misunderstands the problem. Dr. Max Gammon of London, an organizer of the first private teaching hospital project planned in many years, responds to that assessment this way: "Protagonists of socialized medicine will say that this (the present state of the NHS) proves nothing. All that is needed is a little more money and some minor modifications to the basic structure. I suggest . . . that this argument should be rejected; the problem is inherent in the basic philosophy. . . . (T)he implications of a state monopoly in medicine are so malignant that it should be totally rejected."

The central thesis of socialism, Dr. Gammon notes, is that the state is better able to manage the personal resources and deliver the requirements of the individual than he himself is. "The truth is," he concludes, "when the state cares, nobody cares."

The huge administrative force needed to support as massive a project as national health insurance in this country is almost incalculable. Examining the effects of administrative red tape on the British medical system, Melchior Palyi, author of *Medical Care And The Welfare State,* writes that, "From the administrative angle, nationalization raises weighty problems. Bulk-buying was expected to lower the cost of hospital supplies. But governments are poor marketers and the advantage of their buyer's monopoly is canceled by the clumsiness of their maneuvering. British hospitals complain that the poor quality of the 'cheap' supplies increases costs. Under socialism the life of a hospital manager is not easy. There used to be a sort of nation-wide competition in economy of management. Now the economy is of no avail; the savings disappear into the general trough. Economy is actually discouraged; the more money a management requests, the more it is likely to get, provided it keeps in step with the others. But they all try to get the most—which keeps them in step."

Soon after the NHS was created, the British Auditor General reported: ". . . of the total hospital expenditures, 9.9 percent goes in doctors' salaries (specialists), 23.8 percent for nurses, and 26.5 percent represents salaries and wages of 'other officials and employees,' including administrative staffs."

British writer Anthony Lejeune declares that, "A chronic shortage of money, combined with an expensive and frustrating bureaucracy, are characteristic of State-run institutions everywhere, and Britain's NHS provides a classic example. Ten years ago it had more doctors than administrators. Now it has thirty percent more administrators than doctors. . . . The Department of Health and Social Services pours out a relentless stream of new orders; several hundred of these 'Circulars' are issued each year. Paperwork accumulates like a snowdrift. . . . All this nonsense costs money. By way of contrast, many hospitals cannot afford the number of nurses they really need. A paradoxical situation has arisen lately, in which student nurses found they would be sacked if they passed their examinations. Those who failed could stay on in the hospitals while they tried again, but there were no jobs for those who passed, because, in order to save money, the Area Health Authorities had imposed a temporary freeze on the employment of new staff nurses."

Much the same story can be told about the health system of socialized Sweden. While visiting in Stockholm, *The New York Times* correspondent Harry Schwartz stated: "Don't get sick in Sweden. You have never seen such impersonal care and such long waits in your life. Every time you go to a clinic, you see a different doctor. And if you're hospitalized and are seen by a physician three times in one day, it will almost certainly be three different doctors."

If total government medicine would be beneficial, it is reasonable to suppose that limited government medicine would be at least partially so. Thus, the programs government has already entered into—such as Medicare and Medicaid—should meet the burden of proof of providing higher-quality and lower-priced medical care before any more ambitious plans are proposed. But the plain fact is that those who hold that government controlled medicine would provide better, more economical, and higher-quality medical care have, in most respects, failed to provide the real analysis that would lead to such a conclusion.

Let us look briefly at the Medicare and Medicaid programs to determine whether or not they have been successful, and whether or not they have performed as their advocates and sponsors said that they would.

In California, the number of "needy" who have applied for and received admission to Medi-Cal (the state's Medicaid program) had topped 2.4 million by early 1971. That figure represents 12 percent of the state's population. "Medi-Cal's costs have doubled in four years and are still climbing," declared the *San Francisco Examiner*. "The system could bankrupt the state."

Medi-Cal's services are being abused, noted the *Examiner*, "simply because they are free." The early warnings that government-subsidized health programs would produce widespread overutilization were clearly borne out by Medi-Cal's experience. In fiscal 1969-70, 141 claims were filed for

84

every 100 persons enrolled in the program. By June, 1969, a little more than three years after the plan was put into operation, California Blue Cross and Blue Shield, fiscal intermediaries for the program, had already processed more than 66 million Medi-Cal claims.

In 1967, the first full year of Medi-Cal, slightly more than one million Californians were on the program's rolls. By 1970, the number was nearly 2.5 million. Costs soared. In 1967 the program cost the state $600 million; by 1970 Medi-Cal was costing the state $1.2 billion.

The *San Francisco Examiner* complained that support of the Medi-Cal program had driven the average Californian's health-care expenses up to $517 a year by 1970, compared to only $312 per person for the remainder of the nation. "It (Medi-Cal) has become a monster devouring the state's dollar resources," the newspaper stated. "Currently it is consuming an amount equal to the total sum raised by the state income tax."

Under Medi-Cal, an individual was permitted to obtain a wider range of health care at the state's expense than the average working man could afford to purchase. Under Medi-Cal, the taxpayers pay the cost of nursing home care, dental care, home health care, occupational therapy, optometrics, chiropractic care, special duty nursing, psychological drugs, hearing aids, physical therapy—all on a 100 percent payment basis. No limits were placed on the length of hospital stay or physician fees, although private health insurance companies do limit the extent of coverage for the working man who pays for his own health protection. *The Examiner* pointed out that, "The working man's taxes, which support Medi-Cal, are one reason he can't afford more health care."

Unfortunately, California's Medicaid experience is not unique. In early 1970, the Texas Public Welfare Commission announced that it was cutting state Medicaid benefits by some 20 percent in order to stave off an estimated $42 million deficit during the following 17 months. The cutback was averted by a decision of the Texas legislature to transfer $13.5 million, which had been appropriated for the development of two new medical schools, to balance the Medicaid program. Similar circumstances became reality in Massachusetts, New Hampshire, Virginia, Iowa, Louisiana, and Wisconsin.

Medicaid began to be viewed as a failure. The Health Policy Advisory Center, in a 1970 report, stated that

"Medicaid began in 1966 . . . Medicaid began to die two years later." The report observed that New York City, "which embraced Medicaid like a long-lost brother, fell the hardest. . . . By the depth of its fall it reveals most clearly what happened in other cities as well." The report quoted a veteran hospital physician as saying: "Medicaid set health care in New York City back thirty years. Now we're just picking up the pieces."

A grand jury report in January 1972 in New York City charged that about $1 billion in Medicaid money spent by New York City was wasted because of frauds and inefficiency. The report covered a period from May 1966 to the end of 1969, when the city spent more than $1.8 billion on Medicaid assistance. The Manhattan grand jury drew up its report after a two-year investigation with the assistance of District Attorney Frank Hogan.

"Fifty percent of the money spent on Medicaid went down the drain," according to an unnamed high-ranking Medicaid official quoted in the report. "Testimony disclosed the incredibly chaotic manner in which records were kept and Medicaid documents were processed for payment," the report said. It asserted that dozens of examples of "widespread and flagrant abuses" had been discovered and it charged that physicians had billed the city for services and performed inadequate work.

The jury said it had found patients' names forged by dentists on forms used to collect money from the city. Other patients were told to sign blank forms and physicians billed the city for work never performed. It also listed cases of Medicaid recipients passing their identification cards to relatives or friends otherwise ineligible to receive free medical care.

City Councilman Leon Katz made public a report showing that some laboratories had charged under Medicaid for sickle-cell anemia tests on white people. (The disease, as most people know, is almost entirely limited to blacks.)

In a booklet entitled, "The Cost of Medical Care and What You and I Can Do About It," Dr. George E. Shambaugh, Jr., a professor at Northwestern University, described the problem this way:

"Medicare and Medicaid . . . are costing three times or four times as much as the government planners expected. One reason is that the patient, with all his bills paid for him, lacks any incentive to leave the hospital as soon as he is able to. We saw this in VA hospitals, where a fenestration operation required an average of eight weeks of hospitalization, compared to eight days in a private hospital. Another reason is that patients want to be hospitalized for X-rays and other diagnostic tests which their insurance will not pay for on an outpatient basis."

Dr. Sidney Garfield, a long-time promoter of the prepayment group approach to medicine and a founder of Kaiser Permanente argues that government-financed medical care has caused far more problems than it has solved. He states that, "The delivery system functioned fairly well with fee-for-service under which it evolved. It became unbalanced and a so-called 'non-system' under the impact of the poorly planned legislation of Medicare and Medicaid with its elimination of fees, and that result should not surprise anyone. Picture what would happen to air transportation if fares were eliminated and travel became a right. What chance would you have of getting anyplace if you really needed to? Even the highly automated telephone service would be staggered by removal of fees and necessary calls would become practically impossible. The change from 'fee' to 'free' would disrupt any system in the country no matter how well organized, and this is particularly true of medicine with its highly personalized sick-care service."

Eli Ginzburg, Professor of Economics at Columbia University, in a paper presented at the Centennial Celebration of New York City's Mount Sinai Hospital, cautioned: "The only real control over costs is to keep the amount of medical services within bounds; to be sure that essential needs are met but that medical services do not expand beyond."

Expansion, however, is the natural course of government health programs, through administrative bureaucracy, through excessive demand, and through the overuse of facilities. Discussing the Medicaid experience in New York City, Rep. Edward Koch (D-NY) stated on the floor of Congress that, "The abuses have been disgraceful. We can no longer allow our money to be stolen from us. Nor can we allow the health of people to be abused or ignored."

In any consideration of the operation of the Medicaid program, it is incorrect to think that doctors and other providers of health care are the only ones, or even the primary ones, who take advantage of the system. Patients often view the Medicaid program much as they view the totality of the nation's welfare programs, to which it is tied—as a means of obtaining the taxpayers' money for their own advantage.

87

In his book, *The Case For American Medicine*, Harry Schwartz describes the situation in Washington, D.C. in which one doctor "explained that he stopped seeing Medicaid patients in the black area where he works because they were 'unfair to doctors.' He asserted that many of the Medicaid patients who used to flock into his Southeast Washington office had ailments that they could have taken aspirins for. They demanded X-rays, prescriptions, and unnecessary trips to the hospitals. They asked for medicine for friends or relatives and sometimes they even lent their Medicaid identification card to other people who weren't in the program so they could get free care."

Harry Schwartz reports of another Washington doctor who told the local medical society: "I joined Medicaid because I thought it was the right thing to do. Patients I used to treat free now want more frequent visits which they don't need and (they) bug me on the phone." Some doctors, the District of Columbia Medical Society discovered, found it simpler to treat Medicaid patients free of charge, feeling that the small fee they might get from Medicaid was not worth the work, trouble, and irritation of submitting a Medicaid payment claim.

Another view of Medicaid's troubles was given by Dr. Stephen N. Rosenberg, the deputy executive medical director of New York City's Medicaid program. He stated: "Medicaid was founded on the supposition that if doctors could make a living in areas where poor people live, they would move in. A good many did just that. Then the legislature cut back fees 20 percent, cut down on the number of eligibles and required patients to pay 20 percent of their doctor's bill. That pushed the practitioner to the edge, and perhaps over it. Doctors seldom collect that 20 percent. The fee now for a repeat visit to a general practitioner is $4 and change. Doctors feel that it's demeaning to ask a patient for 80 cents, which he usually can't pay anyway. Should a doctor wear a change-maker, like a Good Humor Man?"

Dr. Rosenberg notes that, as a result, "we find doctors who try to make up income by seeing 70 patients a day, which means they give maybe six minutes to each. How much has the system pushed the doctor into that?"

Dr. Rosenberg also pointed to the perverse effects of Medicaid efforts to economize by cutting physician fees: "If a specialist can treat a patient in his office, and we have

88

cut his fee from $16 to $8, he sends the patient over to the hospital where we have to pay $40 per outpatient visit."

Discussing the Medicaid program and the entire concept of government involvement in medicine, Harry Schwartz declares that, "The conventional liberal wisdom today is that Medicaid's problems prove how obsolete private medical practice in the United States is. Some liberals have welcomed the muddle and chaos of Medicaid as prods forcing the United States to a more 'rational' medical system. Usually that more 'rational' medical system is depicted as prepaid group practice. . . . But this is simplistic, naive thinking."

"What the Medicaid semifiasco has shown," writes Schwartz, "is how poorly Congress and state officials coped with the problem of providing medical service for the poor. That failure is hardly encouragement to have these same legislators and bureaucrats expand further their maladroit intervention into the American medical system. The basic flaw of Medicaid as originally conceived was that it gave no incentives for economy to either the buyer or seller of medical services. The more services a seller provided, for example, the more patients a ghetto doctor or dentist saw—the more money he made. But the patients, Medicaid beneficiaries, had no reason to economize either since it cost them nothing to go to a doctor, enter a hospital, or have the dentist work on their teeth. On the contrary, more than a few Medicaid patients learned how to use that mechanism to satisfy nonmedical needs, for example by getting a podiatrist to 'prescribe' ordinary shoes or taking an unnecessary prescription to a druggist and exchanging the prescription for cash amounting to, say, half the sum the pharmacist would be compensated for the medication. This was the worst of all possible worlds in terms of any rational use of resources."

The Medicaid system clearly invited abuses both by providers of health care and by patients, because it had built-in incentives for needless, wasteful utilization. Furthermore, Medicaid is not the only failure of government in the health field. The Medicare program tells much the same story.

Medicare has not only been a failure; it has been a costly failure. The entire Medicare experience has been one of constant actuarial error. According to Robert J. Myers, for 23 years the chief actuary of the Social Security Administration and now a Professor of Actuarial Science at Temple University, disbursements for hospital insurance benefit payments and administrative expenses for the first three years of the program were $11.2 billion higher than the original estimates—an overrun of more than 41 percent.

Within five years after it was adopted the nation's Medicare law was an acknowledged failure. Costs continued to soar as Congress continued to increase the price the aged had to pay to use the program. Administrative expenses— the cost of maintaining the massive health bureaucracy created by the program—totaled nearly half a billion dollars and had more than doubled in the first five years of the program to almost $1.5 billion.

It must be remembered that the Medicare program only covers Americans over the age of 65. National health insurance, which is being proposed by the same individuals and groups that urged the adoption of Medicare, could cover seventeen times as many people. Obviously, the cost of that coverage would be many times higher.

Two facts are clear about our experience with the Medicare program: costs have skyrocketed and the original, "expert" cost projections of both Medicare and Medicaid have had absolutely no relationship to the real costs that have been encountered.

Not only hospital and physician costs went up with the advent of Medicare. Other costs rose, too. In a study prepared for the Social Security Administration, Regina Lowenstein of Columbia University compared utilization of these facilities during a year before Medicare began and during a year shortly after Medicare began. She found a 25 percent increase in the number of hospital days per enrolled persons sixty-five and over. The increases were particularly sharp for several categories. Persons over seventy-five increased their number of hospital days about 70 percent; blacks increased their number of hospital days almost 50 percent; and old people living alone and having under $1,000 annual income more than doubled their use of hospital days.

Some attempted to explain this increase in utilization in terms of a backlog of needed care in the elderly population which many persons could not afford before Medicare; and there is a limited basis for this belief. Dr. Lowenstein's study, for example, found that the rate of cataract surgery more than doubled in the transition period immediately before and after Medicare. The rate at which gall bladder operations were performed during this period tripled. But the trend toward higher utilization of hospitals has continued, and this fact can certainly not be explained on the basis of a backlog of medical care. Both frequency of admissions and length of stay have increased between fiscal years 1967-1971, and the number of hospital admissions per thousand persons enrolled under Medicare increased from 266 to 309, or more than 15 percent. Between 1967 and 1969 the average length of hospital stay increased 10 percent. As a result, between 1967 and 1969 the total number of hospital days paid for by Medicare jumped almost 25 percent. This increase alarmed Medicare officials, who then demanded tighter control of hospital utilization. In the following two-year period the average length of stay in the hospital declined about 7 percent. Although this drop only compensated for the increased rate of Medicare hospital admissions, in fiscal 1971 Medicare paid for approximately 78 million days of hospital care as compared with 61.7 million days in 1967 and 81 million in 1969.

Was all this hospitalization really necessary? While a certain portion of it undoubtedly was, Harry Schwartz points out significant abuses:

Frequently old people who have recovered from an illness or a bout of surgery properly treated in a hospital don't have anywhere to go or anyone to take care of them afterward. With the tightening of Medicare regulations on the use of extended care facilities, the tendency in some areas, for humanitarian reasons that are thoroughly understandable, is to keep them in the hospitals, thus providing expensive custodial care. . . . (T)he availability of seemingly free or cheap hospital care encourages the people involved to use the Medicare mechanism to meet the need.

Medicare, it must be remembered, does not differentiate between beneficiaries who can afford to bear all or part of their health costs and those who cannot. It treats in the same manner people who are in very different situations, offering the same benefits to the aged person who lives solely on his Social Security check and to the one who possesses substantial resources. Thus in many instances taxpayers are bearing the medical costs of men and women who are more than able to pay such costs for themselves.

The unfortunate fact is that although advocates of government involvement in medicine tell us that it will decrease costs and improve quality, the evidence of our own Medicare and Medicaid programs show precisely the opposite—that it will increase costs and decrease quality. At the present time, these same advocates of government med-

91

icine tell us that as a result of the "successes" of Medicare and Medicaid we should embark upon a system of national health insurance, an American version of socialized medicine.

If our medical care delivery system has problems today, with only limited government interference through the ill-fated Medicare and Medicaid programs, it is only a small indication of the difficulties we would encounter were a total program ever enacted. *Current estimates as to the cost of the program of national health insurance suggested by Senator Edward Kennedy of Massachusetts are now over $100 billion!* That, of course, is today's operating estimate, and it must be remembered that cost overruns approaching 100 percent have already been experienced with Medicare and Medicaid, and the cost of those programs is still rising.

As we have seen, socialized medical systems have failed to provide the high level of medical care our own private practice system has produced. Whereas most Americans can count on being hospitalized within a short distance from their homes, for example, the French patient often has to be treated many miles away from home and family. Joan Hobson, writing in *Private Practice,* points out that, "Public criticism of socialized medicine is now so much a part of French life that a weekly radio hour is devoted to a listener-participation program on which dissatisfied patients air their grievances."

British economist Arthur Seldon laid blame for Britain's deteriorating medical care squarely at the doorstep of the government health program: "The NHS stultifies preventive medicine by its ritual dogma that access to medical care should be equal for everyone. This is a recipe for paralysis. Experimentation with preventive techniques cannot set the pace for others to follow if nothing can be done unless it can be done for all. If this had been the rule in the last century, medical science would have been stifled in its infancy. And since a medical service financed collectively by public revenue cannot politically declare the contrary principle—that some people in surgeries (doctors' offices) or hospitals in some parts of the country may have to benefit before other people in other surgeries in other parts—it must at best slow down the rate of innovation of new techniques."

In his book, *Hazardous To Your Health,* Marvin Edwards makes an important point after citing government failures in agriculture, welfare, urban renewal, and education. He states that, "Those who criticize isolated instances of government failure as they occur—and marvel at the frequency of such occurrences—fail to recognize that the fault is in the system itself; that wastefulness, incompetence and inefficiency are an integral part of any attempt . . . for massive government intervention into the highly technical realm of providing medical care for human beings. Government's record in other fields should cause advocates of national health insurance to consider carefully the possible dangers of such a course."

So we have seen that a socialized medical system would be more expensive and less efficient than private, voluntary health care. We can also see that a real threat to individual freedom is implicit in such a system. Even without national health insurance, we have already witnessed serious infringement upon the traditional doctor-patient relationship. One of these infringements is found in the program establishing Professional Standards Review Organizations (PSRO).

This law requires that medical care be "standardized" for Medicare and Medicaid patients. Doctors are forced to comply with a system of guidelines for medical diagnosis, treatment, and care developed in accordance with rules set in Washington, D.C. by the Department of Health, Education and Welfare. In addition, the PSRO program threatens confidentiality which has always been inherent in the relationship of a doctor and his patient.

Under this law, states Dr. Donald Quinlan, president of the American Association of Physicians and Surgeons, "A physician can be forced to turn over to federal employees all medical notes taken in his office or in a hospital, including the most confidential information about his patients. Likewise, it is planned to have massive, detailed, computerized files on patients and doctors which will be instantly available to federal employees as an aid to the surveillance program and for such other purposes as the Secretary of HEW may provide."

Even patients who do not receive federal aid in any form will be subject to having their confidential records examined by government agents in an effort to establish "norms" of medical care. The PSRO examiner is able to search through a doctor's files and records without any court order or search warrant.

The PSRO program, however, may be only the beginning of government control of medical care. Far more serious dangers lie ahead. Consider what is being discussed in England, a country that has traveled farther along this mistaken road than we.

In a June, 1968, symposium on euthenasia that was reported in *The London Times,* Dr. Eliot Slater, editor of *The British Journal of Psychiatry,* stated that even if the elderly did retain their vigor, they suffer from the defect of an innate conservatism. "Just as in the mechanical world, advances occur most rapidly where new models are being constantly produced, with consequent obsolescence of the old, so too it is in the world of nature."

British Professor Glanville Williams presented the argument for euthanasia in front of millions on television. He stated: "At present the problem has certainly not reached the degree of seriousness that would warrant an effort being made to change the traditional attitudes towards the sanctity of life of the aged. Only the grimmest necessity could bring about a change . . . that . . . would probably cause apprehension and deep distress to many people and inflict traumatic injury upon the accepted code of behavior built up by 2,000 years of Christian religion. It may be, however, that as the problem becomes more acute it will itself cause a reversal of generally accepted values."

Lord Longford, who, as leader of the House of Lords, left the Front Bench to speak against an Abortion Bill, said that although he was shocked by the bill he was far more threatened by what he thought lay behind it. To Professor Williams' statement, Lord Longford said: "So the execution time of the old people may not be so very far off."

The prediction was not inaccurate. In March, 1969, a Voluntary Euthanasia Bill was introduced in the House of Lords. *The London Times* for March 24, 1969, opposed it on several grounds, including that it called "the slippery slope: The progress of the law of abortion (where the legal grounds for destroying the fetus have expanded from the life of the mother, to the health of the mother, to the welfare of children already born) confirms the suspicion that euthanasia once legally admitted would be similarly expanded."

Every time government enters any area, serious limitation of freedom results for the people affected. Dr. Klaus Rentzsch practices medicine in Hamburg, Germany. Writing about the socialized medical system in West Germany in *Private Practice,* Dr. Rentzsch notes,

The more social security is guaranteed by the government, the greater becomes the control over social behavior.

One danger of a social security system guaranteed by the state is that personal freedom may be limited because the institution that has to pay for all risks of health may demand that members avoid circumstances which may be a risk of health. . . . A system that gives free medical care and payment for income loss will, of course, try to keep things under control. But control in medicine is a bad thing. Such controls limit the doctor's freedom, his therapy, and even regulate how long a patient stays away from work. All systems of national health insurance believe in this control.

There is every reason for Americans to reject the idea of national health insurance. If we carefully consider the strengths of our private practice system of medicine, compare it to the weaknesses of the socialized medical systems of other countries, and review the failure of our own government programs such as Medicare and Medicaid, that conclusion becomes inevitable. Let us not in the name of better health care for all of our citizens set in motion a series of events that will guarantee the opposite.

The Federal Budget and the Economy

Not since the days of the Great Depression has America faced an economic situation as serious as the one we face today. Regrettably, there are no easy answers; no solutions that do not involve some degree of discomfiture for some people.

For the first time in our history, America is faced with the possibility of inflation and recession occurring simultaneously. For years economists have told us that because of increased federal controls over the economy it would be difficult, if not impossible, to have another collapse like the one that began in 1929. What they did not tell the American people was that these increased controls could so interfere with the workings of the marketplace that prices could rise and productivity could fall simultaneously. That is exactly what happened in 1973 and 1974.

Any time the supply of money increases faster than the rate of productivity, prices will escalate. The reason for that is simple. More money is available to buy fewer goods—relatively speaking—which means that increased demand for these goods pushes up their prices. Or as the classic definition runs, inflation is simply a case of "too much money chasing too few goods."

A number of things can produce rising prices but all deal, one way or another, with this ratio of money to productivity. For instance, when the federal government spends more money than it takes in, the deficit can be made up by increasing taxes, selling bonds in the private market, selling bonds to the Federal Reserve, or printing new money. The first two have minimal impact on prices since they do not increase the quantity of money in circulation. The latter two have a considerable impact because they do increase the amount of money available to spend while failing to provide for a corresponding increase in productivity.

Likewise, if government controls cut down on the incentive to produce, or make it more difficult to produce, the same thing will happen. There will be more money chasing fewer goods. This is why wage and price controls have been notoriously ineffective in holding down prices.

In the situation just described, we have both excessive federal spending and monetization of the debt as well as too much government regulation. This pushes prices up, interest rates up, prevents necessary capital formation to create new jobs and increased production, makes it almost impossible for banks and businesses to plan for the future, and results in massive redistribution of wealth by cheating creditors out of their just due. As a result we have seen a combination of inflation and recession.

Perhaps this problem could have been avoided if we had dwelt a little less on economic theory and a little more on some of the older lessons of history. America has become the most prosperous and powerful nation on earth, not by government doing things for people but by people doing things for themselves. Americans built this country, its business and its industry, by the sweat of their brows. The marketplace, uncluttered by excessive governmental regulation, determined success or failure through consumer democracy. The law of supply and demand ruled and ruled well; efficient producers were rewarded and inefficient ones fell by the wayside. Without undue restrictions, the lure of new markets, at home and abroad, gave the efficient producer the incentive to expand and become still more efficient. Then, with the emergence of interchangeable parts, the assembly line, and new technology, we became the world's foremost agricultural and industrial power. Of course, we were lucky to have an abundance of resources, but the key ingredient was freedom—economic and political.

The Great Depression and the experience of World War II changed things. America survived both to become the preeminent world power economically and militarily. But, at the same time, many Americans who lived through those traumatic years were determined that their children would not have to face the same experiences. The result was that economic security became a goal coequal to economic prosperity.

Since the free market, by definition, involves a certain amount of risk, postwar Americans in their search for economic security sought to minimize those risks by turning to the federal government for protection. Gradually,

97

regulations and subsidies which were begun in the 1930s as a response to the Depression were expanded to provide financial security under very different circumstances than existed during that era. Sooner or later, the internal inconsistency of seeking economic security, which necessitates a growth of federal controls, and economic prosperity, which involves just the opposite, was bound to catch up with us. Unfortunately, in the drive for security many Americans forgot that our nation was built by people taking risks and doing things for themselves, not by government trying to protect them and doing an ever increasing number of things for them.

The first signs of difficulty came about as a result of the rapid increase in federal spending. From a level of $9 billion in fiscal year 1940, federal spending increased to $106 billion in fiscal 1962, to $211 billion in fiscal 1971 and then to $365.6 billion in fiscal 1976. For fiscal year 1977, the Congress has passed a target level of $413.3 billion and the final figure is likely to be somewhat higher than that.

Unfortunately, federal revenues have not been able to keep pace with such spending. Since the end of World War II there have been only seven budget surpluses, totaling $23.4 billion, compared with 22 budget deficits that add up to an astronomical $275 billion. As a consequence, the national debt has soared from $268.7 billion in 1946 to a level of $576.6 billion at the start of 1976. Also, as a consequence, the 115 percent rise in the national debt has been more than matched by a 158 percent rise in the cost of living over the same period.

Alarming as those figures are, the picture for 1977 and beyond is even more grim. The anticipated deficit for fiscal year 1977, which started in January at $43 billion, had jumped by May to $50.8 billion, and is still rising. Such a figure is surpassed—at least for the moment—only by the deficit for 1975 and the World War II produced deficit of $57.4 billion in 1943. Worse yet, it is anticipated that, for the next few years at least, we will see budgets with similar deficits.

Not only do these huge deficits produce large jumps in both the national debt and the cost of living, but they also have a negative impact on the availability of capital for investment. There is only so much capital to go around and, according to Secretary of the Treasury William Simon, governments—federal, state, and local—were expected to require 80 percent of available capital in fiscal 1976 just to cover the deficits projected for that year. If those estimates were correct, that left only 20 percent for business and industry. This eventually will mean higher interest rates and insufficient funds to finance the expansion and modernization programs so essential to increased productivity, higher employment, and economic recovery. And, if the federal deficit reaches $55 to $60 billion in fiscal 1977, which would not be surprising, there will be very little capital for the private sector. Already, it is estimated the nation faces at least a $1.5 trillion capital shortfall over the next decade.

Of course, as I mentioned earlier, the lack of capital is not the only barrier to increased productivity. The proliferation of federal rules and regulations is another major obstacle which, like federal spending, has grown alarmingly in recent years. In more prosperous times the free enterprise system was considered the consumers' best protection against shoddy goods; nowadays, government has taken it upon itself to protect people not only from others but from themselves. One cannot even start a car these days without some buzzer reminding him, in some cases forcing him, to buckle his seatbelt.

Of course, all these things cost money—which means higher prices. In addition, all the red tape and paperwork businesses must put up with in order to get a permit or a license costs millions of dollars that could have otherwise been spent for plant expansion or equipment acquisition. For instance, a recent study done by the Commission on Federal Paperwork, estimated the total cost of federal paperwork at an astronomical $40 billion a year! Moreover, many of the rules and regulations promulgated by various federal regulatory agencies put a damper on competition rather than stimulate it as was originally intended.

Perhaps the best examples of this are the Interstate Commerce Commission, the Federal Communications Commission, and the Civil Aeronautics Board. In their respective areas, each has preempted the free market system by helping determine who gets what piece of the business and how they shall run it. Moreover, both the ICC and the CAB engage in rate regulation that amounts to price fixing just as surely as if a single company had developed a monopoly over the truck, railroad, or airline industry.

For example, not too long ago if one bought an airline ticket in California to fly from Los Angeles to San Francisco, it cost $16.50. Yet, if the same ticket had been purchased in New York, where it became subject to CAB control, the cost was $23. Moreover, it is estimated that, without the CAB, airline fares from New York to Los Angeles and from Washington to Chicago could have been reduced $73 and $19, respectively. I know that if I could save $38 on a roundtrip ticket every time I went back to my district, I would certainly be encouraged to buy more consumer goods and thus do my bit to stimulate productivity.

Instead of a truly competitive system, what has emerged is a system that increasingly shuts new entrepreneurs out and jeopardizes the survival of established businessmen in at least two ways. It denies them the right to do things as efficiently as they might and it adds arbitrarily to their costs and thus the costs of the consumer. To cite an example, one of the representatives from the auto industry recently testified in Washington that the cost of mandated safety features plus emission controls will add $1,200 to the cost of "economy" model cars by 1978. All of this, of course, simply fuels the fires of inflation and leads successively to reduced purchasing power, lowered demand for goods, cutbacks in production, unemployment, and, finally, recession.

Trying to beat inflation by increasing the benefits paid to people under various income support programs or by providing make-work jobs is ineffective because it aggravates the basic problem. Expenditures of this sort contribute to greater deficits; increased deficits mean more inflation; more inflation means more business failures and unemployment: all of which creates a vicious circle that can only end in depression. To put the prime emphasis on fighting recession instead of inflation is to fight symptoms instead of causes. The effort is doomed to failure and all Americans, including the recipients of increased benefits, are likely to come out losers in the long run. A more appropriate remedy would be to increase productivity while reducing the spending deficits that cause inflation.

As long as increased federal spending is combined with expanded governmental regulation of the economy, the ingredients are present for not just a recession but for a major economic disaster. Yet, instead of an all out effort to cut the budget, Congress, which has been controlled by the Democratic Party 40 of the last 44 years, has been leading the charge in favor of rolling up bigger budget deficits. When the previous administration tried to hold down spending, Congress did everything it could to thwart those efforts. Now, when the present administration requests rescissions and deferrals, Congress rejects all but a small percentage of them. Other examples of recent congressional unwillingness to exercise fiscal responsibility include the tax reduction bills passed by the House and Senate in 1975, the support expressed for an even larger public service employment program, the calls for an expanded public works program and the refusal to go along with a reasonable cut in the runaway food stamp program.

The picture is scarcely brighter in regard to cutting back on federal regulation. Today we have 12 departments and 75 agencies strangling business. We have created 20 new agencies just since 1967 and, if that were not enough, Congress is again contemplating the passage of a Consumer Protection Act which, if it takes the form of the bill that was killed several years ago, would create a consumer super-agency with the power to drag other federal regulatory agencies into court. For businessmen who are already at a loss when dealing with federal regulatory agencies, the prospect of one agency's rulings being challenged by yet another agency is almost too much to contemplate. There is no way they can plan for the future if they are left in constant doubt as to what they can or cannot do and when they can or cannot do it. Of course, the ultimate loser will be the very consumer the Consumer Protection Agency is supposed to protect.

In July 1975 and then again in May 1976, I made specific proposals to cut the budget and to reduce, or eliminate altogether, those federal regulatory agencies that help contribute to both inflation and recession. For fiscal 1976 it developed that the President's proposed $52 billion deficit could have been converted into a $900 million surplus just by some prudent cuts in spending. And, for fiscal 1977, practically the same cuts, plus implementation of Congressman Jack Kemp's tax reform bill designed to stimulate capital formation, would result in a budget surplus of almost $42 billion instead of the $43 billion deficit the President originally projected.

There are many good arguments that can be made for a tax reform bill of this nature. On the surface, it would seem that a tax cut at this time would run counter to a policy of reducing the federal deficit, but the proper type of tax cut will more than pay for itself in increased tax revenues generated by the economic recovery thus stimulated. This is what happened when taxes were cut in 1964

101

and the same thing could happen today. Certainly, it is better to give private enterprise a boost and let it create productive new jobs than it is to spend the same amount of money on unproductive make-work jobs, unemployment benefits, or welfare.

Another reason a tax cut is a good idea is that taxes are too high already. The average American pays out approximately one-third of his income in the form of direct taxes to all levels of government and the percentage is rising all the time. In 1974, while food costs were rising 12 percent, housing costs 13 percent, and fuel costs 14 percent, taxes rose 25 percent. If people are to have the money to spend on goods and if companies are to have the capital to produce those goods, then we need to turn the tax trend around so that more money is available to the private sector. There is little incentive to produce when so large a portion of one's earnings are going to the government in the form of taxes.

Congressman Kemp's bill, which I have enthusiastically co-sponsored along with 120 other congressmen, would address these problems decisively. This legislation, which would reduce taxes by at least $28.8 billion, not only would provide the needed stimulus for adequate capital formation but from a budget standpoint, is likely to result in an increase rather than a decrease in federal revenue. Such a conclusion is supported not only by an econometric study done by the economic consulting firm of Norman B. Ture, Inc., but also by the aforementioned experience with tax cuts in 1964 and also the 1973 Canadian experience when that government reduced its corporate tax rate from 49 to 40 percent.

Basically, what the Jobs Creation Act would do is: first allow a $1,000 yearly exclusion—$2,000 for a couple—from gross income of qualified additional savings and investments; second, end the double taxation of common dividends; third, grant a $1,000 exclusion from capital gains for each capital transaction qualifying; fourth, grant an extension of time for payment of estate taxes where the estate consists largely of small business interests; fifth, increase to $200,000 the estate tax exemption for family farm operations; sixth, reduce the corporate tax rate 6 per cent; seventh, permanently increase the investment tax credit by 15 percent; eighth, allow taxable year price adjustments and increase the life class variances for purposes of depreciation; ninth, permit a 1-year writeoff of nonproductive pollution control equipment; and tenth, provide for employee stockownership plan financing. Instead of reducing tax revenue by $22.2 billion as the President's tax package is estimated to do, this proposal is expected to raise revenue by an estimated $5.2 billion over what would otherwise be anticipated. In other words, the Jobs Creation Act, according to some estimates, at least, would raise government revenues from the $351.2 billion level the President has proposed for fiscal 1977 to somewhere in the neighborhood of $378.6 billion.

Another method of tax reform, and one that would be fair to people in all income brackets, would be what is known as tax indexing. Tying such things as tax rates, standard deductions, personal exemptions, depreciation allowances, and interest rates paid by the U.S. Government to the cost of living would give the American taxpayer protection against higher taxes due solely to inflation. As it stands now, wage increases in response to inflation simply push people into higher tax brackets without adding to their purchasing power. As a consequence, an ever increasing share of their income is paid out in taxes.

According to Dr. William J. Fellner, former member of the President's Council of Economic Advisers, personal income tax payments in 1974 increased $8 billion and corporate tax payments went up almost $20 billion, simply on the basis of inflation. However, if Congress were to pass the tax indexing bill sponsored to date by 35 Members, myself included, the savings to the American taxpayer would come to some $17.6 billion.

Tax indexing has one other advantage. It takes away from the government any incentive it might have to promote inflation. With almost $28 billion coming in the year before last as a result of inflation, it is easy to see how such an incentive could develop within the federal bureaucracy. Whether it has or not is another question, but by enacting a tax indexing bill we would make the answer academic.

Obviously, there are other measures that could, or should, be considered within the context of unraveling the mess into which we have enmeshed ourselves. But, by enacting the Jobs Creation Act and tax indexing, we could go a long way towards overcoming the effects of inflation and its handmaiden recession.

The cure for all our ills will not be easy to come by, but if we work on the premises that federal spending must be cut, federal regulation must be reduced, and tax cuts must be used to stimulate economic recovery rather than redistribute income, we will make the greatest progress in the shortest time in dealing with our immediate dilemma. More importantly, we will reestablish the economic vigor and strength that made the United States the envy of the world.

Is Business an Endangered Species?

> Government never of itself furthered any enterprise, but by the alacrity with which it got out of its way . . . The character inherent in the American people has done all that has been accomplished; and it would have done more, if the government had not sometimes got in the way.
>
> —Henry David Thoreau

Three transparently fallacious assumptions, all interrelated, threaten the survival of American business, a free market economy, and, ultimately, our free institutions.

The first is the hysterical claim that our nation is beset with "crises" requiring costly, crash solutions to avert national disaster.

The second is that free institutions—and more specifically free enterprise—is the insidious culprit.

The third, rarely articulated in a forthright manner but implicit in the foregoing assumptions, is that government regulations and control of the American economy can remove the causes of the crises and resolve them.

One need not look far for examples of the "Chicken Little" syndrome. We are told the sky is falling in on us at every turn. The Friends of the Earth hint darkly that all mankind will perish before the end of the century through pollution of our environment. Zero population growth, on the contrary, alerts us to the prospect of billions upon billions of people standing upon one another's shoulders by the end of the century.

Others warn of a crisis in health care or suggest that millions of Americans are starving to death and lacking adequate housing.

To ridicule such absurdities is not to say that we do not have unresolved problems in every one of these categories

105

and more. Further, we all know that hyperbole often attends successful promotion efforts. But the same people who plague us daily with horror stories of this nature are usually in the vanguard of the "truth in advertising" campaign.

"Cherchez la femme," as the French police used to say. Look for the motive. Behind much of this rhetoric are those types whom Margaret Cole once observed "do their donkey work in the shadows." They are ideologues who reject the premises of a free society, the elitists who would play God with our lives.

The natural silly putty for such ideologues are self-serving politicians always eager to find a hobby horse to ride to fame and fortune. These snake oil salesmen, posturing as saviors of the public, are little more than malicious mischiefs. But their ability to exploit an irresponsible media generates the climate of the "big lie," which repeated oft enough comes to gain credibility.

But the greatest threat of all is the sincere, honest, idealistic, misguided reformer. He is the one who, out of a sense of exasperation and a lack of understanding of history, turns impatiently to government to relieve all the ills of mankind. His motives are not self-serving, but generous and charitable. Even so, he represents the greatest threat to free institutions in our society.

Supreme Court Justice Louis Brandeis described him in the Olmstead case:

> Experience should teach us to be most on our guard to protect liberty when the government's purposes are beneficient. Men born to freedom are naturally alert to repel invasion of their liberty by evil-minded rulers. The greatest dangers to liberty lurk in insidious encroachments by men of zeal, well meaning, but without understanding.

God spare us such men.

Those who accept the proposition that we have impending national disasters requiring "crash" solutions are naturally led to find causes before prescribing remedies. With the capable tutoring of the anti-capitalist mentalities, free institutions and free enterprise become convenient scapegoats. To listen to some of the more paranoid allegations against the business community, one would almost suppose that the businessman lives in a world other than our own. The theater of the absurd produced by some of our crisis-mongers accuses the businessman of a calloused unconcern

106

for the air we breathe, the water we drink and recreate in, our wildlife, our purple mountains and our fruited plains. Worse than the businessman's alleged unconcern is the suggestion that he actively promotes pollution of the environment in a reckless pursuit of pelf. The self-righteous have ever been guilty of overlooking human imperfection. Base motives are substituted for ignorance and human frailty. Presumably, such businessmen have found another environment for themselves and their children to live in.

Beyond the conspiracy of wicked businessmen, according to this analysis, is the inherent deficiency of the free enterprise system, which such critics have attacked since the advent of the industrial revolution. There is a romantic longing for the blissful era of medieval feudalism. Such reactionaries would not only repeal the twentieth century —in the name of progress—but would repeal half a millennium. There is a horrifying logical consistency between the goals of people of this persuasion and those of Zero Population Growth, as there are roughly 3 billion more people on this earth today than could be sustained on a feudal economy.

Having defined the crisis and established the cause, the solution that immediately springs into the simplistic minds of the kneejerk statists and collectivists is to launch a preemptive strike by the federal government with massive infusions of taxpayer dollars.

If the fruits of this cacophonous coalition were not so portentous, we might dismiss them with a knowing grin or a bored yawn. But we live at a time when today's lunacy is tomorrow's law. And when national hysteria is thus generated, it is easy to provoke an over-reaction.

Beyond this, there is invariably great waste and excessive expenditure of tax money in fighting crises instead of addressing problems. Further, there is an enormous increase in the role government plays in our lives when we marshal the forces of the federal bureaucracy to attack national issues. After the dismal experience of the past 40 years of federal involvement in such areas as agriculture, welfare, housing, Indian affairs, and the postal system, one might suppose we would have learned some painful lessons of history. On the basis of that history we might safely formulate a law: Problems increase in direct proportion to the degree of attention given them and the amount of money spent on them by the federal government.

The Founding Fathers viewed the role of government in

107

negative terms. Its primary function was to prevent trespass and otherwise stay out of our way.

In a letter to Edward Carrington, Thomas Jefferson wrote, "The natural progress of things is for liberty to yield and government to gain ground." He added:

One of the most profound preferences in human nature is for satisfying one's needs and desires with the least possible exertion; for appropriating wealth produced by the labor of others, rather than producing it by one's own labor. . . . The stronger and more centralized the government, the safer would be the guarantee of such monopolies; in other words, the stronger the government, the weaker the producer, the less consideration need be given him and the more might be taken away from him.

Even as late as the twentieth century, this view of the role of government obtained. Woodrow Wilson held that government's function was to preserve a free field with no favors. Nevertheless, the collectivist pathogenesis dates from this period. Artful advocates of "positive" government called for government to serve as an engine of social reform. "It is the work of the state to think for the people—to teach them how to do, and to sustain them in doing," declared Frank Munsey early in this century. By the 1960's, an Indiana Senator could publicly announce that "The people should depend upon the Government like children depend upon their mothers."

To the extent that many Americans were willing to permit power to gravitate to the banks of the Potomac on the assumption that Washington held magical solutions, irresponsibility was transformed into dependency. The federal breast began to nurse us all.

Today we are beginning to feel the outrageous consequences of the policies of well-intentioned men who lack understanding. American business is bearing the brunt of the attack.

We have been told that selfishness and lack of concern on the part of businessmen are responsible for most of our social ills, from pollution to inflation.

As a result of the analysis that holds that free enterprise and its practitioners are the culprits, and the remainder of the American society are the victims, we have seen the creation of inordinate rules and regulations under which business must operate.

The bureaucratic assaults upon free enterprise that have been instituted thus far, together with those that have

108

been proposed and may be advanced in the future, are a declaration of war against capitalism as we know it.

Before considering the merits or demerits of the proposition that free enterprise is the cause of our problems, let us briefly review some of the constraints now being imposed or proposed against American business.

One of the most shocking and least discussed is a recommendation set forth in a memorandum approved by three top officials of the Equal Employment Opportunity Commission (EEOC) several years ago.

According to that memorandum, any business should be considered in violation of the civil rights statutes if "the community from which an employer moves has a higher percentage of minority workers than the community to which he moves," or "the transfer affects the employment situation of the employer's minority workers more adversely than it affects his remaining workers."

The memo also suggests that the law should be interpreted so that any employer "who relocates to the detriment of the minority work force is clearly in violation of Title VII of the Civil Rights Act." The extraordinary recommendation continues:

It should be noted that it is not necessary for the relocation to have been completed in order for Title VII liability to attach. Section 703(a) states that it is unlawful for an employer to deprive or tend to deprive any individual of employment opportunities.

This memorandum—a recommendation for EEOC to take companies to court on this novel legal theory—suggests that court orders should be sought against businesses planning to relocate, charging them with prima facie violations of the civil rights act. Companies so charged would have to prove an overwhelming business consideration before being permitted to transfer locations.

One business leader commented about this proposal in these terms:

This recommendation to the Equal Employment Opportunity Commission smacks less of civil rights than it does of fascism. It would seem an elementary freedom to be able to relocate one's own company without having to justify it to a bunch of bureaucrats.

Nevertheless this proposal received the support of Stanley P. Hubert, then General Counsel of the Commission, together with John de J. Pemberton, Jr., now Acting General Counsel, and Martin I. Slate, attorney in the General

Counsel's office. This proposal is not yet the law, but it provides some indication of the direction in which government control of business and of the economy may go.

Let us consider briefly some things that are not proposals, but actual facts of business life today.

Under the chairmanship of Miles Kirkpatrick, an appointee of President Nixon, the Federal Trade Commission (FTC) has broadened its powers in an unprecedented manner.

One of many companies which have felt its wrath has been the du Pont Co., makers of Zerex antifreeze. The FTC charged that Zerex was falsely advertised in a television commercial, charges that have since been proven to be untrue. The company lost sales in 1971 as well as public confidence because of unfavorable publicity.

What the FTC did was call a press conference in November 1970 and make a "proposed complaint" against du Pont, alleging, without proof, that the television commercial was misleading, that the antifreeze actually damaged automotive cooling systems and that it had been inadequately tested. The federal agency then publicly threatened to ban the product.

The commercial in question showed a man stabbing a can of Zerex. Streams of antifreeze gushed out and then sealed up. After the FTC charged that this demonstration was phony, newspapers across the country carried stories of the Commission's condemnation of Zerex.

Officials of du Pont were not even informed of the FTC's action before the Washington press conference. Equally important is the fact that the FTC turned out to be wrong. It dropped the charges of false advertising. It dropped the charge that the product could cause damage. The FTC, in fact, found nothing wrong with the product in any way.

To cover its own tracks, however, the FTC issued a formal complaint alleging that the antifreeze had been inadequately tested before it was put on the market and could have caused damage to cooling systems when first sold in 1969. It said nothing of any possible damage to be caused by the product in 1970, 1971, or 1972. It provided no proof of any damage having occurred in 1969.

The financial damage to du Pont, of course, had already been done. Du Pont counted 160 newspaper stories after the initial FTC accusation and only 80, half as many, a year later when the agency admitted that it had been wrong.

110

Twenty front page stories appeared the first time. The FTC's error received no first page placements a year later.

Discussing the current tactics being used by the FTC, Professor Yale Brozen of the Graduate School of Business at the University of Chicago declared:

The FTC has come up with the technique of unilaterally deciding what is deceptive, conducting a trial by press release, and demanding that the advertiser run ads admitting the deception. The burden of proving innocence is left to the advertiser, if he can survive the trial by accusation and publicity—a complete turnabout from our judicial sysem in which an accused is regarded as innocent until proved guilty.

The FTC is now calling on advertisers, industry by industry, to file with it documentary proof of all claims. Perhaps, states Professor Brozen, "the FTC should be forced to substantiate its claims before issuing press releases which greatly mislead consumers."

In the long run, Professor Brozen notes, to advertise at all may become a sin. "The Federal Trade Commission is leveling a barrage of unsubstantiated claims against advertising which, if it prevails, may well cause a withering of advertising."

Government's effort to curtail the efficiency and effectiveness of free enterprise comes in many shapes and forms.

Consider, for example, the Occupational Safety and Health Act (OSHA). This Act invests authority in the Secretary of Labor for the first time to set job safety standards for the bulk of the nation's 80 million working men and women. Only coal miners, railroad workers, and government employees, who are covered by other regulations, are exempt. This Act has opened the door to harassment of business in its daily operation, a harassment that promises to grow greater in the future.

The Act covers every business "affecting commerce," and every aspect of the operation from washroom to storage yards to assembly lines, from the clerk in the shoe store to the farmhand driving a tractor. Although the Secretary of Labor may consult with other federal agencies, he is under no obligation to consult with businessmen; he alone determines what is "safe and healthful employment in places of employment."

Among other things, the Secretary is given authority to enforce safety standards he may issue, and under his broad delegation of power can enter any "factory, plant, estab-

111

lishment, construction site, mine or other area or workplace or environment" to inspect it; close down any operation he finds dangerous; move to cancel government contracts; and ask courts to impose fines and/or jail sentences for violators of his standards.

One wonders what ever happened to the Fourth Amendment guarantees against unwarranted search. One wonders what ever happened to Fifth Amendment guarantees of the security of private property.

Our previous system, based on state-determined standards, education, and cooperation, produced safety statistics that were the best in the world. This, however, has been abandoned in the interest of a nationalized, bureaucratically run system of harassment of private business.

Back in 1972 I proposed a bill that includes some of the amendments necessary for a responsible reform of the 1970 act.

As a result of the 1970 Occupational Safety and Health Act, businesses are deluged with a multitude of so-called health and safety requirements with which they must comply or face sanctions that include civil and criminal penalties and even the closing down of businesses. These requirements have been imposed without any administrative determination that they will improve occupational health and safety, that they are necessary, or that they are the best means of achieving the desired result.

Thirteen amendments are included in the bill I then introduced. The first amendment would exempt small employers, both agricultural and nonagricultural, from the act. Businesses of 25 or fewer employees would be exempted, as they are from the provisions of the Equal Employment Opportunities Act. Another amendment would require the Secretary of Labor to evaluate all of the regulations, distinguish between the various facets of a given general form of business, and determine if the rule should apply to each facet. A case in point are the real differences in the construction business between heavy construction and light residential construction.

Another amendment would require the Secretary of Labor to publish for each present and future rule the maximum estimated cost of compliance and to determine that it is possible to comply. A further amendment would require the Secretary of Labor to provide technical advice and consultation to employers of 100 or fewer employees to assist them in complying with the act. Each of the 13 amendments attempts to restore to individual businessmen at least a portion of the control over their own businesses which the act itself takes away.

Perhaps it is the nature of bureaucrats to be martinets. Of one thing we can be sure, bureaucrats are not bound by the profit discipline of businessmen. As a result, they are inclined to be impractical theoreticians rather than pragmatic realists. Further, they have a vested interest in self-perpetuation and growth. Unlike business imperatives, where a man's progress depends upon his ability to demonstrate efficiency, the prestige of a bureaucratic chief is determined in part upon the basis of how many Indians he has in his department.

But the greatest danger to be apprehended is the often heavy-handed capriciousness of bureaucrats in their war against the businessman and free markets. Since all the presuppositions of bureaucratic interventionism are alien to the concept of free enterprise, it is not surprising to find covert and overt hostility within the bureaucracy. Just as a stagnant pond breeds bacterial life, bureaucracy develops and attracts the germs and parasites that feed at the expense of free institutions.

Herbert Hoover summarized the case most succinctly when he observed that:

In all bureaucracies there are three implacable spirits—self-perpetuation, expansion and an incessant demand for power. These are human urges and are supported by a conviction, sometimes justified, that they know what is good for us. Nevertheless these spirits are potent and possess a dictatorial complex. . . . Power is the father of impatience with human faults, and impatience breeds arrogance. In their mass action, they become veritable exponents of political tyranny.

Perhaps more important is the fact that once our economic freedom is challenged, our political freedom becomes increasingly tenuous. Too few of those who have endorsed a government-controlled economy seem to have considered the intrinsic link between economic freedom and political freedom. Many seem to believe that it is possible to lose our economic freedom while remaining free in other aspects of our lives. Such a view, unfortunately, is repeatedly challenged by the facts of history.

In his important volume, *Capitalism and Freedom,* Professor Milton Friedman points out that:

The kind of economic organization that provides economic freedom directly, namely, competitive capitalism, also promotes political freedom because it separates economic power from political power and in this way enables the one to offset the other.

Professor Friedman continues:

Political freedom means the absence of coercion of a man by his fellow man. The fundamental threat to freedom is power to coerce, be it in the hands of a monarch, a dictator, an oligarchy, or a momentary majority. The preservation of freedom requires the elimination of such concentration of power to the fullest possible extent and the dispersal and distribution of whatever power cannot be eliminated—a system of checks and balances. By removing the organization of economic activity from the control of political authority, the market eliminates this source of coercive power. It enables economic strength to be a check to political power rather than a reinforcement.

Today there are many, in both parties and regardless of their previously stated political and economic philosophies, who would eliminate the checks and balances to which Professor Friedman referred and who would provide government with the power to set the wages of workers and the prices of businessmen—thereby giving government total power over the economic life of the nation. In a recent editorial, *The Wall Street Journal* stated:

Without wanting to sound apocalyptic, we find rather dismaying the ease with which the business community and a Republican Administration have accepted—and often welcomed—the prospect of a controlled economy.

It is important that we deal with the question posed by New Left activists and their older supporters in the Congress, the media, and elsewhere. That is this: Does capitalism produce pollution, decay, fraud, and the host of other problems such critics hope to solve by expanding the power and authority of government?

Those who advance such a view argue that under socialism there would be no pollution of the air, for the state would be in control. With the "people" in control there would be no greed, and thus the proper precautions would be taken to insure pure air, clean rivers, and the like.

This argument makes internal sense, as all ideological arguments do, but it has one major flaw. It is simply not true. A look at the world's environment shows the fallacy of such thinking.

In fact, it is interesting to note that there is a great similarity between the approaches used by those who are fighting environmental and ecological problems in the United States and those who are doing so in the Soviet Union.

Academician Andrei Sakharov published an illegal pamphlet, launched through the Soviet "underground" to demand radical political reforms and blamed the country's economic system for causing damage to the environment and thus "changing the face of the earth."

The issue has moved out of the Soviet underground and into the state-controlled press, much as the question of pollution has moved from being a concern of student activists to being a part of the President's State of the Union message.

An article in *Pravda* pointed to the contradiction between the "unrestrained" growth of industrial production on the one hand, and outdated technology of Soviet industry on the other. The organization of industry was also to blame. The author was saying, in effect, that Soviet industry was so preoccupied with growth targets that it neglected to keep its own house in order—which is what has so often been said of capitalists.

Victor Zorza, the Eastern European correspondent for the British newspaper, *The Guardian*, makes this point:

In the West, the strength of the profit motive is often said to drive capitalists to press on with production regardless of damage to the environment. In Russia, it is the weakness of the profit motive that gets the blame. The *Pravda* article notes that "tremendous material losses were caused" by the failure of the oil industry to develop the necessary procedures to remove water and salt from the oil. The price paid for the oil remained the same, whether these unwarranted constituents had been removed or not.

In the United States, motor vehicles are responsible for 60 percent of air pollution. Russia, which has relatively few autos, has an air pollution problem as well. The Soviet press often boasts that the air in Moscow is cleaner and sweeter than in any comparable capital city. But most of Russia's industry is outside of Moscow. *Pravda* confessed that "We are turning the atmosphere of our major industrial regions and large cities into a dump for poisonous industrial wastes."

It is clear that whatever environmental problems we face in the United States are also being faced throughout the world, in countries that are capitalist and communist and

115

socialist. The fault, it would appear, is not who controls the modern technology, but with the technology itself.

Far too long American businessmen have tended to apologize for their successes, to sit silently by as capitalism was attacked by those who argued that, somehow, government control of the economy would produce a more "equitable" sharing of the nation's resources.

They failed to point out that capitalism was simply freedom applied to economics, that under a system of free enterprise it was the consumer, the individual, who voted with his dollars in the marketplace and determined in this manner exactly what would be produced in the economy. In the socialistic, communistic, and fascistic economies supported by the advocates of collectivism, it is a small band of bureaucrats who make this decision.

Under capitalism, people not only decide for themselves what the economy is to produce, but they are able to procure for themselves a far larger share of that production than under any other system. Capitalism is the best economic system for those at the lowest level as well as for those at the highest. In fact, those at the lowest levels in our own country and in the capitalist societies of Western Europe and of Japan would find themselves in the upper levels of collectivist societies—where a radio, a television, and indoor plumbing are still considered luxuries.

There is no way to increase our standard of living, improve our competitive standing in world markets, ease the problem of unemployment, defeat inflation, and really give consumers the choice they desire except by taking government out of the economy, not giving it control over the economy as we now appear to be doing.

The best consumer advocate is not a new law or government agency, but free enterprise itself. Under capitalism, the consumer votes with his dollars for the kinds of products he wishes to purchase. The jury of American business is not a court of law or a legislative chamber but the millions of free citizens who judge its products and services as they choose between them.

There is an old saying that if you want to be seen, stand up; if you want to be heard, speak up; and if you want to be appreciated, shut up. For too long the business community has apparently wanted to be appreciated. It is high time the outraged businessmen—speaking not just in their own interest, but in the interest of their employees as well as the consuming public—express their sense of indignation

116

over this unrelenting assault upon the concept of a free market. They must get directly involved in this battle and provide the leadership which is so sorely lacking.

Business and industry, if it is to restore economic freedom, must not apologize for itself or for its profits. American business and industry has provided all of our citizens with the highest standard of living in the world. It has done this through economic freedom. The rest of the world, through economic slavery, has hardly been able to feed its people.

The choice is ours, and businessmen must speak up in behalf of economic freedom before it is compromised away in the maze of considerations about what is politically possible. Once freedom is lost, it is difficult if not impossible to restore.

Beyond this, we must guard against leaving the field to the enemy out of a sense of despair over how far down the garden path we have trod. To those who shrug their shoulders and say it is hopeless, that nothing can be done, I would only remind you that this can become a self-fulfilling prophecy if enough Americans believe it. What if George Washington had taken such a point of view at Valley Forge? What if Lincoln had in the dark days of the War Between the States? What if our nation had after Pearl Harbor?

One of the ways in which corporations can make a positive contribution is by educating their stockholders to a better understanding of the principles of a free market economy and why it is the most humane, productive, and morally justifiable system. In addition, stockholders should be constantly alerted to legislation under consideration which does violence to their interests both as stockholders and consumers. Such an educational effort can help to generate those pressures necessary to influence the course of legislation in Washington.

Finally, we should mobilize our limited resources behind rifleshot efforts to affect the greatest changes. There are somewhat over 100 members of the House of Representatives—the body responsible for initiating money bills—who are economy-minded and opposed to the drift toward a regulated economy. At the other extreme there are slightly over 100 members who will vote for virtually any spending measure and who totally support the idea of a controlled economy. Of the 200 odd members in between—all of whom are responsive to pressure—we should identify the 100 closest to our position and focus our efforts on them.

It is wholly unrealistic to suppose that we will ever have

a Congress comprised of talents of the magnitude of those statesmen who laid the foundation of our Republic. Under the circumstances, while still working to upgrade, qualitatively, our representation in the Congress, a more important task is to devise the ways and means of accomplishing our goals with the raw materials at hand. An important aspect of this involves understanding the psychology of the politician. When we have done all this, we should be able to concentrate our efforts more effectively to produce the votes in Congress that will reinvigorate free institutions and preserve the world's last best hope for ourselves and our posterity.

Woodrow Wilson, who was a keen student of history, stated:

> The history of liberty is a history of limitations of governmental power, not the increase of it. When we resist, therefore, the concentration of power, we are resisting the powers of death, because concentration of power is what always precedes the destruction of human liberties.

Today we are witnessing the most unprecedented concentration of such governmental power in our national experience.

On the last day of the convention in Philadelphia in 1787, Benjamin Franklin prepared a speech urging all the delegates at the convention to sign the document that had been drafted. Some members had reservations on the grounds that to deposit the power of the sword and the power of the purse in one level of government was to sow the seeds of ultimate despotism.

Franklin acknowledged that the proposed Constitution was not a perfect document, but that there was a way of remedying defects through the amendment process. Franklin contended, however, that in the final analysis it mattered little what form of government was created because this government, as all governments before it, would degenerate into a despotism when the people needed a despotism.

I am convinced that the American people do not need a despotism today any more than they have in the past and hopefully and prayerfully they never will in the future. To guarantee that future we must unite our efforts and reconsecrate ourselves to that end.

Regulatory Agencies out of Control

Prior to the advent of the New Deal in the 1930s, with a number of specific exceptions, the United States pursued a policy of support for the free market based upon a belief that economic freedom and political freedom went hand in hand, as well as the idea that under a system of free enterprise the nation's goods and services would be most widely and most equitably distributed.

Since the New Deal Americans have pursued a different policy—a policy of government intervention in and regulation of the nation's economy. The initial reason for this departure was the hope that such intervention could help us avoid another great Depression.

In every instance the advocates of intervention and regulation have advanced the view that their policies would best serve the "public" interest. Now we confront a period of economic instability and an economy in which inflation and recession have occurred simultaneously. After a generation of unprecedented intervention and regulation, we are provided a unique opportunity to test the assumptions of the interventionists and regulators.

In an unusual statement for a federal official, FTC Chairman Lewis A. Engman attacked federal regulatory agencies —specifically mentioning the Civil Aeronautics Board and the Interstate Commerce Commission—as being protective of industries they regulate in an unhealthy relationship that unnecessarily raises costs to the consumer and contributes to inflation.

Engman declared, "Most regulated industries have become federal protectorates, living in a cozy world of cost-plus, safely protected from the ugly specters of competition, efficiency and innovation." To correct these problems, he called for re-examination of "every regulation or regulatory policy that contributes to inflation."

It is no accident that government regulation of the economy produces negative results. Liberal reformers who believed otherwise in the 1920s learned a lesson that modern liberals—and their Republican imitators—must now learn anew. Frederic G. Howe, a progressive member of the Wilson Administration, wrote in his 1925 book, *Confessions Of A Reformer*, that he had become distrusting of the government and he now "viewed it as the source of exploitation rather than the remedy for it."

Woodrow Wilson also understood the problems of government control of the economy. In 1912 he declared: "If the government is to tell big businessmen how to run their business, then don't you think that big businessmen have got to get closer to government than they are now?"

The failure of government regulatory agencies is something that has recently become a reality accepted as true even by the strongest proponents of such bodies.

Consider, for example, the record of the Civil Aeronautics Board. Professors Peter Passell and Leonard Ross of Columbia University write that "economic estimates suggest that, without the Civil Aeronautics Board, you could fly from New York to Los Angeles for $95, from Washington, D.C. to Chicago for $33. Current fares on the two runs are $168 and $52 respectively. In general, it seems clear that without the CAB, air fares could be considerably lower throughout the United States and abroad."

Rather than trust the question of air fares to the marketplace, Passell and Ross suggest that "Congress set up independent regulatory commissions with bipartisan membership and lengthy terms . . . [that would] preside over 10 percent of the national economy, including interstate railway, truck, barge and ship transportation; communications by telephone, cable, radio, and television; electric and atomic power; banking, the stock market and cattle investment trusts."

No interstate airline can operate without a certificate from the CAB declaring its "public interest, convenience and necessity." This means that no one can enter the airline business unless the CAB decides that the "public interest" requires it. Interestingly, since it was established in 1938, the CAB has yet to find that the "public interest" would be served by the entry of a single new competitor to the ten major airlines.

Air travel, we often forget, is an inherently cheap commodity. According to statistics compiled by *Aviation Week* magazine, the direct operating costs of a 747 are about one cent per seat mile, or about $25 from New York to Los Angeles. Professor Michael E. Levine, a former CAB staff member, noted that, "The board has . . . operated an imperfect cartel for the benefit of the industry."

What is the answer to high air fares and lack of competition? Professors Passell and Ross state that it is to "Allow free competition. Abolish the board's power to fix minimum prices, and permit any responsible carrier to fly on any domestic route."

In recent testimony before a U.S. Senate subcommittee, Dr. William A. Jordon, a leading critic of air regulation, declared that air fares in the United States are 40 to 100 percent higher than necessary because of the CAB regulation of industry. He contended that, besides making air travel unnecessarily expensive, CAB regulation has sharply cut into airline profits by reducing employee productivity and forcing the airlines to purchase unneeded equipment.

Dr. Jordon is a professor of managerial economics at York University in Toronto. He has worked for four airlines over a 27-year period and his estimates are based on a number of detailed comparisons of federally regulated airlines with intrastate carriers operating within Texas and California, which do not come under CAB regulation. The studies also compared the performance of CAB-regulated airlines with those in Canada and with transport planes operated by the Department of Defense. The studies show that short-haul fares "probably are between 40 to 70 percent higher than they could be without CAB regulations," Dr. Jordon said. This means that, without regulation, the New York-Boston or New York-Washington fare would have been $15 to $17 rather than the $25.93 and $27.78 that was charged at the time.

For flights of medium distance Dr. Jordon estimated that existing fares were 75 to 100 percent higher than they would be without regulation, while transcontinental fares were "around 100 percent higher than they would be without regulation." He said that the total actual savings to all consumers resulting from an end to the CAB's regulatory function would amount to $3.5 billion.

Equally dramatic in its failure to serve the public interest is the record of the Interstate Commerce Commission (ICC). Originally established in 1887 to protect customers and rail lines from discriminatory pricing and rate wars, the agency today has more than 2,000 employees in 78 offices across the country. Not only railroads, but interstate trucking and barge lines have been brought under the agency's jurisdiction. Its stated goal was to end "cut-throat competition" and serve the public. What it has done is end competition almost entirely and serve the joint interests of the large companies and labor unions.

Looking at the record of the ICC, Senator William Proxmire (D-Wisconsin) observed, "The ICC has become a captive of the transportation industry itself. Instead of regulating transportation to avoid monopoly and increased prices, it has established monopolies, reduced competition, and ordered high and uneconomic rates to cover the costs of inefficient producers."

The example of ICC's regulation of trucking clearly illustrates the manner in which the public is seriously harmed by its intervention in what would otherwise be a free market. The ICC has the power and authority to: 1) dictate which truckers can go into interstate business; 2) determine what a commercial trucker can and cannot carry; 3) decide what areas truckers may serve; and 4) permit the trucking industry to fix its own prices.

Each year hundreds of companies apply for operating rights and are turned down by the ICC. Robert Gallagher, a New York attorney specializing in transportation matters, notes that, "The ICC has a disturbing tendency to be protective of large carriers."

In an article entitled "Highway Robbery—Via The ICC," Mark Frazier, writing in *The Readers Digest*, reports that the application of Checker Transportation and Storage is a case in point.

Checker has hauled household goods in South Carolina for 27 years, using licenses owned by a number of giant van lines. Each time the company makes an interstate trip, it must pay an average of 10 percent of the revenues to the big van companies that hold the permits it needs. In August, 1972, Checker asked the ICC for a modest interstate license of its own. A half-dozen nationwide van lines and one regional competitor who already held such permits filed immediate protests. Checker had to spend $5,000 in legal fees to present its case. None of these complainants challenged Checker's service or denied the charge that they shunned the short-haul interstate traffic Checker specialized in. Nevertheless, the commission, after a wait of 20 months, rejected Checker's application —thus forcing the line to continue paying virtual kickbacks for the right to haul goods in interstate commerce. . . .

With regard to the ICC's power to determine what a trucker can and cannot carry, we see a situation in which, according to Frazier:

> . . . some truckers are permitted to carry only unexposed film; exposed film must be hauled by somebody else. Other truckers may transport plastic pipe but not metal pipe. Officials at Quaker Oats, starting a new pizza-making plant in Jackson, Tennessee, have had to face problems with certificate-hobbled truckers. Trucks hauling tomato paste to the plant from California are not allowed to carry pizzas back. Trucks bringing pizza crusts from Denver must also return empty.

As Mike Parkhurst, a former trucker who now edits the trucking magazine, *Overdrive*, notes, "It's as if American Airlines could only carry people from east to west, while United took passengers from west to east."

The unfortunate fact is that cargo restrictions serve the trucking industry by creating a need for more trucking activity: they harm the consumer by dramatically increasing costs. By limiting what one carrier may carry back to his point of origin, the ICC also increased the demand for truck drivers, which of course the Teamsters Union strongly favors. Only the consumers are harmed by the ICC, which serves the interest of the industry and the workers being regulated, not the "public" interest. It is estimated that regulated truckers today travel empty an estimated 30 percent of their miles, triple the percentage for unregulated carriers. These figures are spelled out in a 1970 report on the ICC co-authored by Robert Fellmeth and members of the Ralph Nader research staff.

Equally detrimental to the public is the ICC policy of establishing hundreds of thousands of routes, often specifying to the mile where an individual truck may go. Agency rules, for example, require Cedar Rapids Steel Transportation—hauling sixty truckloads a week to Chicago from St. Paul—to go 90 miles out of the way through Clinton, Iowa. Because truckers are often prevented from taking the quickest and most economic route to their destination, the cost to the consumer is increased, as is the use of much-needed energy resources. Conservation groups such as the Sierra Club estimate that tens of millions of gallons of gasoline are wasted each year as a result of ICC regulations.

Finally, the ICC permits the trucking industry to do what no unregulated private industry is permitted by law to do—set its own prices. Interstate rates are established by 148 "rate bureaus," which are regional associations of truckers. The rates the trucking industry sets for itself are put into effect automatically unless an aggrieved party goes to the expense of asking the ICC to intervene. John Snow of the Department of Transportation says of the truckers that, "They are in a situation that almost every industry would like to be in. They can sit down and veto the rates of their competitors."

Any trucker who tries to lower his rates finds that his position is almost impossible. In his *Reader's Digest* article Mark Frazier writes of the example of the Poole Trucklines of Alabama. "When Poole told customers that it was reducing by 35 percent its rate on hauling paper products," he writes, "the Southern Motor Carriers Rate Conference protested to the ICC that the action was 'unjust and unreasonable.' The commission agreed, forcing the firm to cancel its reduction."

Since 1970 the ICC has exacted more than $3 million from carriers and their customers through the courts for charging less than rate bureau fees.

It is high time that free enterprise be permitted to work in the trucking industry. Professor Thomas Gale Moore of Stanford University notes that when ICC regulations were removed from frozen vegetables in the 1950s, shipping rates dropped 20 percent and more. He sees savings of billions of dollars each year if all rates were set by the free market.

Unfortunately, the trucking industry and the Teamsters Union, which has 125 full-time staff members in Washington, D.C., profit by the regulations promulgated by the ICC. The regulators themselves seem to have a good deal to gain by their continued service to the trucking industry as well. Of the 14 commissioners who have left the ICC for new employment since 1958, 12 found jobs representing the industry they once controlled. The Nader report argues that job-switching between the ICC and the trucking industry has become so frequent that "deferred bribes" have become the norm.

It is not only with regard to trucking that the ICC has done serious harm to the interests of the public. Its activities relating to railroads have been equally damaging. One dramatic example of the manner in which the ICC has caused significant harm by its interventionist policies may be seen by examining the case of the Rock Island Line, which currently is in serious financial difficulty. Its difficulties have been the result not of the failure of free enterprise, but of the refusal of government regulators to permit free enterprise to work.

Aware that it faced an untenable economic situation if it continued to operate on its own, the Rock Island Line petitioned the ICC in 1964 to approve a merger with the Union Pacific. After considering the matter for 10 long years, through countless hearings and 200,000 pages of transcripts, the ICC finally granted "conditional" approval of the merger with estimates running that it would have taken two to four more years for final ICC approval to have been handed down.

But, as the Rock Island waited, it encountered the economic failure it had anticipated. During the past eight years it has lost money, including a record $22 million in 1974. Now, because of the deteriorating financial situation, the merger has fallen through. In a desperate effort to stay alive, the line, which has a 7,500-mile rail system and provides primary hauling for at least 185 companies in the St. Louis area, asked its 10,000 employees to make voluntary loans to keep its trains running. It has also requested a $100-million loan from the U.S. Railway Association, the new federal planning organization created by the 1970 Railroad Reorganization Act, but the loan was refused.

Discussing this situation, the *St. Louis Globe Democrat* editorially commented:

Think of it. Fifteen years to complete action on a merger of two railroads that shouldn't have taken more than a few months! Compared to the ICC, the three-toed sloth moves like a cheetah. If the ICC had been in existence when the West was being built by the railroads, the West would still be Indian country.

Rep. Brock Adams (D-Wash.) recently reviewed the classic case of the Southern Railway System. In 1961 this railroad came up with a new, 100-ton aluminum covered hopper car called Big John, an innovation intended to replace the old 50-ton wooden boxcar whose side doors made it hard to load and whose many cracks and crevices allowed rain and weevils to get in while large amounts of grain spilled out. The new car developed by Southern loaded conveniently through the top and was quickly unloaded when bottom hoppers were opened. It was totally sealed from the elements and its prospects were so good, in fact, that the Southern petitioned the ICC for permission to lower its rate for hauling grain by 60 percent. The ICC turned the request down,

125

claiming it would be unfair competition for truck and barge lines. It took Southern four years of fighting in the courts—up to the Supreme Court itself—to force the ICC to allow it to exploit the advantages of the new car.

To cite an additional case, the ICC issued a 1973 order forbidding railroads to carry more than 20 percent of the grain, which was then moving in huge amounts to the nation's ports, in highspeed 'unit trains,' which provide the most efficient method of transportation. At that time, the ICC's reasoning was that these trains travel only on main lines and this would prevent country grain elevators from having their grain hauled. When the irrationality of this order was discovered, the National Commission on Productivity asked the ICC if it had studied the possibility of using trucks to get grain from the country elevators to the main lines. The ICC replied that it had not. It said that its job was to protect shippers, not concern itself about the efficiency of the transportation system.

Adding all of this up, the *Globe-Democrat* concluded:

The list of the ICC's blunders could go on and on. Nearly everyone who has looked into its labyrinthian labors agrees that this tired old bungler should be cashiered. The ICC is a costly, paralyzing anachronism—a very heavy load on the transportation industry and the American public. It should be assigned to the scrap heap.

Others have come to the same conclusion. According to a study by the Brookings Institution, the economic loss resulting from ICC regulation in 1968 ranged from a low of $3.78 billion to a high of $8.79 billion. While it is a story many have understood for some time, there is now some hope that the flagrant abuses of the ICC, when considered in light of our current economic difficulties, will prove even less acceptable now than in the past.

The latest annual report of the President's Council of Economic Advisers notes that ICC regulation of the transportation industry allows exemptions from the anti-trust laws, presents serious barriers to entry into the trucking business, and promotes costly inefficiencies in the railroad freight transportation, all of which are "inconsistent with an efficiently organized transport sector." One result of the present ICC regulations, according to the report, is: "windfall profits to more efficient truckers and higher prices to consumers." Another: the bankruptcy of numerous rail lines.

In precisely the same way in which the ICC and CAB

limit competition and serve the industries they are meant to regulate rather than the public, so the Federal Communications Commission tends also to serve the regulated industry rather than the consuming public. The Communications Act of 1934, which established the FCC, allows that body to restrict licensing, oversee programming, and strictly regulate pay television. The regulations enforced by the FCC maintain the monopoly of the major television networks and prohibit any real competition in this field.

These restrictions state that: 1) No subscription television may exist unless four "free" stations already exist in a given area; 2) subscription television cannot show series programs, movies that are two to ten years old, or sports shows that have been on "free" television in the last five years; and 3) a legislated minimum of free programming must be shown. These restrictions specifically deny subscription television, whether cable or over-the-air, the chance to compete with "free" television for popular programming. Perhaps even more important, they compromise our First Amendment rights. Freedom of speech and of the press seem not to apply equally to the electronic media and the printed media. In fact, the Department of Justice calls the FCC's jurisdiction over cable television "highly questionable" and states that some of its rules have "no reasonable basis." If changes were made in these arbitrary rules, it is certain that every community in the nation would have more choice with regard to television viewing. The result would be the kind of diversity a free society should welcome.

Another major area in which added diversity is possible is that of frequency allocation. Under current regulations, the FCC allocates stations on the basis of the Commission's own evaluation of the public interest. The result has been inefficient scattering of stations so that only two areas, the Los Angeles and New York metropolitan areas, have six VHF stations, although it is technically feasible for every community to do so. An entirely different, more beneficial result would occur if the free market, not a government agency, could restructure the distribution of frequencies. One way to do this would be to auction available television frequencies to the highest bidder. The industry, through the price system, would be allowed to decide how the frequencies should be distributed. Beyond this, the FCC should relinquish its control over cable television and permit the television industry to operate competitively.

It is clear that many interests would oppose such reforms

127

as these. The National Association of Broadcasters, for example, has waged an expensive campaign against pay television. Why? Because, so-called "free" television costs brings in $4.1 billion annually in advertising fees. Pay TV will only work if it gives the viewing audience the programming it is willing to pay for. Obviously, the television networks now in existence prefer a government-controlled monopoly to free competition. Again, only the public is the loser.

To correct the problems inherent in the conduct of the FCC, Senator William Brock (R-Tenn.) has proposed an act to "de-regulate" television. Its main features include the following:

1. All remaining stations will be auctioned to the highest bidder over a reasonable period of time. Thus, we will at least use the available supply.

2. Ownership will be complete (no renewal licensing) and only misuse by obscenity, etc., will be grounds for losing one's license.

3. Sale of stations or even portions of a station's frequencies will not be restricted, provided the buyer is technically competent to operate a station.

4. Copyright privileges will be extended to cover television in the same way as written material. The rights may be sold or given to whomever the originator wishes.

5. Cable television will be freed of restrictions other than copyright and obscenity laws.

6. Subscription fees and/or advertising will be allowed for any over-the-air broadcasting.

7. To guard against future unnecessary intervention, the FCC direction to work for "public convenience, interest and necessity" will be interpreted only in the sense of technical quality.

Senator Brock's proposal should receive the serious consideration it deserves. By any standard the public interest is being served poorly by the FCC, although the major networks are being served well. The FCC works to protect their monopoly standing.

When FCC Chairman Richard E. Wiley was asked to identify his major achievements during his year as chairman, he produced a list of 25 items, including final action on a long-standing case dealing with land mobile communications (mobile radios for business firms), conclusion of a four-year study of children's television and creation of task forces to cut down regulation of cable television. Chairman Wiley conceded that the commission takes too long to decide cases.

"People are concerned in this country about regulatory delay," he said. "If you get sent to hearing today, unless you're a rich guy it's almost like losing. It will take years." In fact, the hearing process at the FCC commonly takes from two to six years.

What the federal government has done in this area, beginning with the Radio Act of 1927, is to nationalize the airwaves. In effect, the federal government has taken title to the ownership of all radio and television channels. It then proceeded to grant licenses for use of the channels to various privately owned stations. Stations, since they receive the license grants, do not have to pay for the use of airwaves. Thus, the stations receive a significant form of subsidization, which they naturally seek to maintain. The federal government, as the licensor, asserts the right to regulate the stations in every aspect of their business, including editorial content. Over the head of each station is the threat of nonrenewal or suspension of its license. Freedom of speech on radio and television is, as a result, always questionable.

Murray Rothbard in his book *For a New Liberty* contrasts the way television and radio is controlled by the FCC with a similar form of hypothetical control over newspapers as follows:

> What would we think, for example, if all newspapers were licensed, the licenses to be renewable by a Federal Press Commission, and with newspapers losing their licenses if they dare express an "unfair" editorial opinion, or if they don't give full weight to public service announcements? . . . Or consider if all book publishers had to be licensed and their licenses were not renewable if their book lists failed to suit a Federal Books Commission? . . . An abstract constitution guaranteeing "freedom of the press" is meaningless in a socialist society. The point is that where the government owns all the newsprint, the paper, the presses, etc., the government—as owner—must decide how to allocate the newsprint and the paper, and what to print them on. The solution for radio and television? Simple: treat these media precisely the same way the press and book publishers are treated . . . the government should withdraw completely from any role or interference in all media of expression. In short, the federal government should denationalize the airwaves and give or sell the individual channels to private ownership.

If television stations were granted this type of independence, the large networks would no longer be in a position to put pressure upon the FCC to outlaw the competition of pay TV. Discussing the concept of "free television" advanced by the networks to defend their own monopoly position, Professor Rothbard points out that "free television" is not really free. He writes:

. . . the programs are paid for by the advertisers, and the consumer pays by covering the advertising costs in the price of the product he buys. . . . The television advertiser, for example, is always interested in a) gaining the widest possible viewing market; and b) in gaining those *particular* viewers who will be most susceptible to the message. Hence, the programs will all be geared to the lowest common denominator of the audience, and particularly to those viewers most susceptible to the message; that is, those viewers who do not read newspapers or magazines, so that the message will not duplicate the ads he sees there. As a result, free television programs tend to be unimaginative, bland, and uniform. Pay television would mean that each program would search for its own market, and many specialized markets for specialized audiences would develop—just as highly lucrative specialized markets have developed in the magazine and book publishing field.

It should be clear to all those who will look objectively at the data that regulatory bodies such as the CAB, the ICC, and the FCC, serve not the *public* interest, in whose name they were created, but, instead, the very private interests they were intended to regulate—the truckers, the airlines, and the radio and television networks. Just as government regulation *directly* harms the public in these fields, so a host of other government regulations, imposed by a number of different government agencies, harm the public in other ways—both directly and indirectly.

The fact that government regulations, even those which may be of some benefit, cost the taxpayers billions of dollars each year is still not clearly understood. A June 30, 1975 estimate by *U.S. News & World Report* puts the figure at $130 billion a year. A study published in February 1975 by Professor Murray L. Weidenbaum of Washington University (St. Louis) helps explain this phenomenon. For example, Dr. Weidenbaum points out that government regulations under the Occupational, Safety and Health Administration (OSHA), require that any cuspidors on the premises be cleaned daily as well as that a lounge area adjacent to women's toilets in work facilities be provided. Furthermore, Dr. Weidenbaum notes that the public is generally unaware that "all government regulatory activities generate costs as well as benefits."

The study, published by the American Enterprise Institute, goes on to list "29 major pieces of regulatory legislation which imposed non-productive costs on business during the period 1962-1973." Dr. Weidenbaum states that, "there has been a shift to more, rather than less, government intervention and, if this reduces innovation and productivity, it's something to be concerned about." One of the areas dealt with in the study is drugs. Regulations imposed by the Food and Drug Administration, according to the study, delay the introduction of effective drugs by approximately four years, leading to higher prices "on the order of $200 to $300 million a year."

Dr. Weidenbaum declares, "A second managerial revolution is now under way—a silent bureaucratic revolution, in the course of which the focus of much of the decision making in the American corporation is shifting once again—from the professional management . . . to the vast cadre of of government regulators." Professor Weidenbaum believes that attention should be focused on this cause of inflation for two reasons: "1) The government is constantly embarking on new and expanded programs which raise costs and prices in the private economy and 2) Neither government decision makers nor the public recognize the significance of these inflationary effects. Literally, the federal government is continually mandating more inflation via the regulations it promulgates. These actions of course are validated by an accommodating monetary policy."

Rather than burden the public treasury with the full cost of cleaning up environmental pollution—which would mean a Congressional vote for added expenditure—we now require private firms to devote additional resources to that purpose. Instead of spending federal funds to eliminate traffic hazards, which would require members of Congress to vote for huge expenditures, we require motorists to purchase vehicles equipped with various safety features that appreciably increase the selling price.

Exactly the same is true with regard to the effect of regulations promulgated by such bodies as OSHA and the Consumer Product Safety Commission. Concerning these, Professor Weidenbaum notes, ". . . every time CPSC imposes a standard which is more costly to attain, some product costs will tend to rise. The same holds true for the actions of the Environmental Protection Agency, the Food and Drug Administration, and so forth."

Although many believe that imposing costly regulations upon private business somehow aids the public without costing it anything, such is not the case. The higher prices paid by consumers throughout the American economy represents the "hidden tax" that is simply shifted from the taxpayer to the consumer. Dr. Weidenbaum concludes:

As these government-mandated costs begin to visibly exceed the apparent benefits, it can be hoped that public pressures will mount on governmental regulators to moderate the increasingly stringent rules and regulations that they apply. At present, for example, a mislabeled product declared an unacceptable hazard often must be destroyed. In the future, the producer or seller perhaps will only be required to relabel it correctly, a far less costly way of achieving the same objective.

In February 1975 President Ford's Council of Economic Advisers called for substantial reductions of federal regulation in the transportation, natural gas and financial industries. Concluding that existing controls by agencies such as ICC and CAB are "imposing significant costs on the economy," the Council advocated the formation of a national commission to study the question of regulatory reform. "Precise estimates of the total costs of regulation are not available," the Council said, "but existing evidence suggests that this may range up to 1 percent of the Gross National Product, or approximately $66 per person per year."

While this estimate seems a bit conservative, the President's economic advisers did state that there has been a marked trend in recent years toward more rather than less government intervention in directing the operations of many companies. In the process, federal regulators have tended to protect those firms already in business at the expense of innovation and at increasing cost to consumers. To prevent bankruptcies, the council said, regulatory agencies "are thus prone to protect firms from competition—frequently to the detriment of efficient service."

As an example, the Council cited the Civil Aeronautics Board, established in 1938. No major airline has gone bankrupt since then, although several airlines "at the brink of bankruptcy" have merged with stronger lines. Regulation by the CAB has resulted in air service that is below optimum standards in both quality and price. With fares regulated in Washington, airlines tend to compete only on a basis of scheduling, over which the CAB has no control. The Council declared that, "The result is 'excess capacity,' and efforts to raise the regulated fares in order to assure a return on investment greater than the industry's perceived cost of capital serve only to set the stage for further battles over how to fill all the empty seats."

In the current regulatory environment, the Council stated, the airlines have not earned windfall profits nor suffered dramatic losses, "but the traveling public has paid higher fares because of the regulation-induced excess capacity," developed at a time when the CAB encouraged more competition on many routes than there was business to support. This excess capacity, the Council argued, provides more frequent departures, less crowding, and a better chance of getting seats on preferred flights, but at a value to the nation's economy "almost surely less than its cost."

In surface transportation, the Council criticized the lack of challenges by the ICC to truck rates set by cartels which have antitrust immunity. If the trucking industry could be opened up to new firms with free rate competition the result would be lower shipping costs.

Railroads present the opposite problem—a lack of freedom to exit from the business. ICC regulation, the Council concluded, has prevented rail firms from dropping unprofitable services that truck competition brought about and "impaired that overall financial position of the railroads."

For financial institutions, President Ford's Council said that more competition could be created by allowing thrift institutions, such as savings and loan associations, to issue checking accounts. An even more important reform would be elimination of regulatory agency control over interest rates that banks and savings institutions can pay to attract funds. In the field of natural gas, the Council warned that over-regulation by the Federal Power Commission has led to shortages of supply—because the government has tried to control the price of a commodity too rigidly, thereby reducing incentives for industry efforts to find new producing wells.

The call for regulatory reform is now being heard across the country and many individuals and publications who once supported the concept of government regulation of various aspects of our economy are now admitting that such regulation has been a failure. In an editorial entitled "The Need For Regulatory Review," the *Washington Post,* in its issue of February 10, 1975, commented:

We suspect that much of this regulation no longer serves the purpose for which it was created and needs to be either eliminated or drastically changed. The ICC, for example, was created in 1887 primarily to protect the public against the monopoly power of the railroads. For a long time now, its primary role has been to protect the railroads against competition from other carriers of freight . . . the ICC may be a classic example of an agency that has outlived its useful life by several decades. As far as we can tell, only it and the industries over which it has jurisdiction defend the way in which surface transportation is now regulated.

The *Post* continues:

The economic problem of this kind of regulation is staggering. There is a growing body of data that suggests it costs far more—not just to the government but in unnecessarily high prices for consumers—than the value of the benefits the regulation brings. The President's economic report says one study puts these costs of government regulation of the surface transportation industry alone at $4 billion to $9 billion a year.

Despite the temporary dislocations that might be entailed in radical reform of government regulatory agencies, the *Washington Post* believes that this is the time for reform. The *Post* concluded its editorial by stating,

. . . this seems to us to be the time for Congress to get on with it. If it is true . . . that the hand of government regulation is now a major drag on the economy, and it certainly appears to be true in some areas, ways can be found to ease the transition of business back toward a less regulated situation. To do that, Congress may have to upset some of the theories that have dominated government policies for decades and will have to face up to some of the entrenched special interest groups. But we can think of few greater contributions this Congress could make to a proper celebration of the nation's Bicentennial than a full dress reappraisal of what government is doing in the way of regulating free enterprises and of why it is doing it.

The fact that the *Washington Post* and many other liberal publications and legislators have now come to understand the regressive nature of our regulatory agencies, and the manner in which they work against rather than in behalf of the public interest, is certainly to be welcomed.

Let us hope they will come to understand that such agencies are not negative accidentally but inherently.

Unfortunately, some advocates of "regulatory reform" mean by this term not a return to the free market but, instead, the creation of new regulatory agencies to oversee the ones we have at the present time. Those who advance this viewpoint should remember that government regulations, even before they are actually administered, have a negative effect upon the economy. One impact of federal regulation is what has become known as the "announcement effect." For some time, economists have pointed out the existence of this effect with regard to government spending or taxation. What happens is that potential government contractors may start preparing to bid on a project even before Congress has appropriated funds for it, or consumers may increase their expenditures while a tax cut is still being debated.

The role played by OSHA provides a case in point. In Illinois, the rumor that OSHA might impose more stringent standards for migrant worker housing caused strawberry farmers to reduce their production. The *St. Louis Post-Dispatch* of June 11, 1974, quoted Lester Pitchford, the largest grower in the Centralia area, as stating that, "We don't know if OSHA is coming or not, but when it was even rumored, it put strawberry production out."

The basis for the concern in this case was the possibility that farmers would have to provide migrant workers with the same amenities as permanent workers—100 square feet of living space (the present state standard is 60 square feet), with flush toilets and showers in each room. Some Illinois strawberry farmers concluded that the capital investment required could not be justified for a two-week harvest. According to James Mills, an official with the Illinois Department of Public Health, a basic problem is the lack of distinction under OSHA regulations between long-term and short-term migratory farm worker housing. Centralia farmers, he was quoted as saying, "just can't compete and, if OSHA puts the pressure on them, they'll get out of the migrant business completely and go strictly U-Pick" (consumers pick the fruit for their own use for a fee).

The very men and women meant to be helped by OSHA regulations have been the ones most clearly hurt—by losing their jobs. In addition, all Americans are hurt by the higher prices they are forced to pay. Now, OSHA has assigned a social scientist to explore the idea of extending occupational health surveillance to management personnel, supposedly to consider psychological stress among executives. *NAM Reports,* for July 29, 1974, indicates that the National Institute for Occupational Safety and Health has recommended that it test and certify all personal protective equipment, thus excluding competent private laboratories from the testing process. The institute's proposal also calls for an "absolute guarantee" that a product it had tested would not fail in the marketplace.

In the name of environmental control and safety, federally mandated costs average $320 per new automobile. With new car purchases totalling about nine million for 1974, American motorists paid approximately $3 billion extra for the governmentally imposed requirements. In addition, the added weight and complexity of the mandated features have increased the operating costs, particularly the fuel costs, of vehicles. The cost of the new catalytic converters that were required on 1975 automobiles was estimated at $150 per vehicle. Recent information indicates that the converters are themselves failures, causing more problems than they correct.

It seems clear that government regulation of industry, particularly in the safety area, has been insensitive to the notion of discovering the least costly way of achieving objectives. Professor Roger L. Miller of the University of Washington has described the problem in these terms:

Now they seem to be insisting that Detroit should begin producing what amounts to overly expensive tanks without giving much thought to some alternatives that are just as effective, while less costly to society. Modification or removal of roadside hazards might eliminate as many as one quarter of all motor vehicle fatalities. Another 10 percent or so occur when automobiles collide with bridge abutments, or with pier supports or overpasses.

In addition, 60 percent of drivers in fatal, single car crashes are drunk, as are 50 percent of the drivers at fault in fatal crashes involving two cars or more. Professor Miller asks the obvious question: "Why should the many who purchase autos end up paying for increased safety in order to prevent fatalities involving the drunken drivers?" He suggests that a far less expensive alternative might be more vigorous legal prosecution of drunken drivers and drunken pedestrians.

Whether we are discussing the Consumer Product Safety

Commission, the Environmental Protection Agency, OSHA, the CAB, the ICC, the FCC, or any of the myriad governmental regulatory agencies, we find a similar story—regulation in behalf of the public that, in the end, costs the public a great deal of money and does the public a significant amount of harm. Only when the American people recognize that this is the inevitable result of government regulation will we begin to really solve the problem.

The regulatory agencies which we have at the present time are, in fact, remnants of the philosophy of the Progressives. Discussing this movement in his book, *The Bewildered Society*, George Roche III writes:

The Progressive Movement, which dominated the American scene in the years from the turn of the century to United States entrance into World War I, was not primarily a liberal movement . . . in contrast to former American efforts at reform, progressivism was based on a new philosophy, partly borrowed from Europe, which emphasized collective action through the instrumentality of the government. . . .

The new political theory of the Progressives borrowed most heavily from bureaucratic thought. The ideal was to achieve a professional staff of government workers who presided over the operations of society in an essentially non-partisan manner. The old distinction separating executive, legislative and judicial functions were now to be set aside in favor of "the public man," the leader who could take charge of a modern, highly specialized government. Constitutional interferences which stood in the way of this public man were regarded as anachronisms from a previous and less enlightened age.

What the Progressives seemed not to understand properly was that the more they used political authority to defend or restore individual values, the more they created a political and social condition that left steadily less room for the individual. Dr. Roche declares, "The Progressives were bound to fail in their attempt to destroy a power monopoly by creating a power monopoly."

The effect of the regulatory agencies established initially during the Progressive era has not been to serve the public, but to serve the vested interests they were created to regulate. A number of historians have made it clear that the primary effect of the new regulatory agencies was to give dominant business groups a greater control over their respective economic interests than they had previously en-

137

joyed. In fact, Professor Gabriel Kolko, in his volume *The Triumph Of Conservatism,* insists that it was the dominant business groups themselves who shaped and promoted the "Progressive" reforms as a means of continuing their own dominance.

Professor Kolko writes:

It is business control over politics (and by "business" I mean the major economic interests) rather than political regulation of the economy that is the significant phenomenon of the Progressive era. . . . Political capitalism is the utilization of political outlets to attain conditions of stability, predictability and security—to attain rationalization —in the economy.

In the Progressive era, government became an ally rather than a foe of entrenched interests, both those of big business and of the large labor unions. Political regulation of economic affairs proved to be designed in most cases by the very interests presumably to be regulated. That is why, when today we discuss the possibility of eliminating such agencies as the ICC, the major defenders of this agency are the trucking industry and the Teamsters Union—the groups to be regulated who have turned that agency into one that pursues their own interests, and opposes "public interest."

The classic symptoms of monopoly have been an absence of price competition and an inability for new competition to enter the marketplace. Nothing could be a more accurate description of a government-regulated industry. As we have already seen, agencies such as the FCC do nothing more than permit the already established giants in the communications field an absolute monopoly of the market by means of government licensure. The CAB does precisely the same thing for the airlines, and the same can be discovered in other regulated sectors of our economy.

Discussing this unfortunate situation, Professor Yale Brozen of the University of Chicago comments:

The regulatory agencies not only prevent those in the transportation industry from competing with each other —they also protect those in the industry from the entry of additional competitors. You cannot get into the trucking business, the airline business, the bus business as you would enter retailing or manufacturing. You must be certified by the CAB if you wish to enter the airline business. The CAB has not certified an additional scheduled airline in the continental United States since it began operating in 1938. The ICC will certify an additional common car-

138

rier truck company to operate on a given route only if it can be demonstrated that adequate truck service is not available on the route in question. The only major city in which you can start a taxi business simply by applying for a taxi license and demonstrating that you carry the necessary public liability insurance and have safe equipment and drivers is Washington, D.C. All other major cities stop any additional taxi operators from entering the business. They even prevent taxi operators from increasing the size of their fleets. Transportation regulation very effectively protects transportation companies from new competition and produces the exact opposite of the situation which our anti-monopoly laws were designed to produce in other industries.

Unfortunately, many businessmen prefer government regulation to the risks of the free market. James M. Roche, writing in *The Michigan Business Review*, expresses this view: "Business and government can ill afford to be adversaries. So mutual are our interests, so formidable are our challenges that our times demand our strengthened alliance. The success of each depends upon the other."

The old warning by economist Friedrich Hayek that socialism in its radical form was not nearly as dangerous as socialism in its conservative form is worthy of serious reconsideration. As George Roche has noted, "When the advocates of state power and the advocates of corporate bigness form an alliance, the resultant form, however conservative, is still socialistic."

While we may understand the reasons for business and labor support of the regulatory agencies that have grown up in the years since the Progressive era, there is no reason for those who are truly concerned with the public interest to accept them. Only by permitting the free market to work, by eliminating government-created monopolies, can we give each citizen the opportunity to vote with his dollars for the goods and services he seeks. The regulatory agencies as they exist today not only eliminate competition but, in that they give government total power over vital sectors of the economy, challenge the very concept of individual freedom as well.

This last point was made by the distinguished economist Wilhelm Roepke, in his book, *The Social Crisis Of Our Time:*

An economic system, where each group entrenches itself more and more in a monopolist stronghold, abusing the power of the state for its special purposes, where prices and wages lose their mobility except in an upward direction, where no one wants to adhere to the reliable rules of the market any more, and where consequently nobody knows any longer whether tomorrow a new whim of the legislature will not upset all calculations, an economic system in which everyone wants to live exclusively at the expense of the community and in which the state's budget finally comes to about half of the national income: a system of this kind is not only bound to become unprofitable and thus bound to intensify the scramble for the reduced total profit, but it will moreover in the end suffer a complete breakdown. This is usually called the crisis of capitalism and is used as an occasion for new and revolutionary interventions which complete the ruin and corruption and finally present us with the inexorable choice of either returning to a reasonable and ethical market system or of plunging into the collectivist adventure.

The American society has the opportunity to turn away from its self-destructive policies of governmental regulation of the economy. The place to begin, as many in Washington now believe, is with the abuses of the regulatory agencies. Unless we take these steps now, it may cost us much more to do so in the future. With our economy uncertain, with unemployment and inflation an ever-present danger, we can ill afford the counter-productive role being played by regulatory agencies in Washington. Hopefully, an aroused society, carefully examining the available data, will come to this inevitable conclusion.

The Bloated Bureaucracy

In recent years most Americans unavoidably have become aware of the role being played in our society by nonelected government officials, men and women whom we have come to refer to as "bureaucrats." As government involves itself increasingly in our lives, more and more of the rules and regulations under which we must live are made by individuals other than our elected representatives in the Congress. These myriad rules and regulations are the creation of government bureaucrats.

Professor Charles Hyneman identified the problem inherent in bureaucratic government in his book, *Bureaucracy And Democracy*. He writes, "It is in the power of these men and women to do us great injury, as it is in their power to advance our well-being. It is essential that they do what we want done, the way we want it done. Our concept of democratic government requires that they be subject to direction and control that compels them to conform to the wishes of the people as a whole whether they wish to do so or not."

Yet, too often our elected representatives abdicate their responsibility. They permit these nonelected officials to make laws through regulation. Compulsory seat belts, for example, were imposed by bureaucrats at the Department of Transportation, not by the Congress. And it took an act of Congress to reverse this bureaucratic ruling.

The men who wrote the Constitution considered Congress to be the most important branch of government. It alone, was given the power to declare war. Congress—more specifically the House of Representatives—was given the power to initiate all bills resulting in the expenditure of money. The executive branch was to carry out the laws passed by the legislative branch. On policy matters, Congress was meant

141

to be supreme; the executive was to be precisely what the term meant, the "executor."

In his relevant book, *The Political Culture of the United States,* Professor Donald Devine of the University of Maryland, says that the American political tradition ". . . stresses the importance of limiting the sphere of government. Thus, the tradition emphasizes restrictions both for minorities and even for popular majorities. . . ." Professor Devine goes on to say that, "The first and most basic institutional rule of the . . . tradition is that the legislature predominates."

Political philosopher John Locke also was emphatic on the position of the legislature. In his *Second Treatise,* a volume which had a profound impact upon the men who wrote our Constitution, Locke stated, "There can be but one supreme power, which is the Legislature, to which all the rest are and must be subordinate."

According to Locke, the legislature is subordinate to the people, but among the institutions of government, the legislative branch is supreme. It is the legislative institution "which has a right to direct how the force of the commonwealth shall be employed for preserving the community and the members of it." The legislative power is best put into "the hands of many who assemble to make laws but who do not administer them."

Our government was created as one of strict checks and balances. In *The Federalist Papers,* James Madison wrote, "In framing a government which is to be administered by men over men, the great difficulty lies in this: you must first enable the government to control the governed; and in the next place oblige it to control itself." Madison continued, "If it be a fundamental principle of free government that the legislative, executive and judiciary powers should be separately exercised, it is equally so that they be independently exercised."

Today, unfortunately, the will of the Congress is not being exercised. Far too often, the Congress passes a law, sets forth a policy goal, appropriates a sum of money and then is ignored by the executive or by the new "fourth branch of government," the bureaucracy. Often the Congress is actually scorned by both. The statement by a State Department official after his transfer to the Department of Agriculture reflects what appears to be a prevalent view in the bureaucracy: "The bureaucrat has a program to carry out that he believes in. The question of whether or not Congress has authorized it is not so important to him. He figures that if Congress really had the facts and knew what was right, it would agree with him. So he goes right ahead getting away with as much as he can. I've attended lots of these meetings within the department where budget questions and the like were decided and I never heard a respectful word spoken about Congress in one of them."

This startling view is unfortunately supported by the actions of the bureaucracy in a multitude of examples. And this contempt for the Congress has little bearing on the party affiliation of either the Congress or the executive. The Internal Revenue Service (IRS), for example, has regularly disregarded the legal prohibition against wiretapping. The Communications Act of 1934 says that "no person" is allowed to "interpret and divulge" telephone conversations. The Supreme Court, as early as 1939, ruled that Federal agents may not legally tap telephones. None of this, however, has stopped the IRS, which in violating these regulations has become a virtual lawmaker itself.

The Highway Beautification Act is another example of bureaucracy rampant. In 1965 Congress authorized a program to set aside and beautify certain areas along the nation's highways, to screen junkyards and control proliferation of billboards. What, in fact, has happened? In 1967 Rep. Jim Wright pointed out that, "In the city where there isn't much natural beauty, Congress decreed that any standards on size, spacing and lighting of billboards would comply with customary usage. Hideous, outsized or abnormally cluttered signboards would come down, but the others would stay. The Federal Bureau has utterly ignored this requirement. It has promulgated standards which, if followed, would destroy approximately 80 percent of all the properties owned by legitimate outdoor advertising firms throughout the whole country. This, obviously, is not conforming to 'customary usage.' It would throw many thousands of people out of work and cost the government an estimated $2.9 billion, much of it needlessly." Even after the effect of these administrative decisions had been called to the attention of the bureaucrats by Congressmen (who wrote the law), the bureau persisted in making its own policies. The agency established by the Congress decided that it knew better than the Congress what was in the public interest.

In the Economic Development Act of 1965, another example, Congress clearly stipulated that no government loans would be made to start new businesses in fields where the present demand is "not sufficient . . . to employ the efficient capacity of existing competitive commercial and industrial enterprises." EDA Administrators, notwithstanding this injunction, authorized federal loans that would have the effect of creating artificial competition and resulting unemployment for existing firms.

Much of the blame for the growing power of the bureaucracy may properly be assigned to the willingness of the people's elected representatives to abdicate their own legitimate authority. It is not enough to argue that a power-hungry executive and bureaucracy has usurped Congressional authority. More often, Congress has delegated its authority to others. In the Gulf of Tonkin Resolution, for instance, Congress told the President that he could do whatever he found necessary with regard to fighting a war in Southeast Asia.

During President Nixon's first administration, Congress passed what was, in effect, an economic Gulf of Tonkin resolution—declaring that the President could do whatever he found necessary with regard to fighting a war against inflation by giving him *discretionary* wage and price control authority. Thus, Congress turned the power granted to it by the Constitution over to the executive. This is not what it was elected to do.

There are several potential flaws inherent in delegation of authority to someone else. The most important flaw may be uncertainty that this "someone else" is acting on the basis of what is best for the country, rather than on the more partisan basis of what he believed to be in his own self-interest. We should not lose sight of the counsel of James Madison, who observed, "There is nothing inherently wrong with monarchy as a system of government, provided you get an angel for a king."

Experience indicates that many in political life too often choose policies on the basis of their reelection value, rather than their value in solving real problems facing the country. But this approach, used by men whom we elect and can recall at the next election, is a shortcoming we can at least partially correct. But when the approach is used by a pay board, an administrative commission, or an executive advisor *appointed* by the President, the authority of which is simply a delegation by Congress (which Congress has no real right to delegate), then how do voters express their anguish and dismay? They cannot. In large measure, they are not in control of their own government.

In *The Decline and Fall of the Roman Empire*, Gibbon

144

reminds us: "Augustus was sensible that mankind is governed by names; nor was he deceived in his expectations that the Senate and people would submit to slavery provided that they were respectfully assured that they still enjoyed their ancient freedom." Our problem is not that we are ruled by evil men, or that evil men are abdicating their authority and responsibility. Adlai Stevenson once said of a politician of particularly rancid practices: "If he were a bad man, I wouldn't be so afraid of him. But this man has no principles. He doesn't know the difference." This may be the real crisis of American politics, in both the executive and legislative branches; we are losing our ability to tell the difference.

Since 1887 when Congress created the Interstate Commerce Commission, more and more commissions have been established, covering a wide area of the nation's economic and social activities. In most instances Congress had delegated the power to "issue such regulations and orders as it may deem necessary or proper in order to carry out the purposes and provisions of this act." The practice of delegating to administrative agencies and commissions the power to issue rules and regulations and apply them to specific cases has grown significantly in recent years. Twenty new regulatory agencies have been created just within the past eight years, bringing the total to 75, exclusive of regulatory departments.

Legislators often recognize the need for delegating legislative powers as a means of reducing their workload and taking care of technical matters beyond their competence. What has happened, however, is that administrators are often carrying out not the wish of Congress, but their own wishes. In many respects, the growth of administrative lawmaking has challenged the constitutional function of Congress as the legislative branch of government. The commissions and administrative agencies created by the Congress, possess executive, legislative, and judicial powers. Often they use these powers intentionally to *circumvent* the will of Congress; not only that, but to impose their own will and their own code of moral and social values on society.

To cite one example, the majority of members of Congress oppose school busing to achieve racial balance, as do the majority of the American people of all races, as indicated by every poll taken on the subject. Nevertheless, the buses are rolling.

In their efforts to end racial, ethnic, and sexual discrimination, government agencies have become involved in enforcing racial and sexual quotas in hiring—most openly in the construction industry, through the Philadelphia Plan, but in universities and businesses as well through insistence upon so-called "affirmative action" programs.

Professor Paul Seabury, writing in *Commentary*, expressed the view that bureaucrats at HEW are not fighting discrimination by their (unsanctioned) interference in the academic world but are calling for it. He writes:

A striking contradiction exists between HEW's insistence that faculties prove that they do not discriminate and its demand for goals and timetables which require discrimination to occur. For there is no reason to suppose that equitable processes in individual cases will automatically produce results which are set in the timetables and statistical goals universities are now required to develop. If all that HEW wishes is evidence that universities are bending over backward to be fair, why should it require them to have statistical goals at all? Do they know something no one else knows, about where fairness inevitably leads?

How is the presidential appointee in Washington to control (or even find out) what the Civil Service employee in Atlanta or Seattle or Des Moines is doing? The appointee, of course, answers to a President who, in turn, answers to the voter, every four years. But the Civil Service employee, responsible neither to an elected nor appointed official, answers to a code or scale that says "once you get to second base, no one can send you back to first base, let alone tag you out." The captains, the managers, the coaches, indeed even the owners of the franchise may change. But, alas, the players remain the same.

When Sargent Shriver was head of the Office of Economic Opportunity and the Peace Corps, he tried to learn what was really happening by forming an independent office of evaluation; reports did not come from the very people involved. The *Washington Monthly* commented, "The traditional bureaucrats didn't like Evaluation because Shriver's inspectors ruined the whole elaborate sanitizing system that made information gradually more palatable as it passed from the field up the line. The sanitizing occurs in all government agencies, largely because if your report to your boss doesn't enable him to write an optimistic report to *his* boss, then your boss will be out of a job, and so presumably will you."

The bureaucrats' role now is not only to hide the facts from the public, this report continues, "but also to keep them from fellow bureaucrats up the line. When bad news gets into the papers, the superiors will read it, too. If the heat is on and there might be leaks in the pipes, the best thing to do is not send such adverse information through. Both the public and the agency's directors end up suffering from the same ignorance."

Congress cannot legislate intelligently if it does not understand what government agencies are really doing. Often those government employees who have made an effort to help Congress understand the truth end up out of a job. State Department official Otto Otepka, for instance, lost his job as a result of his testimony before a Senate committee. The nonelected officials above him did not want him to tell the elected representatives of the people what was really happening in the Department of State. Similar examples can be found in other agencies.

In many respects, Congress itself is largely responsible for allowing bureaucrats to become lawmaking and law-enforcing agencies unto themselves. Harold Seidman, who spent 25 years observing the bureaucracy from the Bureau of the Budget, in his book, *Politics, Position and Power,* says that bureaucratic bodies provide examples of how Congress transfers its own overlapping powers to the Executive branch. "When jurisdictional problems could not be resolved," he states, "the Congress in 1966 created two agencies—the National Highway Safety Agency and the National Traffic Agency—to administer the highway safety program. The President was authorized to designate a single individual to head both agencies. All that was gained by creating two agencies—where only one was needed—was to give two Senate committees a voice in the confirmation of the agency head."

Another case is the U.S. Travel Service, a Commerce Department program funded over the years at between $3.5 and $4.5 million. It is designed to attract foreigners to vacation in the United States. "We did a study of the travel service," says Fred Simpich, general counsel of the Commerce Department in the last year of the Johnson Administration, "which showed that it had a zero effect on the travel patterns of Europeans. . . . If the economy is good, they come to the United States. If not, they don't."

It is the rare bureaucrat who admits it when programs accomplish nothing, but cost a great deal; he risks his job by doing so. One result of this situation is that when an agency comes before the Congress for its annual appropriation, it

147

invariably reports that the agency has been working effectively and efficiently—that it needs additional funding. Members of the congressional committee rarely know whether such witnesses are telling the truth or not. Usually, they acquiesce and provide additional funding. As a result, the government continues to grow, budgets become more and more out of balance, government becomes less and less efficient, and the potential for abuse escalates.

For too long, Congress has relied upon the very men who were conducting particular government programs to be the ones to decide whether such programs have been successful and have been administered properly. For them to say that programs had been unsuccessful and were conducted inefficiently would be to indict themselves.

If Americans feel helpless to control their government, it is this trend toward bureaucracy that is largely responsible. In 1910, Louis Brandeis told Walter Fischer, the incoming Secretary of the Interior, "I have but two suggestions to offer: approve no documents the contents of which you do not understand; sign no letters which you have not read." Fischer replied tersely: "You ask the impossible." How much more true are Fischer's words today? Even in 1910 it was recognized that elected leaders and their appointed officials were virtually out of control of the vast complex of government machinery beneath them.

It has often been asked whether an extensive government bureaucracy can be run efficiently. On what basis, for example, can Congress decide whether a given administrator has been doing a good job or a poor one? When an agency comes before Congress with a request for the budget for the following year, what sort of analysis can be used to decide whether the request is proper, or too high, or too low?

In his book, *Bureaucracy,* economist Ludwig Von Mises points out the essential difference between the management of a business and of a government bureaucracy:

Business management, or profit management, is directed by the profit motive. The objective is to make a profit. As success or failure to attain this can be ascertained by accounting not only for the whole business but also for any of its parts, it is feasible to decentralize both management and accountability without jeopardizing the unity of operations and attainment of their goal. . . . In public administration there is no connection between revenue and expenditure. Bureaucratic management is the method applied to the conduct of administrative affairs the

148

result of which has no cash value in the market. Bureaucratic management . . . cannot be checked by economic calculations.

When government moves into areas previously occupied by private enterprise a valuable test of efficiency of the operation is lost, for the goal is no longer profit making but "public service," a goal whose effect may not be determined in any economic way. In such a system there is little to prevent individual bureaucrats from seeking to obtain an ever larger share of the national budget for their own departments, and any question of efficiency becomes a challenge to the validity of the program itself.

Bureaucracy is not only a threat to democracy in the sense that it exercises control over our lives to a great degree while being subject to less and less control by the elected representatives of the people. Another challenge to democratic government is found in the current bureaucratic trend. More and more Americans are directly dependent upon the government and its agencies for their livelihood; when they vote it is for candidates who promise an increase in such unearned dividends.

Our current system has been compared with similar systems in Germany and France prior to the fall of democracy in those countries. At that time a large part of the electorate was dependent upon the state as the source of their income. They were the public employees, the recipients of unemployment checks, of retirement and disability (Social Security benefits) and farmers who were directly or indirectly subsidized. Their main concern was to get more and more for themselves from public funds.

Von Mises observes, "They did not care for ideal issues like liberty, justice, the supremacy of the law and good government. They asked for more money, that was all. No candidate could risk opposing the appetite of the public employees for a raise. . . . Representative democracy cannot subsist if a great part of the voters are on the government payroll. If members of the Parliament no longer consider themselves mandatories of the taxpayers but deputies of those receiving salaries, wages, subsidies, doles and other benefits from the treasury, democracy is done for."

The reasons for growth of government are many. The prevailing political doctrine in the United States since the days of the New Deal has been "Spend and spend, tax and tax, elect and elect." We have been told repeatedly, over the course of more than 40 years and under the administrations

149

of seven Presidents, that the answer to most of our pressing domestic problems is the additional expenditure of funds by the federal government. This approach has been advocated for problems as diverse as agricultural surpluses, educational inadequacies, urban decay, mass transportation, drug addiction—even the control of rats in our large cities.

Those who advocate the panacea of federal government programs—and their corresponding huge bureaucracies—fail to point out that previous programs have failed to solve the problems at which they were aimed. Despite the huge sums of money spent on agriculture, the farm problem persists. Despite large expenditures on urban renewal, the poor remain poor. Despite Washington's involvement in almost every area of social concern, problems remain and, in many cases, are worse than ever as a result of federal intervention. In a number of instances, government involvement has complicated the existing situation or has come up with an entirely new dilemma.

Part of the dilemma is that the American people have too little control over their own government. The machinery of the national government is becoming a virtual rule unto itself, controlled neither by the citizens who are called upon to pay taxes nor by their representatives in the Congress, who are elected precisely for that reason.

The striking fact appears to be that a professional national bureaucracy seeks to manipulate society in the manner it deems best. In many instances, it is a "public be damned" philosophy and it is often employed with a vengeance.

What has developed is a total breakdown of the system of checks and balances, and separation of powers. The federal agencies, of course, administer their rules and regulations, which is the executive function. But in issuing rules, regulations and guidelines (often in direct defiance of Congressional intent) they become policy makers thus performing the legislative function. Furthermore, they have the power to prosecute and serve as judge, jury, and executioner of their own cases. This is the judicial function. So all three functions of government are combined in one body and that body cannot be held accountable at the polls.

More and more, those who enter government service appear not to want to carry out the will of the people, but seek to impose their own will upon the people. This point was made about the growing number of intellectuals in government by Eric Hoffer, the self-taught longshoreman who has written such volumes as *The True Believer* and *The Ordeal of Change*: " . . . it's disconcerting to realize that businessmen, generals even—men of action—are less corrupted by power than intellectuals. You take a conventional man of action—he's satisfied if you obey. . . . But not the intellectual. He doesn't want you to just obey. He wants you to get down on your knees and praise the one who makes you love what you hate and hate what you love. In other words, whenever the intellectuals are in power, there's soul-raping going on."

In recent days we have seen many former advocates of centralized government power express concern over the results produced by such policies. Such important liberal spokesmen as Richard Goodwin, Daniel Moynihan and Kenneth Clark, to name three, are now calling for new coalitions with conservatives and expressing the view that Americans are less and less in control of a government meant to represent their own interests and wishes.

In a speech before the National Board Meeting of Americans for Democratic Action several years ago, Daniel P. Moynihan, later U.S. Ambassador to the United Nations, told his fellow liberals:

It is necessary to seek out and make much more effective alliances with political conservatives . . . liberals must divest themselves of the notion that the nation can be run from agencies in Washington . . . liberals must somehow overcome the curious condescension which takes the form of sticking up for and explaining away anything, howsoever outrageous. . . . We must begin getting private business involved in domestic programs in a much more systematic, purposeful manner. Making money is one thing Americans are good at, and the corporation is their favorite device for doing so. What acrospace corporations have done for getting us to the moon, urban housing corporations can do for the slums. All that is necessary . . . is to enable enough men to make enough money out of doing so. . . .

Black liberals are also expressing a similar view. Dr. Kenneth E. Clark, black psychologist and faculty member at the City University of New York, said that blacks should consider alliances with white conservatives. He noted that, "Bill Buckley is one of the straightest thinkers I know on the issue of race." Conservative Buckley, for his part, stated that the proposals of liberals such as Daniel Moynihan represent "a Magna Carta for American liberals," and has agreed that there is much common cause to be made by the two groups.

As previously mentioned, there are numerous examples of the failure of bureaucratically controlled programs to solve the problems at which they are directed. Education is but one example, however illustrative.

Between the years 1952 and 1972, while the school population was doubling, school personnel trebled and expenditures rose 700 percent. Yet over the past 12 years, ACT and SAT scores have fallen each year with the most precipitous drop this past year. Moreover, we are now offering remedial reading courses at the college and university level.

The unfortunate, and bureaucratically stimulated, fact is that whenever a problem is discussed in political terms, the goal is to find an "answer" that may be implemented in specific legislation, implying that every problem has a legislative remedy and that government, in effect, can successfully involve itself in all areas of concern.

The growth of the bureaucracy in recent years has been unprecendented—a fact of which too few Americans are aware. The time may soon be at hand when more than half of our population either works for the government or is dependent upon the government in some other way for its livelihood.

From 1952 to 1972 the public payroll multiplied more than fourfold, from $35 to $150 billion. The 330 percent rate of increase exceeds somewhat, if not spectacularly, the simultaneous 247 percent growth in employee compensation in private industries (from $161 to $557 billion). This more rapid expansion in government consists of two major factors: (a) the number of public employees grew 52 percent, those of private jobholders only 35 percent; (b) average annual earnings per full-time employee advanced 183 percent in government, 146 percent in private industry. In 1952 the average worker in private employment was 5 percent ahead of the public employee in wages ($3,430 compared to $3,279); by 1972 he had fallen 10 percent behind the government worker ($8,440 compared to $9,264).

As Roger Freeman points out in *The Growth of American Government*:

> There is now *one* person working for government for every *four* employees in private industry producing the multitude of goods and services needed, consumed, and used by 210 million Americans or exported. The sixteen million persons drawing their wages from public sources

152

possess, with their families, a significant voting power, which they use to exercise influence on pay decisions by the legislative and executive branches of the government they serve.

Dr. Freeman continues, "Considering that now about one person in every four in the United States obtains his livelihood through *workless* pay from the various social welfare programs, this constitutes an organized and powerful bloc of those who have a direct and strong stake and interest in pushing government programs to ever higher levels." The bureaucracy has grown at a rate significantly higher than the growth of the total U.S. population. In addition, even those agencies which have less work to do, have many more workers at much higher salaries to do it. Consider these examples, cited by Dr. Freeman:

• Employment in the Department of Agriculture went up 47 percent between 1952 and 1972 (78,000 to 115,000) though the number of farms in the U.S. dropped by 45 percent (5.2 to 2.9 million).

• The Internal Revenue staff grew 28 percent between 1952 and 1972 (56,336 to 72,085), almost parallel to the number of tax returns filed, which went up 26 percent (from 89 to 112 million). The number of tax returns per employee, however, dropped from 1580 to 1554—during a period of the most intensive mechanization and computerization. In addition, audits declined from 4.4 to 1.7 million and delinquent notices from 19.8 to 8.8 million.

• The number of government employees working in a particular area and the accomplishments recorded in that area have been shown to have little relationship to one another.

• In the past twenty years we have seen an increase of 129 percent in the number of employees working in the field of police protection, while the U.S. population was increasing only 33 percent. There were 1.6 police employees per 1,000 population in 1952, 2.8 in 1972. Despite this sharply increased protection ratio, crime has soared. Between 1952 and 1972, the U.S. population grew 22 percent, the number of police employees grew 84 percent—nearly four times faster—while the estimated incidence of crime jumped 309 percent, from 1.4 to 5.9 million.

Roger Freeman comments:
We must recognize that, in contrast to private industry, where competition and the profit goal impose pressure for greater efficiency and a natural and generally reliable gauge of productivity, governmental programs have built-in

153

counterproductive trends. It is a natural tendency for a public employee to want to handle fewer cases—pupils, tax returns, welfare families, crimes—in the belief that he could do a better job if he had a smaller workload, and most certainly have an easier life. For the supervisor there is a definite gain in stature, position—and even grade—by having a larger number of subordinates. This and the ideological commitments to the program goals and methods of their professional fraternities provide a powerful and well-nigh irresistible incentive for empire building.

In a review of recent academic studies of governmental bureaucracy in the *Public Administration Review* (March-April, 1974), Kenneth F. Warren concludes: "The authors' consensus . . . is that American bureaucracy is guilty of the gross mismanagement of the public interest. The real accountability crisis is that even if our bureaucrats act inefficiently and against our interests, as is too often the case, we cannot realistically hope for administrative abuses to be checked by the present 'watchdog' system."

In an earlier volume, *Democracy and the Public Service*, Frederick C. Mosher found that professionalism in governmental bureaucracy and the power of the civil service pose a distinct threat to democratic control; that is, they are self-serving rather than serving the public interest. Perhaps the sharpest criticism came from Richard S. Rosenbloom in the *Harvard Business Review* (September-October, 1973): "The largest employer group in the United States has shown the least concern for worker productivity. This seems absurd in a society that prides itself on management and efficiency, but the fact appears to be indisputable. . . . Not only is productivity in these groups lagging, but little is being done about it." Rosenbloom adds, "One is less surprised at the absence of evident productivity growth in government when it is recognized that none of the major forces operating in the private sector applies in government."

The growth in government salaries has been far in excess of the growth of salaries in the private sector. In 1962 an employee in private industry earned on the average $116 more than a federal employee (earnings were $5,081 and $4,965 respectively). Relative positions had changed very little in the preceding ten years; the difference in 1952 had been $85 (earnings were $3,430 and $3,345 respectively). Between 1962 and 1964, however, positions were reversed, due to the Federal Salary Reform Act of 1962 and subsequent action. In 1964 a federal employee was on the average

$101 *ahead* of his counterpart in private industry (earnings were $5,605 and $5,504 respectively). In the succeeding eight years, when federal pay was supposed to move parallel to private wages, federal employees made their most substantial absolute and relative progress. In 1972 they were on the average $1,783 ahead of workers in private industry (earnings were $10,223 and $8,440 respectively). Between 1964 and 1972 average earnings of federal workers rose $4,618 while average earnings in private industry rose only $2,936.

Average annual earnings per full-time employee of all governments (federal, state and local) increased by $975 *more* than in private industry, adjusted to constant dollars. Private earnings increased 56 percent between 1952 and 1972, governmental earnings 79 percent, which is 41 percent faster. In relative terms, average annual earnings in government equaled 96 percent of earnings in private industry in 1952, 110 percent of earnings in private industry in 1972.

Most Americans are unaware of another aspect of the extraordinary benefits bestowed upon public employees, such as the huge pension commitments that are being entered into. Public employee retirement payments multiplied more than ten times between 1952 and 1972—from $831 million to $8,562 million—although salaries only quadrupled. At present rates, public employee pensions will more than triple in the current decade. In some cities certain agencies already pay out as much in pensions as in current salaries and their number is increasing.

Federal employee retirement funds held a balance of $28 billion in 1972 with uncovered liabilities well over twice that. State and local employee retirement funds owned $68 billion worth of assets in 1972, only a fraction of their long-range obligations. *The actuarial value of all public retirement commitments is in the hundreds of billions.* In contrast to the strict accounting for direct federal, state and local debts, no comprehensive records are kept of the "contingent" retirement obligations of governments.

Public retirement schemes are so generous that in some public systems a worker can retire on half pay after twenty years, regardless of age, while few private systems distribute benefits before age sixty. In addition, private pensions and annuities are usually based strictly on actual contributions which are in turn related to the wages received during the earning career. Under federal civil service retirement rates pensions are based only on the highest years.

It is interesting to consider the fact that while the benefits of Social Security recipients are now annually adjusted for inflation by the consumer price index, retired federal employees receive an additional 1 percent pension increase every time their checks are adjusted for changes in the cost of living. At the time of the passage of that provision in 1969, the General Accounting Office warned of its tremendous long-range spiral effect. Congress, nevertheless, approved the measure.

Bureaucracy is, as we have seen, growing apace. Bureaucrats are earning more money than those in comparable positions in private enterprise. During our recent economic difficulties, while private firms laid off employees, government at all levels put more people to work. Today, government employs one in five workers—up from one in seven little more than 15 years ago. This does not count jobs in private industry, particularly in defense, which stem from government contracts.

The result is that nearly three in every ten dollars of income Americans receive—29 percent—comes from government. Of the $345 billion dollars paid to people, nearly half is in the form of wages and salaries. Almost as much comes as Social Security payments, unemployment compensation, welfare benefits and veterans' benefits. The growing toll of government upon the taxpayer is also clear. Thirty seven cents of every dollar of national income is taken in taxes, up from 28 cents two decades ago.

Bureaucracy has grown not only in size and cost, but in its power. Nonelected government administrators have taken unto themselves more and more power, something previously reserved for the elected representatives of the people. One example may be seen in the operation of the Environmental Protection Agency (EPA), which *Reader's Digest* editor John Barron notes "threatens to grow into the most fearsome bureaucratic monster of all." Under a broad grant of power conferred by the National Environmental Policy Act, the Clean Air Amendments, the Water Pollution Control Act and the Noise Control Act, EPA has claimed for itself authority which many believe to be unprecedented in our history. Professor Irving Kristol has written, "If the EPA's conception of its mission is permitted to stand, it will be the single most powerful branch of government, having far greater direct control over our individual lives than Congress or the Executive or state and local government."

In his *Reader's Digest* article, "Too Much Government By Decree," Barron highlights the nature of the power which bureaucrats at EPA have assumed for themselves:

- EPA asserts the right to veto construction of almost anything that might generate a substantial volume of traffic.
- As of January 1, 1976, unless Congress intercedes, local communities may not permit development of a major shopping center, hotel, stadium, or factory without approval from Washington.
- In Gary, Indiana, U.S. Steel attempted to meet EPA requirements by building two new installations of non-polluting furnaces. But initially their output was limited by factors beyond the company's control: a power failure that damaged its furnaces, the coal strike, and a construction strike. Then, U.S. Steel asked in the fall of 1974 that EPA permit it to keep its one remaining open-hearth installation in operation six months more. It was told that the installation could be kept open for three months with a $2,300 fine for each day of operation. Instead, the company closed the installation, and hundreds of workers lost their jobs as a result.
- An infestation of tussock moths in 1972 defoliated 174,000 acres of Washington and Oregon forests. To prevent further damage, state officials and conservationists pleaded with the EPA to allow a carefully controlled spraying of DDT. The EPA, however, refused even a temporary removal of its arbitrary ban against DDT. Unchecked, the multiplying moths by the summer of 1973 had afflicted 700,000 acres of timber. Faced with opposition from Congress and a lawsuit, the EPA, in February, 1974, relented and authorized the use of DDT. Helicopters sprayed the forest, and the infestation ended. The devastation inflicted by a doctrinaire bureaucracy, however, remains.

Even more alarming is the charge that the EPA's ban on DDT is a prime factor behind the encephalitis epidemics of the summer of 1975 and the reemergence of bubonic plague and malaria in the United States.

The remedy to this situation is clear. Barron puts it this way:

The remedy lies in Congress, which created the problem in the first place. Congress should reappraise each federal agency, with a view to outright abolition of those that have obviously outlived their usefulness. It should withdraw from the others the vast grants of arbitrary power that it has bestowed. And Congress should define the powers left to bureaucracies in language so clear and explicit that no officials can expand their power beyond Congressional intent. . . . Finally, broad national policies required to protect consumers, workers, minorities and the environment should be implemented through specific legislation rather than bureaucratic fiat. If the people don't like the results, then—in the next election—they can remove the members of Congress responsible. That is why the American system has always provided that power must be exercised by elected representatives instead of by bureaucrats who have earned the vote of no one. If freedom is to survive, power must remain in the hands of elected representatives.

The problems we face with the current bureaucracy are diverse. On the one hand, we have the arbitrary use of power in instances such as that provided by the EPA. On the other hand, in many agencies, although the need for a particular job has disappeared, the job remains. A particular case that illustrates this general problem received a good deal of publicity in June, 1975.

At that time a rare federal bureaucrat, Jubal Hale, who had spent the past four years listening to Beethoven records, urged Congress to abolish his $19,693 a year executive director's job.

"I want you to do it as quick as you can," Hale told a Senate committee considering a bill to eliminate the Federal Metal and Nonmetallic Safety Board of Review. The committee was reviewing this and other bodies that appeared to have no discernible functions. The Board, established in 1971 to hear appeals from mine operators ordered to shut down by the Department of the Interior, has never heard an appeal. Moreover, Hale testified that the Board each year sent a one-page report to Congress saying it had nothing to do. Nevertheless, the Congress has continued to fund the Board. Hale said in an interview that he has so little to do that he spends nearly all of his time listening to Beethoven records and reading. When he was asked, "Is there any reason to continue the Board other than to improve your cultural life by listening to Beethoven records?" Hale replied: "I don't think you've got any choice but to abolish the Board."

As Mr. Hale's testimony became a subject of increased discussion many members of the Senate and House expressed their shock at the state of affairs he described. Senator

Abraham Ribicoff, Chairman of the Senate Committee on Government Operations, declared, "The startling revelation with regard to this Board is not simply that it has no work to do, but rather that it apparently has never had any work to do."

Unfortunately, the Federal Metal and Nonmetallic Safety Board of Review is hardly a unique case. Also unfortunate is the fact that few bureaucrats exist who would join Jubal Hale in complaining about not having enough work to do. Anyone familiar with the working of our bureaucracy knows that this case represents only a small tip of a very large iceberg.

The bureaucracy is far more than simply a costly burden to be borne by the taxpayers. It is, in addition, a vocal and powerful advocate for the further growth of government and for those programs which will cause such growth. Economist W. H. Hunt notes:

> A particular instance of an institutional barrier to the sort of reforms which many economists believe to be desirable is a civil service inflated through the adoption of . . . "welfarism." In the opinion of some economists, civil servants under contemporary conditions tend to have a built-in bias in favor of discretionary controls and against the coordination of the economic system through accountable entrepreneurial planning. . . . The prejudice in this case may indeed frequently be influenced by a sense of pecuniary interest: less government means fewer civil servants.

There is a real contradiction in the desire of many Americans to turn over to government control ever increasing portions of their own lives while at the same time complaining vocally about governmental corruption and inefficiency. This condition was the subject of comment in the nineteenth century by Herbert Spencer in his important essay, *Over-Legislation,* and his statement is reflective of mid-twentieth century America as well as that of nineteenth century England. When state power is applied to social purpose, Spencer remarks, its action is invariably "slow, stupid, extravagant, unadaptive, corrupt and obstructive." He devotes several paragraphs to each count and shows further that the state does not even fulfill efficiently what he calls its "unquestionable duties" to society. It does not efficiently adjudge and defend the individual's elemental rights. Consider our own mounting crime rate and the inability of government to deal effectively with it. Spencer sees no reason to expect that state power will be more efficiently applied to "secondary social purposes."

Pointing to the anomaly of leading newspapers regularly opposing corruption and mismanagement by the state while calling for an extension of state supervision, Spencer declares, "While every day chronicles a failure, there every day reappears the belief that it needs but an Act of Parliament and a staff of officers to effect any end desired. Nowhere is the perennial faith of mankind better seen."

The problem of bureaucracy has become much greater since the time of Herbert Spencer. Today, nonelected government administrators constitute a fourth branch of government never envisioned by the authors of the Constitution. That fourth branch, at the present time, seems effectively out of our control. To the degree that it remains out of our control, the future of a free society is directly threatened. Only if we adequately understand the real basis of the threat which bureaucracy poses can we act effectively to reverse this trend. Thus far, such understanding seems remote.

Public Employee Unions

In recent months we have witnessed a strike by transit employees in San Francisco, of sanitation workers in New York, of police in Baltimore, and of teachers in cities throughout the country. In almost all instances of strikes by public employees, local and state laws are being broken. Political leaders have repeatedly acquiesced in these tactics of blackmail and are showing union leaders that violation of the law pays significant rewards.

As previously noted public employees not only receive wages and benefits higher than those received by men and women in private business and industry, but they are also the beneficiaries of generous pension programs. Professor Roger Freeman comments:

> The public is almost always unaware of the huge commitments that are being piled up—and when it learns of them it is far too late to do anything about them. Because pension boosts create a sizeable long-range obligation for the community, former Mayor Frank P. Zeidler of Milwaukee suggested that they ought to be subjected to a referendum. This might offer at least some safeguard to the taxpaying public. Sam Zagoria of the U.S. Conference of Mayors proposed that controversial new public employee contracts be placed on the ballot, which could act as a restraining influence and might take decision-making officials at least partially off the hook.

Yet, at the very moment when federal workers are the recipients of such generous benefits, there is an effort to force all of them into labor unions, whether they wish to join or not. Legislation now before the Congress would impose compulsory public sector bargaining on all governments. If passed, this would mean putting the U.S. Government in the position of having to negotiate as an equal with a private organization, in this case a labor union. Second, workers

161

would be forced to grant monopoly bargaining privileges—that is, individual public employees would be compelled to accept union officials as their "exclusive representatives" in dealing with their own government. Third, compulsory membership will be imposed where all public employees, including those who do not wish to join or pay money to the union or lose the right to work for their own government.

This legislation is dangerous, both for those workers who will be forced into unions against their will and to the American society as a whole, which will be subjected on a federal level to the "public be damned" attitude which increasing numbers of public employee unions have presented on state and local levels.

Discussing this legislation, Senator Jake Garn (R-Utah) asked:

. . . whether the government—by its nature a monopoly and protector of all citizens' rights and liberties, has the authority legally or morally, to transfer any of its function to a private, independent organization. When public officials acting under authority granted to them by other public officials give union organizers the right to say who will perform public service and how those services will be performed, do not we have a situation in which the authority of government has been divested from the public?

Laws against strikes by public employees are widespread, but have proven to be totally ineffective. This was not always the case. When he sponsored the Wagner Act as a charter of freedom for workers, Franklin D. Roosevelt said: "A strike of public employees manifests nothing less than an intention on their part to prevent or obstruct the operations of government until their demands are satisfied. Such action, looking toward the paralysis of government by those who have sworn to support it, is unthinkable and intolerable."

Yet, there are now hundreds of public workers' strikes every year—their number has grown from 15 in 1958 to more than 400 in 1970 and 388 in 1973. Governors and mayors are unwilling to fire and replace public employees even though the law, in many instances, mandates it.

The Courts have also changed since Judge T. Alan Goldsborough in December 1946 sentenced the United Mine Workers Union to a fine of $3.5 million and John L. Lewis to $10,000 for disobeying an order to postpone strike action. The conviction was upheld seven to two by the U.S. Supreme Court because "the course taken by the union carried with it such a serious threat to orderly constitutional government, and to the economic and social welfare of the nation, that a fine of substantial size is required in order to emphasize the gravity of the offense. . . ."

Today, a typical situation was that of a District of Columbia Superior Court, which imposed fines and jail sentences against leaders of striking Washington teachers in September 1972—but vacated them on the following day. When a state superior court ordered a picketing ban in a San Francisco municipal strike in 1974, the mayor refused to enforce it because he "would not act as a strike breaker." The Mayor's actions the following summer in acquiescing to the demands of an illegal strike of San Francisco policemen confirmed the fact that laws against municipal strikes in that city would not be enforced.

In many respects, New York City has set the pattern for smaller municipalities. In the Condon-Wadlin Act, New York State has a strict law against strikes by public employees, but it was never enforced because officials deemed it too severe and punitive. After a 12-day subway strike in 1967, Governor Nelson Rockefeller sponsored its repeal and replacement by the more lenient Taylor Act. But a few months later, in February 1968, when the Mayor of New York City was attempting to hold firm against striking sanitation workers, the governor intervened. Instead of carrying out the mandate of the Taylor Act or calling out the National Guard as the Mayor had requested, he capitulated to the demands of the strike leaders.

What public employee unions have learned from all this, Roger Freeman points out, is that "strikes against government, though they are a felony under federal or state law, can be undertaken with impunity. Moreover, such unlawful strikes pay off in fat wage agreements because no public official has the courage . . . to uphold the public interest."

The critical financial position of New York City has largely been brought about by the role played by its municipal unions. Labor leaders, rather than the elected representatives of the people, more and more are making the key decisions about the manner in which the city of New York is to be run, how many employees are to be hired, what the conditions of their employment are to be, and what compensation should be provided. In fact, Victor Gotbaum, the chairman of New York's Municipal Labor Committee, declared, "There's no question about it, we have the ability, in a sense, to elect our own boss."

The New York Times, long a friend of organized labor, has recognized the role union leaders have played in destroying the financial structure of the city. In its editorial of July 9, 1975, entitled "Captive Politicians," *The Times* notes:

The effect of this extraordinary union clout can be readily seen in the astonishing spectacle of captive politicians falling all over each other in Albany and City Hall to impose still higher taxes on the overtaxed citizens of New York City in order to preserve their union jobs . . . it is the municipal union chieftains themselves who are anti-labor in the sense that it is the laboring men and women who work in but not for the city who will bear the brunt of the taxes required to sustain and sweeten what are already the most liberal municipal pay and fringe benefits in the nation.

The unfortunate fact is that the entire concept of democratic government is being challenged by municipal employee unions. Governmental decisions are no longer being made by elected officials, who may be removed by the voters if their performance is not approved. Instead, many of these decisions are now made by union leaders.

In a July 8, 1975, editorial, entitled "Union Ruled City," *The Times* states:

. . . one thing is clear: New York is working for its unionized civil service workers, not vice versa. The real power in the city is held by the municipal unions. Last week's illegal sanitation strike, a wretched charade in which every step was apparently orchestrated by the union leadership, with the Beame administration a benign co-conspirator, was the end product of three decades in which one New York mayor after another systematically fostered the growth of centralized union power. The rationale always was that strong, secure unions would bring cooperation for a more efficient civil service. Instead, it delivered into union hands ironclad control over every essential civic department, with a precipitous increase in personnel and payroll and a steady shrinkage in standards of performance.

The negative impact of public employee unionization is evident throughout the country. In Massachusetts, for example, Rep. Barney Frank, a member of the state legislature, declares, "I plan to make public employees the Number One issue in my next re-election campaign. I don't. think there's any bigger issue."

The problem faced by his state was described in these

terms by Robert G. Kaiser in the *Washington Post* of September 2, 1975:

* An unprecedented and lavish campaign by two national unions working together to organize virtually every worker on the state's payroll.
* A financial crisis that may lead to extensive layoffs from the state government, a prospect that appears to be mobilizing public employees and pushing them toward new militancy.
* A group of new managers at the Metropolitan Boston Transit Authority whose first priority is to reduce the power of entrenched unions and make the work force of the large and money-losing transit system more responsive to management.

Rep. Frank, a liberal legislator and former aide to Mayor Kevin White, thinks that public employees are or will soon become so unpopular with the public that politicians will be able to win votes by campaigning against them. "The balance has tipped much too far in the direction of the public employee," Frank said. "The mistake we made was to give them collective bargaining on top of civil service. Now they are triply protected. I'm not so worried about the money they earn, but productivity—you just can't get any. . . . The value of government is supposed to be that people benefit from it. But now the only benefit is to the people who run the government. . . . You can't hire them [public employees], you can't fire them, you can only yell at them." The attitude expressed by Rep. Frank in Boston can be duplicated throughout the country, wherever public officials and the public itself has been faced with a well-organized union of public employees.

Perhaps the most dramatic examples of public employee union irresponsibility thus far may be seen in the police strikes that have plagued a number of cities. Also to be observed in these events is the irresponsibility of public officials who have acquiesced in the illegal strikes and have made it clear that such violation of the law brings not punishment but reward.

Consider the police strike that rocked the city of San Francisco in August 1975. Police refused to work for three days. Mayor Joseph Alioto, at that time a lameduck officeholder, at first ordered the policemen fired for ignoring a court order to return to work. However, then he granted them the 13 percent raise they wanted with only one proviso—that the increase take effect October 15 rather than be

165

retroactive to the previous July 1. A first year policeman's pay was already $16,044 a year.

While Mayor Alioto's capitulation was hailed by the striking Police Officer's Association, the city-county Board of Supervisors voted 9 to 0 with one abstention to reject the agreement. The supervisors denounced the mayor's tactics as "dictatorial." They had called for a much lower wage offer, but Alioto said that wages saved during the strike and other money-saving steps would reduce the difference. The mayor capitulated in precisely the same manner to an illegal strike by the city's firefighters.

"It is a total capitulation to the people who are supposed to uphold the law, and who violated the law," said Dianne Feinstein, president of the Board of Supervisors and a candidate to succeed Alioto. After October 14, 1975, starting salaries for city police and firemen were $18,816. Prior to his capitulation Mayor Alioto used stern rhetoric. He declared that, "The spectacle of New York is too well known to all. San Francisco can go the route of New York City unless we call a halt to unreasonable expenses right now." Supervisors note that police and fire salaries have increased 35 percent in the past five years. The acquiesence of San Francisco to this illegal strike did bring many critical comments across the country, a further indication of the public mood concerning this subject.

The Wall Street Journal noted on August 21, 1975, that "San Francisco's police strike is but another of the recent assaults by public employee unions on the budgeting and management processes of cities and states. This may be the wave of the future, but it cannot be a viable future. . . . Policemen, to a degree greater than any other public employee, represent legal authority. Since police strikes are almost universally illegal, they are a jarring symbol that legal authority has broken down." If the traditional function of cities still maintain their validity, *The Journal* stated:

This trend cannot continue. . . . Since Ur of Chaldea, and perhaps even earlier for all we know, the concentrated populations we call cities have served the very useful function of facilitating manufacturing, trade and commerce. Cities can tolerate a great deal of disorder as long as their basic reason for being is not threatened. The alienation and militance of public employees poses such a threat. . . . Our primary message is addressed to the public employee unions and their leaders. If they persist in their extra-legal assaults, they may indeed conquer some cities. New York is practically subdued. But it will be a Pyrrhic victory. Without enterprises that give them a reason for being, those conquered cities will be only hollow shells.

Mayor Alioto was criticized very harshly by the traditionally liberal and pro-labor *New York Times*. In an editorial on August 23, 1975, *The Times* commented:

. . . when most of San Francisco's police and firemen struck . . . Mayor Alioto forgot all his brave words. He spurned a request by the city's Board of Supervisors that he ask Governor Edmund G. Brown, Jr. to assign state troopers to patrol the city—a move that would have given the community's 670,000 people more security at the same time that it strengthened its leverage at the bargaining table. Instead the Mayor 'mediated' the pay dispute by giving the strikers twice as much as the supervisors had authorized them to get—the unions' full 13 percent demand . . . Alioto . . . in betrayal of his own precepts . . . has reinforced the conviction that unions in control of vital public services can compel the community to capitulate by holding a strike gun at its head. This is not only the road to municipal bankruptcy; it is the road to anarchy. It is a death knell to democracy.

The *Phoenix Gazette*, in an editorial, expressed the view that, "As Alioto's capitulation chillingly attests, the suggestion that high-riding public employee unions can indeed bring an end to the American system of representative government is not at all far-fetched." In a similar vein, *New York Times* columnist William Safire, discussing the San Francisco police strike, commented:

An entire city was kidnapped and held for ransom; the ransom was paid, and now the extortionists patrol the city's streets, making sure nobody else breaks the law. Whenever policemen put their guns to a city's head, they create a police state. . . . Public employees are not slaves with legitimate grievances, they have no obligation to grunt and sweat under a weary life. They have the option of looking for jobs in the private sector, where competition is keener and raises less automatic.

It is interesting to note that the Supreme Court, which has been ordering employers to bargain with unions for many years, has refused to recognize a union organized to represent the 50-member police force assigned to the Court itself. Court officials have cited a 1962 Presidential order that, while encouraging union activity by federal employees, exempted security units where "national security requirements and considerations" were involved.

The union for which the Supreme Court guards sought recognition is the American Federation of Government Employees, which has organized, among others, the police force of the Department of Defense. Perhaps the rules the Supreme Court sets for itself should be considered of equal applicability to the remainder of the American society.

The increasingly aggressive behavior of public employee unions has produced a significant change in public opinion concerning the entire idea of the right to strike by groups such as policemen and firemen. A Louis Harris poll of September, 1975, indicates that by 50 to 45 percent, the American people now believe that policemen should not have the right to strike, a turnaround from the slim 47 to 46 percent plurality who felt differently in 1974. Harris concludes that "This current feeling against strikes by the uniformed services is only one part of a generally negative turn in public opinion about unions of government employees."

Among other findings in this poll are these:

• By 86 to 8 percent, the public feels that "people who work for the government have working conditions as good or better" than people employed in private business.

• By 84 to 7 percent, the public believes that government employees "have pension and retirement benefits as good or better" than those employed by private business.

• By 76 to 15 percent, the public feels that those working for the government "are paid just as high or higher salaries" than people employed in private business.

• By 56 to 28 percent, the public believes that "government employees have as good or better chances to express grievances over work."

• Significantly, by 52 to 38 percent, the public also does not believe that people working for government "work as hard or harder" than people employed in private business.

Equally interesting is the result of another study, conducted by the Opinion Research Corporation of Princeton, New Jersey, for the Business Roundtable. This study discovered that there is very little difference between the views held by the public as a whole and by union members in particular on key questions involving such controversial matters as the use of union dues to support political candidates and the right of policemen and firemen to strike.

Union members appear to be at odds with their leaders

with regard to many important questions. According to the Opinion Research survey, 72 percent of both the general public and union members favor antitrust laws to control union monopolies. The rank and file of labor is not asking for any special privileges. Where 79 percent of the general public says that the use of union dues in political campaigns should be outlawed, 76 percent of the union membership is of the same opinion.

When it comes to the use of union personnel in political campaigns, labor has a more permissive attitude than the general public. A majority of both groups, however, would still ban partisan political activity on the part of officials on union time: 63 percent of the general public disapproves of this practice, as does 53 percent of union membership.

As recently as 1973 a majority of union members favored granting unemployment benefits to strikers. But today, 54 percent of organized labor opposes this practice because it subsidizes one side in a dispute and hurts collective bargaining. This is only slightly lower than the general public figure of 58 percent. And 46 percent of union members are even against extending welfare benefits to strikers.

Concerning strikes by the police, 71 percent of the total public opposes such strikes as do 59 percent of union members. A majority in both categories is also against strikes by firemen, prison guards, hospital employees and federal employees.

On compulsory unionism for public employees, 70 percent of the total public is against it. A majority of union members—57 percent—agrees with the general public on this. Columnist John Chamberlain expresses the view that, "It is the 'bourgeois' attitude toward the closed shop that still prevails with labor and the general public alike . . . a good thought for AFL-CIO President George Meany to keep in mind."

The claim on the part of public employees and their union leaders that they should have and do have both the right to bargain collectively and the right to strike is something new and unique in the history of labor relations in the United States.

In a democratic society, the elected representatives of the people are the ones with the legal responsibility to determine the laws and to see to it that government employees carry out these laws properly. Now, union leaders claim for themselves the right to bargain for government employees, not only with regard to salary and working con-

169

ditions but also about the nature of their work. Many critics have charged that such labor leaders are really challenging the concept of the sovereignty of government itself.

While we are told today that the concept of the unionization of government employees is perfectly consistent with the philosophy of representative government, that view is highly questionable. Few Americans, at earlier periods, felt that this was the case. Many, however, felt the two—representative government and unions of government employees—were in total contradiction to one another.

A New York State Court, for example, spelled this out in a 1943 opinion:

To tolerate or recognize any combination of Civil Service employees of the government as a labor organization or union is not only incompatible with the spirit of democracy, but inconsistent with every principle upon which our government is founded. Nothing is more dangerous to public welfare than to admit that hired servants of the state can dictate to the government the hours, the wages and conditions under which they will carry on essential services vital to the welfare, safety and security of the citizen. To admit as true that government employees have power to halt the functions of government unless their demands are satisfied, is to transfer to them all legislative, executive and judicial power. Nothing would be more ridiculous. (*Railway Mail Association v. Murphy*, reviewed on other matters in *Railway Mail Association v. Corsi*, U.S. Supreme Court, 1945.)

In the legislation presented to the Congress by Rep. William L. Clay (D-Missouri), and supported by organized labor, the preamble sets the scope of collective bargaining. This document repeatedly used the phrase "and other matters of mutual concern." This language clearly reflects the demands of such groups as the American Federation of Teachers and the American Federation of State, County and Municipal Employees (AFSCME) that a proper subject for collective bargaining, above wages, hours and conditions of employment, should be government policy itself. To implement this approach AFSCME has been involved in demonstrations against the war in Vietnam as well as other matters of government policy.

The Clay Bill would compel government employees to join a union whether or not they wished to do so. By doing so, the constitutional rights of government employees would clearly be challenged. In his book dealing with the question

170

of public employee unions, *The Municipal Doomsday Machine,* Ralph de Toledano points out, "A 'right' becomes compulsion unless it is coupled to an equal right to desist. Under the First Amendment, the guarantees of free speech and free association include the rights not to speak and not to associate—but these are denied by the Clay Bill in the clearest derogation of the Bill of Rights since the enactment of the Alien and Sedition Acts in the early days of the Republic by a vindictive Congress."

The legislation before the Congress would, if passed, eliminate the Civil Service system in which merit is to be the sole criterion for government employment. Author De Toledano declares:

> It is the determination of Big Labor and its allies in the Congress to destroy both the civil service system and the right of Americans, if qualified, to government jobs. . . . Since an exclusive representative will have the right to bar from employment any individual who is not a member of the union, Section 10 (b) goes far beyond anything in the National Labor Relations Act by reimposing an outlawed closed shop. The civil service system opens the door to government employment for all qualified citizens. The Clay Bill slams that door shut by allowing unions to set up their own standards of employment that supersedes those of previous government statutes. A union can decide that only brown-haired males, five-feet ten inches in height, who swear eternal fealty to George Meany can qualify for membership in the union. Under the Clay Bill, all government within the United States will have to bow to what the unions 'prescribe'—and have prescribed in the private sector. (In the past, unions have barred blacks from membership, thereby depriving them of the right to work.)

The leaders of the public employee unions that exist at present do not hesitate to break the law. In May, 1969, Mr. Jerry Wurf, head of AFSCME and presuming to speak for all public employees, threatened, "They do not want to engage in strikes, but they will if that is the only answer. They do not want to engage in civil disorder, but they will if that is the only answer. To win or reinforce bargaining rights for public employees, AFSCME has staged 75 illegal strikes in the past two years."

A police strike in Baltimore in 1974 caused "a terror in the community," according to Maryland Judge James W. Murphy. Fortunately, Maryland's reaction was different

171

from that of Mayor Joseph Alioto of San Francisco a year later. Maryland's Governor Mandel and Baltimore Police Commissioner Donald Pomerleau took a strong stand. Some of the police ringleaders were fired and others were demoted or otherwise disciplined, in spite of threats of vengeance from AFSCME.

While trouble stirred in Baltimore, AFSCME leaders threatened to "shut down the state of Ohio." Beginning with a strike at the Lebanon Correctional Institution, the illegal walkouts multiplied. *The New York Times* of July 16, 1974, reported: "Since then employees at five other penal institutions, five mental health facilities and a facility of the Ohio Youth Commission have walked off their jobs in protest because the Ohio General Assembly did not pass a wage increase for state employees."

Beyond its illegal strikes and desire to control the very government by which its members are ostensibly employed, AFSCME uses its dues to engage in partisan political activity. Mr. Wurf does not hesitate to admit this is the case. In a written deposition in the case of *Mamie Adams, et al. v. City of Detroit* on July 26, 1973, Wurf wrote the following:

The American Federation of State, County and Municipal Employees, AFL-CIO (hereinafter AFSCME) receives revenues in the form of per capita tax payments . . . Per capita tax revenues so received are comingled in the general fund of AFSCME and used for its programs and activities, including political action and legislative action programs. . . .

In carrying on its political action programs and activities AFSCME utilizes its officers and salaried staff personnel. A portion of the salaried time and reimbursed expenses of staff personnel and of the costs of office space, office supplies, telephone and telegraph, printing and general overhead and administrative expenses of AFSCME are either directly related to its political action programs or provide administrative support for such programs and activities. . . ."

Mr. Wurf admits that public employee unionism is a "revolutionary" departure from traditional American thinking on the subject and notes, "the old concept of government sovereignty is fast fading away" and that unions are "coequals" with government in the ordering of public affairs —virtually a fourth branch of government, on a par with the executive, legislative and judicial branches.

In the area of teaching, for example, we must ask ourselves whether a teacher, indebted to and controlled by a union such as the American Federation of Teachers, can retain his objectivity in his classroom presentation of labor-related questions. The answer seems to be that he cannot.

In January 1970 the United Federation of Teachers distributed to its members in the New York City high schools a study guide entitled *The ABC's of the G-E Strike—A Teaching Unit for Secondary School Teachers.* The guide was prepared by Jeannette Di Lorenzo, a junior high school social studies teacher and District 15 representative of the UFT. It was clearly an effort to indoctrinate students in the issues of the strikes that AFL-CIO unions were waging, and to enlist their support for the strikers.

The summary of Lesson Four of this document speaks for itself:
1. The AFL-CIO maintains that the legitimate demands of labor unions in America are not the cause of inflation. 2. Businesses and corporations which increase prices on products despite the fact that their profits are already very high contribute to inflation. 3. The workers of America depend on their trade unions to win them a living wage and do not want to see their unions destroyed. 4. The unions in America will not permit the collective bargaining process to be destroyed. The government, the courts, and the public generally recognize the importance of collective bargaining in determining wages. 5. A consumer boycott was started against G.E. on November 28, 1969, to help the G.E. workers with their strike. . . .

In a television program in April, 1974, Bill Moyers asked a number of important questions about the role of the teachers unions, particularly in New York City: "Organized teachers in New York have come far since those days. . . . Every triumph increases Albert Shanker's influence and power. But his victories mirror the predicaments of success. Do his teachers owe their first loyalty to the classroom or to their local chapter? Are they trade unionists first and professionals second? Do increased teacher benefits spell better education? . . ."

The American Federation of Teachers has widely disseminated what it calls a "Bill of Rights" for teachers. The document includes a great deal of cynicism. In Article XIII, for example, it said that, "Since teachers must be free in order to teach freedom, the right to be members of organizations of their own choosing must be guaranteed." The document does not indicate that if a simple majority of teachers vote for representation by the AFT this "right" becomes compulsion for the other 49 percent.

Ralph de Toledano expresses this view:

If teaching is a profession, as the AFT's Bill of Rights repeatedly urges, then a teacher's function is to teach. To date, the unionization of education has debased teaching to the point where Johnny can no longer read or add, condemning the children of those with low income to perpetual penury. If teaching is a profession, then teachers must be part of the community, sharing in community purposes. In the past, dedicated teachers considered it part of their job to encourage bright students and help slow ones, but Shanker opposes this unless it is done at time-and-a-half. The AFT and other teacher unions claim for themselves the present prosperity of that profession although salaries were sharply rising long before the Albert Shankers had injected themselves into the picture. What, then, has unionization accomplished? Among other things, it has brought to the surface a union demand that "seniority"—a pejorative term when applied to the Congress— be the rule in the filling of school supervisor posts, not ability but union time-serving. That, and hatred of school boards and other democratically elected officials.

Perhaps the most important issue involved in the entire question of public employee unions is the question of where governmental sovereignty is meant to reside and whether or not such unions are challenging the very idea of rule by law.

When compulsory unionism is applied to the public sector, a situation is created in which a small minority within the total body politic assumes what is, in effect, independent governmental control over the vast majority of citizens. In the private sector, compulsory unionism deprives industry of due process and individual working men and women of their freedom of association. This, of course, is bad enough. In the public sector, however, the people themselves are deprived of the sovereignty guaranteed by the Constitution.

Woodrow Wilson once commented ". . . The business of government is to see that no other organization is as strong as itself; to see that no group of men, no matter what their private business is, may come into competition with the authority of society."

Our entire legal tradition leads inevitably to the conclusion that governmental sovereignty and public employee collective bargaining are incompatible. In the case of *City of Springfield v. Clouse* (356 Missouri 1239), the Missouri Supreme Court stated:

> Under our form of government, public office or employment never has been and cannot become a matter of bargaining and contract. . . . This is true because the whole matter of qualifications, tenure, compensation and working conditions for any public service involves the exercise of legislative powers. Except to the extent that all the people have themselves settled any of these matters by writing them into the Constitution, they must be determined by their chosen representatives who constitute the legislative body. It is a familiar principle of constitutional law that the legislature cannot delegate its legislative powers and any attempted delegation thereof is void. . . . If such powers cannot be delegated, they surely cannot be bargained or contracted away, and certainly not by any administrative or executive officers who cannot have any legislative powers.

Those who advocate public sector unions and collective bargaining attempt to make an analogy between the public and private sector. If collective bargaining is an acceptable procedure in the private sector, they argue, it should be equally acceptable in the public. This overlooks the very important differences between the two. Industry is the servant of the marketplace, government is not. Unions in industry must, at some point, consider the correlation of wages, prices, and profits. In government, this is not the case. Beyond this, if the United Auto Workers strike against Ford, the individual citizen can purchase a Chevrolet—or a Toyota, Volkswagen or Volvo. Government, by its very nature, is a monopoly. We do not have competing police departments, fire departments, or armies. *A strike of those in the public sector is not really a strike against government but a strike against the people themselves.* Taxpayers are deprived of essential services for which they have paid and, without police, fire and military protection, they are left helpless before any potentially aggressive force.

In his important essay, "Sovereignty and Compulsory Public-Sector Bargaining," (*Wake Forest Law Review*, March 1974), Professor Sylvester Petro proposes that:

> Governmental sovereignty and public-sector collective bargaining are contradictory, as well in practice as in logic. The contradiction is so corrosive, indeed, as to dissolve into meaninglessness. Sovereignty *means* the supreme and

unchallengeable power of compulsion. How can a genuine sovereign be *forced* by a private person or agency to do something and remain sovereign? . . . compulsory public-sector bargaining laws are incompatible with governmental sovereignty and constitute a fatal threat to popular sovereignty as well. They can make no contribution to the peace or to the productivity of society. They point in the direction of anarchy, and of all the dread consequences of anarchy and disorder.

The leaders of public employee unions do not hesitate to give the warnings of critics such as Professor Petro the substance required to make their case clear beyond any doubt. Jerry Wurf, for example, has insisted on a "power relationship where public officials and policymakers respect you as equals and deal with you." This, of course, is the private-sector analogy once again. Taken to its extreme, we reach the point advocated by Walter Reuther in which unions should sit with management to determine what will be produced, how it will be produced, how materials will be allocated, and so on. Wurf has proclaimed his hostility to the Civil Service merit system and has declared that public employee unions "must make it unmistakably clear that where there is a conflict between the desires of the parties, as evidenced by the collective bargaining agreement, and merit system rules and regulations, that the contract shall prevail. . . . This, in effect, would establish a new "Spoils System."

What negotiators on both sides are doing in the case of a public employee union, Ralph de Toledano argues, are "usurping the legislative function of setting public policy on wages, conditions of employment, qualifications for employment and any other matters taken up in the contract. In short, by the very process of collective bargaining in the public sector, the union asserts and imposes its sovereignty over government and the *res publica.*"

To those who argue that "binding arbitration" would be the appropriate answer to public employee union strikes, de Toledano says, "Compulsory arbitration is subversive as well of the commonweal as of the principle of governmental sovereignty. It takes the legislative process one step further away from those who alone can legitimately exercise it. Arbitrators are accountable and responsible to no one, least of all to the popular sovereign—the people." Such arbitrators become, as the court declared in *National League of Cities et al. v. Hon. Peter J. Brennan,* "more powerful in the disposition of community resources, gain greater control of the taxing process, than the citizens and their elected representatives possess." It seems clear that public sector collective bargaining and unionization are not compatable with either representative government or the nature of the sovereignty which is necessary for a decently ordered society to exist.

As the leaders of public employee unions flex their muscles with a variety of strikes by policemen, firemen, teachers, and sanitationmen, the demands are becoming increasingly excessive. Consider the latest expressed intention of labor leaders—the unionization of the U.S. Army.

At the present time, a top-level committee of the American Federation of Government Employees is hard at work studying methods for conducting a campaign to organize soldiers, sailors, and airmen. Clyde Webber, president of the union, wants the union's constitution amended at its 1976 convention to allow the inclusion of servicemen as union members. "Servicemen need somebody to represent them, that's for sure," Mr. Webber says. "We think we could perform a useful service in doing that."

AFGE officials say that there is not any doubt that the U. S. Constitution's First Amendment already guarantees servicemen the right to join unions. These officials also interpret Pentagon regulations as giving unions the right to represent servicemen in limited ways.

When *The Wall Street Journal* asked Pentagon officials for their reaction to the idea of the unionization of the armed services, the reactions were uniformly negative. An Army General stated the following: "Sheer horror! If you analyze the meaning of military discipline, you can't tolerate any organization that competes with the chain of command. The day we do that is the day the Army begins to lose its effectiveness."

William Brehm, Assistant Secretary of Defense for Manpower Affairs, declared that, "A military organization can't be democratic; it must be based on command authority."

The Union's general secretary, Leo Pellerzi, sharply differs with this analysis. He declared that, "It is a volunteer army and that means people are selecting a military career as a means of livelihood and not patriotic reasons. Servicemen today aren't responding to an attack on the country. They want to be paid."

The 1969 presidential order that gives unions the right to negotiate contracts and process grievances for civilian federal employees, including those in the Defense Department, does specifically bar them from providing those services for uniformed military personnel. An army labor expert, however, says that this prohibition has to be "distinguished from the right of soldiers to join unions under the Constitution," and a top Civil Service Commission official agrees. In fact, an Army policy statement issued in mid-1969, when radical anti-war groups were attempting to build "servicemen's unions," conceded that "In view of the constitutional right to freedom of association, it is unlikely that mere membership in a servicemen's union can constitutionally be prohibited." The policy memorandum also declares, however, that "commanders aren't authorized to recognize or to bargain with a 'servicemen's union.' "

Thus, according to both union leaders and lawyers for the Pentagon, the First Amendment's "right of the people peaceably to assemble, and to petition the government for a redress of grievances" provides sufficient legal justification for a servicemen's union.

The entire notion of unionization of military personnel should be objectionable to those who believe in the sovereignty of government as well as in the need for a strong national defense, one not dependent upon the whims and desires of labor leaders who have never been elected by the citizens to represent them. Discussing this idea, Senator John Tower (R-Texas) declared that, "Recent events in New York City have provided us all with graphic illustrations of the havoc that can be wrought by public employee unions unmindful of the public interest. . . . Imagine an army in which enlisted soldiers refuse to carry out orders from superior officers until they have been cleared by a shop steward or agreed to at a union meeting."

Discussing the proposal for unionization of the armed forces the *Indianapolis News,* in an editorial of August 18, 1975, asked, "Will union power, rather than the actual nature of the jobs, determine such matters as minimum crews for artillery pieces and tanks? Will the featherbedding that helped wreck the railroads be forced on the military as well? . . . The movement must be stopped before it gains momentum. . . ."

It is clear that unionization of public employees and the entire notion of collective bargaining in the public sector leads inevitably to the threat of strikes and to widespread public disorder and disarray. Some advocates of compulsory unionization of public employes argue that strikes can be made illegal. In practice however, this is of little consolation as events in New York, San Francisco and other cities have shown only too well.

In his article in the August, 1975, issue of *The Freeman*, "Compulsory Public-Sector Bargaining: The dissolution of The Social Order," Professor Sylvester Petro responds to this argument:

All competent scholars in the labor law field are aware that anti-strike injunctions are almost impossible to enforce, even in the private sector, where, at least, the forces of government are available to attempt to induce respect for the court orders. But what prospect is there for enforcement of a court order against a public-sector union when all civil servants are unionized, as they will be if compulsory collective bargaining laws prevail universally in this country? Who is going to enforce an injunction against a strike by a policeman? the National Guard? the Army?

Dr. Petro continues:

The situation is even grimmer than the foregoing analysis suggests. In fact, public-sector strikes do such enormous harm in such a brief time that court actions aimed at enjoining them are usually an exercise in futility. Even before the legal papers are filed, the greater part of the damage done by a good many public-sector strikes is already done. The strikers have the community over a barrel. It has to give in. According to one study of events in the experimental laboratory of our subject, the City of New York, the vast preponderance of the public-sector strikes called there never reach the courts at all. The harm they do is so vicious that the striking unions are in a position to extort, as part of the price for going back to work, an agreement from the city authorities not to prosecute the strike, despite its illegality!

It should be clear that compulsory public-sector bargaining is not compatible with our entire idea of representative government and rule by law.

In a recently published book, *The Unions and the Cities,* Harry H. Wellington, the new Dean of the Yale University Law School, and Yale Law Professor Ralph K. Winter, Jr., express concern over the power of public employee unions to dictate public policy—such as school curriculum or the size of classes. They offer a number of proposals to curb the power of such unions. For example: "To curb excessive wage demands, the law might require that the terms of a contract be submitted to a referendum." Dean Wellington favors out-lawing certain kinds of strikes by public employees but admits that such a ban is "impractical." "Employees," he states, "would strike in spite of it, as they have time and again."

It will not be easy to challenge the power of public employee unions in our large cities. These organizations have become more and more entrenched and difficult to dislodge from their position of power. That they should never have been recognized in the first instance now appears to be clear to many who once believed that such organizations would be beneficial to the community.

What we can learn from this experience, however, is not to compound upon the national level the difficulties we seem unable to deal with on the state and local levels. If police strikes plague us in New York and San Francisco, let us not set into motion a policy which can produce a strike of the Army, Navy and Air Force in the future.

The very idea of a free society becomes increasingly a mockery if the United States Government finds itself in the position of compelling its own employees to join a private labor organization as a condition of governmental employment. Such proposals must be vigorously opposed. If they are not, the chaos of New York and San Francisco will be repeated in every city and town in the United States. This is a state of affairs which the nation cannot afford.

A Time for Reform: Some Proposals

After 43 years of experimentation with liberal proposals leading to a recrudescence of feudalistic welfare statism, it ought to be apparent to all that such proposals work contrary to the interests of a free people and that the programs established by them are badly in need of reform. For too long we have been looking to government and the coercive sector rather than to individuals and the voluntary sector for solutions to problems, overlooking the historical record which shows that big government creates more difficulties than it solves. Moreover, despite the generous impulses behind such programs, they have almost invariably done the greatest violence to the people they were intended to help.

What follows therefore is an outline for reversing the trend toward increasing coercion through reforms that will not only work but will enhance individual liberty. In the year of the Bicentennial, nothing could be more fitting than a rededication to the principles of individual liberty and limited constitutional government upon which our country was founded and which made it the envy of the world.

In proposing such reforms, the author is quick to acknowledge that a moral and spiritual regeneration is the bedrock upon which we might lay the foundation for at least two more centuries' preservation of the world's last, best hope. But one must simultaneously concede that environment does indeed have an impact on behavior. To be paranoid in a police state, for example, is to be normal. Thus, in proposing reforms of our laws, the objective is to attempt to begin restoration of a climate that would minimize coercion and dictation, liberate the creative and productive energies of a free people, and facilitate the renaissance of a society that is righteous, responsible, and humane.

181

Budget Reform

For the free enterprise system to operate at peak efficiency, and to end the inequity of taxation through inflation, excessive federal spending must be curtailed. Budget deficits not only absorb investment capital that could otherwise be used to increase productivity, but they mean more dollars in circulation with which to buy goods and services. The result, "more money chasing fewer goods," has been a prescription not only for inflation but, as we saw in 1974 and 1975, for unemployment, high interest rates, and recession as well.

The relationship between deficit spending and inflation is easy to document. During the eight-year period from the end of 1967 to the end of 1975, the figures show that, in response to deficit spending, the national debt went up 67.6 percent. Turning the coin over, the figures also show that, for the same eight-year period, the cost of living went up 63.7 percent. The similarity in numbers is more than just coincidence.

To say that the politicians are to blame for such profligate spending is one thing. Stopping them is quite another matter. For years, Congress has authorized and appropriated on a bill-by-bill basis with little regard for the bigger budget picture, thus appeasing various special interest groups while ignoring the larger public interest. Finally, as a reaction to the impoundment dispute and the Watergate mess, Congress decided to assume a share of the responsibility for developing an overall budget but, despite good intentions, the corrective legislation did not go far enough. Instead of establishing a mandatory ceiling that, once set, could not be raised, Congress changed the bill to permit the ceiling to be raised if it could not resist its penchant to spend more. Thus, the bill is only as effective as the willpower of Congress, and history shows that isn't very strong.

By going back to the original concept of one set ceiling with which expenditures would have to be made to conform, some backbone could be added to the Congressional budget-making process. At least, Congress would have to consider spending priorities more carefully and say no to some special interest groups periodically; both actions would be steps in the right direction.

Another needed improvement involves curtailing the power of Congress to authorize new budget authority for more than one year. Much of our present difficulty stems from the fact that Congress, partly to delay any possible adverse reaction, spreads expenditures for an expensive program over several years without taking into account what affect the practice will have on future budgets. Therefore, not only should budget ceilings be set several years in advance, but Congress should not be permitted to obligate funds for more than one year at a time. By taking such a step, controllability would be applied to a major portion of the budget that is now uncontrollable.

Still another reform that would discourage profligate spending involves requiring that each piece of legislation passed carry with it a taxpayer's price tag. If such a proposal were adopted, every taxpaying family would be told how much a particular program would add to their tax bill before it was enacted into law. In addition, government should be required, as a part of its annual budget, to tell the taxpayers not only how much it expects to take in and pay out in that year, but also what liabilities it has incurred that taxpayers will have to pay off in future years. This practice would enable Congress and the American people to make a rational judgment as to whether they prefer to pay higher taxes or cut back on government expenditures.

The best way to accomplish this objective would be to require the federal government to adopt the accrual accounting system which most American businesses use—a system that gives a full picture of the financial strengths and weaknesses of any particular fiscal entity. The recent fiscal debacle in New York City demonstrates clearly enough the need for such a reform. Moreover, full disclosure of federal finances is consistent with the trend towards more open government and greater government accountability demanded by liberals and conservatives alike.

While all these steps will help bring about reduced federal spending, the simplest and most effective way to balance the budget, as is necessary, is to pass a constitutional amendment requiring a balanced budget in addition to systematic repayment of the national debt over a 100-year period. Enactment of such a measure would ensure fiscal responsibility and would ease the pressure on existing capital markets. The only exception to the balanced budget provision would be in a time of war or national emergency, in which case the House and Senate, each by a two-thirds vote, could suspend it for up to two years.

While cutting the budget sufficiently to bring it into balance may not be easy, it can be done. When President

183

Ford first proposed a $52 billion budget deficit for fiscal 1976, I instructed my staff to look into ways of cutting the budget; after considerable study, it developed that not only could the budget be balanced but, even after adding $1 billion for weapons research and development, a surplus of $900 million could be realized. The cuts would be accomplished by revamping and reducing subsidy programs, by postponing projects not urgently needed, by cutting back on foreign aid, by reducing personnel costs in the defense budget, by eliminating programs and agencies that are counterproductive, and by rolling back most other spending to fiscal 1974 levels. Using the same criteria, an even bigger surplus—$41.8 billion—could be realized for 1977 if we coupled constructive tax reform to the spending cuts.

Thus, the argument, often offered, that the budget cannot be balanced, lacks merit. Just as Congress had the power to vote the programs that unbalanced the budget and resulted in a 12.2 percent inflation rate in 1974, so too does it have the power to vote the measures that will bring the budget back into balance in the future. All that is lacking is the willpower but that, at least, is something the American voter can correct.

In a broader perspective, this struggle between citizens and their government over fiscal responsibility will not be ultimately resolved until government is denied the means of expanding the money supply and thus inflating the currency. Reducing expenditures and balancing the budget are necessary and vital steps, but the best way to keep the problem from recurring is to return the nation to the gold standard. As the distinguished monetary expert, the late Ludwig Von Mises once said, "the essence of the gold standard consists of the fact that it makes the determination of the monetary unit's purchasing power independent of the measures of governments. It wrests from the hands of the economic Tsars their most redoubtable instrument. It makes it impossible for them to inflate."

In an October 2, 1974, speech in Indianapolis, Indiana, the distinguished Senator from Arizona, and one of the great contributors to the cause of individual liberty, Barry Goldwater, made reference to this quote and then added some salient points by reiterating several prophetic statements by Herbert Hoover. Hoover, he noted, once said that "Currency convertible into gold . . . is a vital protection against economic manipulation by the government. As long as currencies are convertible, governments cannot easily tamper

184

with the price of goods and, therefore, the wage standards of the country." Moreover, Hoover had added, governments "cannot easily confiscate the savings of the people by manipulation of inflation and deflation."

In short, fiscal responsibility is a moral issue as well as a political and economic one. Inasmuch as inflation is a hidden tax, reintroducing the gold standard will protect us from not only the loss of our wealth but also the erosion of our liberty.

Tax Reform

Since the health of our free enterprise system is dependent on adequate financing for productive endeavor, changing the tax structure to encourage capital formation is as important as amending the budget process to prevent excess spending. Even though a balanced budget would decrease the competition for the capital that is available, it is most important, if the economy is to expand and employment is to grow, for the total amount of available capital to increase. To put it another way, businessmen should not only be able to borrow sufficient money for capital investment, but should be able to use more of their company's earnings for the same purpose.

Last year's rise in the unemployment rate, coupled with a 7.5 percent drop in industrial productivity since 1973, underscores the need for meaningful tax reform that will permit increased capital expenditure for equipment replacement, technological improvements, and plant expansion. Without such improvements, U.S. firms will lose ground in domestic and world markets, resulting in increased unemployment. The recent example of Canada is illustrative. Faced with many of the problems plaguing U.S. firms, the Canadian government reduced the corporate income tax rate from 49 percent to 40 percent to encourage reinvestment and accelerate productivity.

In the United States, however, the tax rate for corporations remains at 48 percent and, in many instances, U.S. firms cannot depreciate facilities and equipment as can firms in foreign nations. Thus, reform of the tax structure to permit greater capital formation is all the more in order.

Of the ideas that have been proposed, two seem to have particular merit. One is the aforementioned Jobs Creation Act, sponsored by Congressman Jack Kemp and co-sponsored by 120 other members of the House, which focuses primarily on business. The other is known as "tax indexing" and is oriented more towards the individual taxpayer. While passage of either would be most beneficial, the two are not mutually exclusive; enactment of both would give the economy the stimulus it needs to increase productivity and employment.

As noted in Chapter Six, the Jobs Creation Act has nine specific provisions aimed at stimulating capital formation. Among the most significant are 1) excluding dividends paid by domestic corporations from gross income; 2) increasing the investment tax credit to 15 percent; 3) reducing the corporate tax rate by 6 percent; 4) increasing the asset depreciation range from 20 to 40 and 5) permitting a complete one-year write-off of required, but nonproductive, pollution control facilities and equipment. All in all, these and the other changes would result in an increase of $74.6 billion in capital outlays during the first year alone.

Contrary to what some might think, an econometric study done by Norman B. Ture, Inc. a Washington based consulting firm, indicates that implementation of the Jobs Creation Act would result in a first-year increase in tax revenue of $5.2 billion. Moreover, the study also showed that over a three-year period this act would increase the GNP by almost $250 billion, employment by almost 11 million, capital outlays by almost $82 billion and tax revenues by just over $25 billion. Corroborating these findings in the Canadian example, where the aforementioned reduction in the corporate tax rate brought about a $250 million increase in tax revenue rather than the $450 million tax loss originally anticipated.

An approach of this type makes far more sense than spending billions of dollars for public service jobs that do not result in productive, permanent employment. It is also far better than having millions of people collecting unemployment compensation or, worse yet, welfare. Furthermore, by increasing productivity, employment, and tax revenues, such a measure will represent a positive contribution to the war on inflation.

The second reform, tax indexing, addresses two problems —the inflation tax and the problem of capital formation. The measure would tie the income tax rate, personal exemptions, the standard deduction, depreciation, and the interest rate on U.S. savings bonds to the cost-of-living index. By doing so, more money would be available for capital investment and, in addition, people would not be penalized

186

for having received a wage or salary increase to compensate for increases in the cost of living. As it stands now, a wage earner finds his percentage of tax increasing while *real income,* as measured by purchasing power, remains constant or even declines. And since Congress does not vote directly on this "inflation tax" increase, it represents a form of both taxation without representation and taxation by misrepresentation.

What makes the "inflation tax" even more attractive to profligate politicians is that it not only does not require affirmation but it even permits Congress to "reduce taxes" and thereby appear to be a "Good Samaritan" to the taxpayers. These kinds of reductions have been going on for years and constitute an unofficial tax indexing of sorts, but they are usually incommensurate with the inflation rate, delayed in their applicability, and timed more to suit the politicians than the taxpayer. What is needed, instead, is an automatic tax indexing feature, which would make *real* rather than *earned* income the basis for taxation and would remove whatever vested interest government might have in promoting inflation.

Enactment of positive capital formation and tax indexing measures would be a tremendous step towards the necessary goal of bringing the growth of the money supply back in line with the growth of productivity. However, over the long term, the measures must not be our sole objectives. For just as balancing the budget is not the ultimate check on fiscal irresponsibility, neither is capital formation or tax indexing the ultimate response to a system of taxation which is inherently weak from both a moral and an economic standpoint. What is needed is a basic reform of the tax code —one that not only makes it simpler but also ensures that everyone pays his fair share.

From humble beginnings back in 1913, the federal income tax code has grown, mostly in recent years, into a million-word monstrosity of almost unfathomable complexity. Just describing all the deductions, exemptions, credits, and exclusions requires over 6,000 pages of fine print. Further, rarely do two people, even two experts, agree on how much is owed by someone with anything more than the simplest of returns. As a result, people have not only been frustrated in filling out their returns but have developed the feeling that the so-called loopholes, whether they be used by the very rich or the very poor, have enabled some people to escape paying their fair share of taxes.

As an alternative, therefore, we might prudently examine the idea put forth by Professor Milton Friedman in 1966 and recently endorsed in large part by Treasury Secretary William Simon: to eliminate all deductions, exemptions (except for possibly personal exemptions), exclusions, and other items so often viewed as tax loopholes and substituting, in their stead, a flat rate of tax. If this had been done in 1975, each and every taxpayer would have had to pay only 10.5 percent of his income to Uncle Sam. If, to ease the burden on the lowest income people, a $1,500 exemption were allowed everybody, the tax rate would only come to 14.9 percent. Such a system would not only be more equitable, it would save countless hours and a considerable amount of money otherwise expended in filling out returns and in monitoring the system through the IRS.

Beyond that basic change, which would return government to its more appropriate role of collecting revenue for its operation rather than redistributing income, capital formation could be given additional stimulus by further reductions in the corporate income tax. Going to the extreme, if corporate income taxes had been totally eliminated in 1975 and a flat-rate individual tax without exemptions had been adopted, the same revenue could have been generated by taxing all individuals at a rate of 13.9 percent. Even if personal exemptions were doubled under such a system, a 19.7 percent tax rate would compensate for the loss of corporate tax revenue. As indicated by the studies done on the Jobs Creation Act, reducing corporate taxes has a double advantage: it stimulates economic activity and it increases employment. The latter, of course means higher individual income for more people and hence a greater sharing of the tax burden amongst more people. Both government and the individual taxpayer come out ahead in such an arrangement. Moreover, since corporate taxes are simply a business cost passed along to consumers in the form of higher prices, simplicity and equity argue for such a reform.

Finally, there should be a ceiling on the total amount of taxes one is required to pay to the federal government. If spending were systematically reduced, and if greater economic activity and employment were the consequence of providing for more capital in the private sector (and hence more revenue to government), one could reasonably expect the time in the forseeable future when a 10 percent total tax would be realistic. The Bible notes that man owes a tithe of his earnings to God. Caesar should ask for no more.

Along with overspending, over-regulation ranks as perhaps the most serious of the federal excesses. With the creation of 24 new agencies in the last fourteen years, there are now 12 departments and 75 agencies (not to mention the hundreds of commissions and bureaus) in the federal government, bureaucracies which, instead of making life easier for the average American, cost him an estimated $130 billion a year. Worse yet, the size and power of these agencies has grown to the point where they constitute a fourth branch of government, having the most profound implications for the survival of our system of justice and self-government. We have permitted the fusion of legislative, executive, and judicial functions in the unelected branch of government and have trampled upon such constitutional rights as freedom from unwarranted search and protection against loss of our property without due process of law.

By virtue of the fact that most individuals or businesses either cannot afford to fight a government civil suit or find it cheaper to pay the fine, instances of compliance by coercion are becoming the rule rather than the exception. In the process, the delicate balance of power between the individual and his government has been tipped steeply in the direction of the latter and, if it does not tilt back in the other direction soon, both individual freedom and the free enterprise system are in jeopardy. Thus, the power of the regulatory agencies to apply unfair rules and regulations must be curbed.

While the ultimate solution is to reduce the size, scope, number, and influence of the regulatory agencies, two interim proposals have great potential for reducing abuses under the current system. They are the Legal Compensation Act and Congressional veto power over federal rules and regulations. The Legal Compensation Act, which I introduced early in 1975, would give individuals and businesses a viable alternative to coerced compliance by compensating successful defendants in civil suits filed by any department, agency, or commission of the United States government. The other measure, which I have co-sponsored, would give Congress 60 legislative days to veto any bureaucratic rule or regulation, thus providing a mechanism for heading off regulatory abuses before they became a problem.

The legal compensation measure provides that a reasonable attorney's fee and other reasonable litigation costs *must* be paid by the government every time it files a civil suit subsequently proved to be lacking in merit. If enacted, this legislation would not only remove an unjustified penalty levied against those who currently contest a case, but it would serve to curb the activities of overzealous bureaucrats within the regulatory agencies.

By virtue of the fact that compensation payments would become a matter of public record, enactment of this legislation would give the American people a quantitative measure of agency error for the first time. With such a yardstick available, agency bureaucrats would be discouraged from filing unjustified suits aimed at achieving compliance on a "lesser of two evils" basis. Conversely, those being sued by a regulatory agency would be encouraged to contest a civil suit they believed to be unjustified. The cost of compensation should be offset by a reduction in the number of unjustified cases filed while the benefit, in terms of restoring faith in our system of justice, should be incalculable.

The proposal to give Congress the power to veto proposed rules and regulations is certainly complementary to the legal compensation bill, in that it would forestall certain regulatory practices that would otherwise result in suits. Further, it would remind the agencies that their function is to interpret and implement existing law, not to make new law of a type Congress did not envision or intend. Moreover, if this concept were extended to existing rules and regulations, Congress could correct obvious misapplications or abuses of the intent of the law by the regulatory agencies. Certainly, the results of the legal compensation measure, should it be enacted, would help Congress in making these determinations.

It should be noted that the legal compensation concept can and should be made applicable to the Internal Revenue Service. Since the IRS can bring the same types of pressures to bear on individuals as the regulatory agencies can on businessmen, fairness dictates that successful taxpayers in IRS tax liability cases be compensated for their attorneys' fees and other litigation costs, including accountants' fees. Also, in a further effort to keep the IRS bureaucrats from engaging in harassment for reasons of personal advancement, self-vindication, or political advantage, IRS procedures should be refined to insure greater confidentiality of IRS records, to provide for advance notification to the taxpayer of an intention to audit, and to explain the reasons for such an audit. Recent history, to say nothing of consistency, speaks eloquently to the need for such measures.

Vetoing unjustified rules and regulations before they go

into effect and compensating for them after they are in effect is not a total answer however. That lies in the elimination of the vehicles of over-regulation (OSHA, EPA, ICC, CAB and others), and that can only happen when the American people realize that excessive regulation is not only counterproductive to the economy but a threat to their freedom. For over 150 years, consumer democracy regulated the free enterprise system well enough to make us the most prosperous nation on earth. If given a chance, there is no reason to believe it wouldn't do just as well for another 150 years.

Labor Union Reform

Just as the rise of the federal bureaucracy has tipped the balance of power in favor of government, the federal government has, through sins of omission and commission, put management at a disadvantage in dealing with labor unions. If the free-enterprise system is to regain full vitality, excesses of labor union power need to be curbed just as surely as excesses of bureaucratic zeal.

Under current law, labor unions are accorded preferential advantages for the benefit of their members, but at the expense of certain groups in particular and consumers in general. For one thing, the unions are allowed to engage in practices that, if employed by management, would be considered in restraint of trade and therefore illegal. A second advantage, written into the National Labor Relations Act, guarantees labor union membership in 31 states by requiring an employee of a unionized company to join the union in order to keep his job. A third factor is legislation such as the Davis-Bacon Act, which requires construction workers on federal projects be paid at the highest wage rate (meaning union scale) prevailing in the surrounding area. Still another facet of the problem is minimum wage legislation, the primary objective of which is to keep young people from successfully competing with union members for jobs. Then, there is the Social Security earnings limit, which is intended to force the elderly out of the work force just as the minimum wage law does to young people. Finally, abuses such as food stamps for strikers cause the American taxpayer, contrary to both his own interest and a spirit of equity, to provide assistance to labor unions in achieving their objectives. Put together, these special advantages add up to higher costs for the producer, higher prices for the consumer, inflation, and unemployment in that order.

191

To correct the problem, numerous reforms are not only in order but long overdue. First, Congress should pass a bill ending the exemption labor unions now enjoy from the antitrust provisions of the Sherman Act. If monopolistic practices, such as industry-wide price fixing, are illegal for management, then similar practices such as industry-wide wage fixing and restraint of trade should be made illegal for labor unions. Not only is such a standard both fair and consistent, but it is essential if future wage-price spirals are to be averted.

The second reform, equally necessary, would give every American, not just those in 19 states, the right to work at a job without having to join a labor union. Such a right is not only consistent with the principles of freedom of association, but its implementation would make labor union leaders more responsible to their membership. Without the ability to compel people to join a union and pay dues, union leaders would be far less likely to make exorbitant contract demands or to engage in partisan political activities for fear of losing members and financial support. The resulting decline in strikes and inflationary wage settlements would be of as much benefit to rank-and-file union families as to all other consumers.

Related to this issue is the problem of using unions dues for political purposes, such as voter registration drives and get-out-the-vote drives. Since in union shop states the employee has no choice but to pay the dues and no control over the political purposes to which they are put, he is, for all practical purposes, being forced to financially support political causes and candidates that he may disagree with. It is bad enough that many people are forced to join a labor union and required to support its normal activities; compelling them to support political activities they may personally oppose is not only unnecessary but is morally wrong.

The fourth area of reform involves repealing other special interest legislation that benefits unions at the expense of the taxpayer and the consumer. Certainly, the Davis-Bacon Act, which adds millions of dollars to the federal budget each year in the process of subsidizing the construction trade unions, is that type of legislation and, had it been signed into law, the *common situs* picketing bill (legalizing the secondary boycott in the construction industry) would have fallen into the same category. The only argument in favor of either is that it makes it easier for unions to coerce non-members into joining a union, something that is economically shortsighted and morally wrong.

A final reform involves repealing the minimum wage law. While such legislation ostensibly helps all workers by assuring them a wage of at least $2.30 per hour, what it really does is freeze people (the unskilled, minority group members and the inexperienced) out of the job market altogether. According to a 1969 study published by Yale Brozen in the *Journal of Law and Economics*, minimum wage laws threw three times as many teenage black Americans out of work than nonblacks. With unemployment at its present high rate, particularly for teenagers and minority groups, such legislation is clearly not in the national interest but in the special interest.

For similar reasons, repealing the earnings limit for Social Security recipients should be next on this list of labor union reforms. The reduction of benefits for people in that category who earn over $2760 a year is not only intended to keep senior citizens from remaining in the job market. It also represents a form of governmental thievery. After all, the senior citizens affected have paid into Social Security all their lives expecting a return after they reach 65; appeasing the labor unions hardly constitutes justification for denying them the full measure of that return. Moreover, to do so denies senior citizens, many of whom are on small fixed incomes, the right to combat the effects of inflation and improve their lot.

Finally, requiring the American taxpayers to subsidize the organizational objectives of one group of people involved in a dispute with their employers (as is the case when striking workers can receive food stamps) is not fair either to them or the employer. If anything, the taxpayer's interest lies in keeping consumer costs down, not in having his tax dollars used to drive them up. Moreover, such taxpayer assistance unfairly gives strikers both the incentive and the wherewithal to draw out their disputes, an advantage not accorded the employer and, again, not in the national interest.

Moving over to the public sector, the last decade has witnessed rapid growth in the power of public employee unions with even graver consequences for American society. Precisely because there is no ready alternative to government employees providing public services, no public employee union should be permitted the power to represent exclusively any group of public employees nor should it be permitted to bargain collectively for them. If such powers are granted, governmental sovereignty will be compromised. The public employee union will become a unique group; one able to work its will on government without having to ask the voters for support. This means that determination of levels of taxation and budget priorities will have passed from the people's elected representatives to vested special-interest groups.

To prevent such a situation, collective bargaining, exclusive representation, and binding arbitration should be denied public employee unions. Further, the trend toward monopoly in public sector unionism should be discouraged by enactment of legislation giving every federal employee the right to work for the government without having to join a union. Passage of such legislation will give the employee more freedom and the public some hope—hope that it will not be held hostage to the demands of the labor union bosses.

Taken as a whole, these reforms will in no way affect the right of an individual to join a labor union or the right of the union to seek improved wages and benefits for its members. What these reforms will do is eliminate any unfair advantages the unions enjoy and make them compete on the same basis as anybody else. Rather than singling out a group for special treatment, these reforms will help ensure that all groups receive a fair shake within the context of our free enterprise system.

Welfare Reform

One of the items most responsible for the big budget deficits in recent years has been the rapid growth in spending for social welfare programs. A record $24.8 billion was paid out in 1975, for Aid to Families with Dependent Children (AFDC), Medicaid, and relief programs run by state and local governments. Two of the best examples of this increase and two desperately in need of reform, are AFDC, which increased 8.3 percent in 1975 (more than 11.3 million persons in 1975), and the food stamp program.

In 1965, these two programs cost the federal government $1.18 billion and $36 million respectively. In fiscal 1976, the respective figures will be $4.7 billion and $6.8 billion, a 297 percent increase in expenditures for AFDC and a 17,889 percent increase in the cost of food stamps. Yet, instead of getting people off the poverty rolls, these astronomical increases in expenditures have had the opposite effect; enrollment in AFDC has jumped 159 percent in the last ten years, while the number of people collecting food stamps has gone up more than 4200 percent!

The runaway nature of the food stamp program gives the clearest indication of why reforms are desperately needed. At its outset ten years ago the food stamp program provided benefits to one person in 439. Now, despite the existence of AFDC, the school breakfast and lunch programs, unemployment compensation, and a variety of public service jobs programs, one American in eleven is collecting food stamps and the number continues to rise every month. In fact, it has been estimated that, unless reforms are enacted, one American in four can be considered eligible to collect food stamps. Obviously there has been no increase in poverty to parallel this increase in food stamp recipients. In fact, quite the opposite is true. While 19 percent of all Americans were below the so-called poverty line in 1964, only 11.6 percent were below it in 1974. Moreover, disposable per capita income, corrected for inflation, has increased from $3,009 to $3,981 over the same period, demonstrating that, instead of of an increase in poverty, what we have really witnessed is an increase of those not really in need of welfare who have taken advantage of loopholes to collect it anyway. College students whose parents are wealthy are but one example. Strikers are another. Still others can be found among those who have juggled their finances so as to parlay child care expenses, high tuition payments, large utility bills and lavish housing costs into maximum benefits.

To correct such abuses, the National Food Stamp Reform Act, modeled along the lines of the successful state reform program initiated in California under Governor Reagan, has been introduced with nearly 100 co-sponsors. Included among its 41 provisions are such needed improvements as: 1) basing eligibility on gross rather than net income, 2) eliminating all those whose gross income exceeds the official poverty levels, 3) ending categorical eligibility of public assistance recipients (to reduce duplication of benefits), 4) limiting the amount of property a recipient can have to retain eligibility and evaluate it on the basis of market value, 5) eliminating the voluntarily unemployed—such as college students and strikers—from the rolls, 6) requiring the able-bodied with no children under six to register for and actively seek work, 7) establishing precise criteria to prohibit people from technically splitting households to gain greater benefits, 8) counting all other types of public assistance as part of gross income, 9) improving food stamp accountability procedures, 10) requiring all recipients to have a photo identification card, 11) replacing food stamps with countersigned warrants similar to travelers cheques, and 12) requiring monthly income reporting. These and the other changes should produce a savings to the American taxpayer of $2 billion in the first year and more in future years, and would simultaneously permit an increase in the food allowance for the truly needy of 29 percent.

Regarding AFDC reform, another successful California welfare reform provides the necessary direction. The proposed National Welfare Reform Act is based on a California welfare reform that has reduced caseloads in that state by 8,000 per month since early in 1971. To accomplish the objective of getting the non-needy off the welfare rolls and on payrolls, the bill provides for: 1) eliminating all those whose gross income is more than 150 percent of the needs standard; 2) deducting work-related expenses before using the $30 and ⅓" formula for exemptions; 3) providing for a standard work-related expense option; 4) barring illegal aliens and strikers from getting welfare benefits; 5) standardizing the sanctions against the able-bodied recipients who refuse to look for or accept employment; 6) requiring military personnel to forward support payments to their families; 7) banning assistance to those voluntarily leaving work (such as college students); 8) requiring the use of a standardized identification card; and, 9) mandating that stepparents who claim adopted children as dependents must support them. Cumulatively, these and other changes will save the American taxpayer about $1.1 billion a year in federal taxes, plus another billion or so in state taxes, to say nothing of their value in rebuilding the concept of a "work ethic."

Inasmuch as passage of these two measures would reduce subsidized indolence and save the taxpayers considerable money both should be adopted without delay. However, even larger savings could be achieved, to say nothing of greater community input, if full responsibility for these programs, as well as many others, was turned back to the states. As things are now, the federal treasury supplies all the money for food stamps and 55 percent of the welfare costs, while the states establish eligibility standards within the broader context of federal legislation. Under this proposal, first articulated by Governor Reagan in the fall of 1975, the states would take over full responsibility, not only for administering the programs but also for raising the money to fund them. Thus, one layer of bureaucracy would be eliminated, efficiency improved, local decision-making enhanced, and accountability accentuated.

The federal tax cut that would be made possible by transferring these programs to strictly state administration would more than cover the additional state taxes that might have to be paid. This raises a final point: if the taxpayers of a state believed that all or part of some program either lacked merit or had little applicability in their area, they could do away with it, either in part or in toto. The result would be better programs, albeit fewer of them perhaps, and government closer to the people—which is where it belongs.

Another program presently administered by the states under the aegis of federal law, but funded by the federal government, is unemployment compensation. While not considered a welfare program, even though its beneficiaries contribute little if anything to its financing, unemployment compensation is likewise in need of reform. Under the present system, too many people not in need, desirous of a paid vacation, or unwilling to settle for anything other than the "perfect" job are living off employer's tax dollars that could otherwise be used for capital investment and jobs creation purposes. As a consequence, the program should be converted into one utilizing private unemployment insurance not unlike life or health insurance. Such a plan then would enable people to protect themselves suitably but, by making them more responsible for their own destiny, it would reduce the potential for abuse and ease the burden on the taxpayer.

While subsidies to non-needy individuals have received the most criticism from conservatives, subsidy programs to businesses, municipalities, transportation systems, and agricultural groups should be equally suspect. New York, with more self-discipline, could take care of its own problems. The railroads, freed from excessive governmental regulation, could get along without federal assistance. Likewise, recent farm income figures have shown that farmers are better off with less government intervention than they are with more government assistance. Thus, both logic and consistency dictate that conservatives should be aiming to cut back all subsidy programs, not just a select few. Both the government and the governed operate more efficiently when the former keeps hands off the latter and the latter does not expect a handout.

Postal Reform

When one contemplates that just over 20 years ago it cost only three cents to ensure the prompt, reliable delivery of first class mail, the need for postal reform becomes self-evident. In fact, postal rates have increased 117 percent

197

in the last five years, business mail deliveries have been reduced in East Coast cities, rural post offices have been threatened with closings, the letter-sorting error rate has increased from 1 percent to 7 percent, delivery time for mail is longer instead of shorter, and, according to recent testimony by the General Accounting Office, the Postal Service flirts with insolvency. Moreover, with the signing of a new labor contract, postal costs are expected to increase another $1 billion per year by 1978. As a consequence, the General Accounting Office has projected that mailing a first class letter will cost 19¢ by the end of 1976, 30¢ by the end of 1977, and 36¢ by the end of 1984. Of course, with each rate increase, mail volume declines, precipitating the need for further rate increases.

Ironically, it was concern about rising costs and declining efficiency that prompted Congress to adopt the Postal Reorganization Act of 1970 establishing a quasi-governmental corporation to run the Postal Service. The idea was to combine business management techniques with efficiency of scale in the hope that the Postal Service would be self-sufficient by 1977. But Congress forgot to add the one ingredient without which no corporation operates at either peak proficiency or optimum cost: competition. Instead of repealing the Private Express Statutes, which permit the Postal Service to enjoy a monopoly over the delivery of first class mail, existing law was left intact thereby giving management no incentive to be more efficient and labor no reason to hold back on its demands for higher wages and fringe benefits. Not surprisingly, the result has been bureaucratic mismanagement and wage increases almost twice those given other federal workers.

A prime example of bureaucratic mismanagement was the decision to automate by investing $1 billion in bulk mail centers. First of all, these centers have not appreciably speeded up service. Instead, they have produced repeated instances of mail traveling hundreds of miles and many days to reach a destination only a few miles away. Second, with labor contracts that make it all but impossible to lay off postal employees the full benefits of automation can hardly be enjoyed. These two factors provide an explanation for the otherwise incongruous fact that, while the percentage of mail processed by machine has increased from 23 percent to 60 percent over the last seven years, labor costs *have gone up* from 81 percent to 86 percent of total Postal Service expenditures.

As far as wage demands are concerned, it is instructive to

note that not only have the wages of postal workers increased 60 percent since 1970—as compared to 38 percent for other federal employees—but that the average postal worker makes about $3,000 a year more than his or her counterpart in the federal government. And under the latest labor contract, this trend is likely to continue, despite the fact that the volume of mail is likely to decline.

Adding to the frustration the average American feels with regard to the Postal Service, is the fact that, insofar as first class letters are concerned, there is no alternative. Where there has been an alternative, such as in the delivery of parcels, people have turned with increasing frequency to private delivery firms which can do the job quicker and cheaper. United Parcel Service (UPS) is an excellent example. Despite the 10 percent subsidy granted the Postal Service for the delivery of parcels, UPS has, in just eighteen years, captured over one half of the parcel delivery business in the continental 48 states by providing cheaper, quicker, and safer service. And they have not simply "skimmed the cream" by just serving big cities. A look at the UPS rate structure shows that it costs an urban customer no more to get a package delivered to a rural area than it does to a city an equal distance away.

United Parcel is by no means the only example of a successful private competitor to the postal service. At least 20 other firms (such as the American Home Delivery Co., New York City; the Florida Postal System, Miami Beach, Florida; the American Postal Corporation, California; and the Consumer Communication Corp., Columbus, Ohio) in the country are competing with the Postal Service delivering magazines, circulars, and packages—with more entering the market all the time. The example thus set has, in turn, prompted the President's Council on Wage and Price Stability to announce, on January 16, 1976, that ". . . permitting competition in the Postal Service's first class [mail] service probably would result in significant benefits to the economy and the mail user."

That announcement, backed up as it is by the 1974 Report of the House Subcommittee on Environmental Problems Affecting Small Business, to the effect that the first class mail monopoly should be ended, has generated tremendous interest in the possibility of repealing the Private Express Statutes. Over the last five years the author has repeatedly introduced just such legislation; I am happy to note that 31 other Congressmen plus three Senators have joined me in the effort. Such legislation, if enacted, would not necessarily mean the end of the Postal Service. Rather, it would be the beginning of a new era when people would be free to shop around and take advantage of the quickest, cheapest service available.

The presence of such alternatives would certainly give the Postal Service an incentive to improve. Moreover, additional alternatives prompting greater utilization of service, would give postal employees a bigger market in which to offer their services; that would mean more jobs, a greater chance for promotion, and more opportunities for salary advancement. About the only serious objection that can, and has, been raised is that private firms would take the lucrative inter-city business and leave the Postal Service with the responsibility for the more expensive rural delivery. This in turn would mean higher rates and more subsidies from the taxpayer. However, the fact that UPS serves all 48 states in the continental United States and does not charge more for delivery to rural areas than to urban areas, argues convincingly against the validity of such a position. Moreover, some estimates indicate that if private enterprise were given the job of delivering all mail to the rural areas *free of charge* to the postal user, the annual subsidy required would be only $600 million as opposed to the $1.5 billion the Postal Service has requested in subsidies for 1977. The difference between these two figures speaks eloquently for rather than against, the case against continuing the government monopoly. Finally, repealing the Private Express Statutes would free government from the unsupportable contradiction of prosecuting monopolies on the one hand while sponsoring them on the other.

Given all the evidence, there is no valid reason why private enterprise should not compete with the Postal Service. In the long run, such competition would benefit all concerned.

Educational Reform

While the controversies over forced busing, objectionable textbooks, and federal aid requirements are significant to any discussion of educational reform, they are all symptoms of a larger, and more crucial question—who should control the schools? Traditionally, this control has been vested in the hands of the parents and the local community, but in recent years the bureaucrats in Washington, through a carrot-and-stick policy involving grants and guidelines, have been extending their influence over the nation's schoolchildren.

The impetus for this shift has come from an erroneous but growing belief on the part of bureaucrats that they, rather than the parents, know what is best for the student. But, by any test of logic—be it proximity of interest, emotional attachment, or freedom—a much more convincing case can be made for ultimate parental control over pupil education. Moreover, unless the case is made, and the trend toward bureaucratic control is reversed, the future of limited government in America is bleak indeed.

In my view, the best way to achieve greater parental control over the education of children is to adopt what is commonly known as the voucher system. Under such a system, the money for a student's education each year would go directly to the parents in the form of a voucher that would be presented by the parents to the school in which they wanted their child educated. That school would then provide the student with the best education it could.

Adoption of such a system would introduce a needed element of competition into our public schools. In order to attract the vouchers necessary to justify their continued operation, schools would have to improve their over-all curriculum or specialize in certain areas. Also, there would be an incentive for them to be more economical. And most important, parents and students would have a wider range of choices from which to select the type of education best suited to their needs. Further, schools would have to satisfy the constituency they serve with their overall performance or risk the loss of enrollment to other schools that would be willing to do so.

For instance, if a student had a particular manual skill, the parents could use their voucher at a school with a strong vocational-technical program. If the parents did not like the caliber of instruction or the textbooks used in a particular school, they could elect to use their voucher at another school the next year. Likewise, if having the child attend a school close to home was deemed most convenient or important, the voucher could be used at that school. With all these options, the battles over forced busing and textbooks would disappear, while quality education would be enhanced.

Given these advantages, what is most surprising is that the voucher system has yet to get beyond the test stage. Not only would it encourage the schools to do a better job of educating our children, but it would ensure that parents, rather than the state, have the final say over the job they do.

Given the fact that the Social Security System not only has inequities but suffers from an actuarial deficit approaching $3 trillion, there is little question about the need for some type of reform. As things stand now, the Social Security Trust Fund, out of which benefits are paid, will probably run out of money by 1980 unless changes are made.

If the current structure were to be retained, it is estimated that a 50-100 percent increase in payroll taxes would be necessary to keep the system solvent by the year 2000. With so substantial a tax increase, the likelihood of a taxpayers' revolt is probable, particularly since the contributor to Social Security has no guarantee of a benefit return commensurate with the amount of his or her contribution. In fact, the Supreme Court has ruled that the contributor has no guarantee of any benefit at all.

This raises a crucial point: rather than being an insurance program designed on an actuarial basis, Social Security simply transfers income from one generation to another. Thus, if a succeeding generation cannot meet its obligations to its elders, the system will default and those who have contributed to it in expectation of a return will be out of luck. One of the great weaknesses of Social Security is that the contributor has no firm assurance, other than his belief in the future, that his contributions will be paid to him when he retires. The present system therefore might be called anti-social insecurity.

The possibility that future generations may be unwilling to shoulder the burden assigned to them by their predecessors is not the only difficulty. Unforeseen circumstances such as an economic slump or changes in living patterns must also be taken into account—as social security planners are discovering a bit too late. While everyone anticipated that the postwar baby boom would mean a dramatic increase in senior citizens shortly after the turn of the century, few people expected the recent decline in the birthrate. As a result of this combination of events plus increased longevity, the latest riddle to present itself is financing a program whose scope will be broadening at the same time its base will be diminishing.

With all these uncontrollable factors, serious advocates of Social Security reform should look beyond the expedient of a temporary increase in payroll or income taxes to the possibility of restructuring the Social Security system to provide genuine security for the elderly. One small step in the right direction has already been taken with the enactment, in 1974, of the Private Pension Reform Act. If its imperfections can be corrected, particularly in the area of burdensome paperwork, this legislation should result in private company pension plans and individual income retirement accounts becoming the bulwark of our retirement system. Social Security should then revert to its original role providing supplemental retirement income.

However, these developments are a long way off. Even if they do come to pass they do not obviate the need to protect the investment of those who have invested in Social Security. That obligation can only be fulfilled by finding a way to liquidate the unfunded liabilities Social Security has accrued and by putting the system on an actuarily sound basis.

Of the multitude of ideas to reform Social Security several should be given serious consideration. One such idea involves the issuance of U.S. Retirement Bonds (in the amount of current contributions plus interest) to each contributor to Social Security, with the further requirement that from that point on, wage earners contribute 10 percent of their earnings to the purchase of Retirement Bonds. Return on investment would be computed at either the rate of interest on long-term U.S. Retirement Bonds or the rate of growth in the GNP whichever was higher. Thus the contributor's investment would be protected against inflation.

Enactment of a reform program along these lines would effectively solve the problem of rapidly rising payroll tax by eliminating that tax altogether. Moreover, senior citizens would be assured of getting back a commensurate return for their investment. Some difficulties are involved, such as financing the retirement bonds of current contributors and absorbing the capital that the future sales of retirement bonds would eventually accumulate, but they are minor compared to the advantages inherent in having an actuarily sound system.

As a matter of fact, one way to solve the problem of investing accumulated capital, a problem well down the road, would be to allow private insurance companies, banks, or other outlets to join the government in issuing retirement bonds, and then let the people decide for themselves which would be the better investment. Thus, free enterprise and competition would be introduced, the range of individual choice broadened, and the stage set for the day when the Private Pension Reform Act of 1974, reaches its maximum potential. At that point (if not sooner), when all workers could have a private pension plan or income retirement account of their own, the requirement that one purchase government retirement bonds could be dropped, provided one opted for, and developed, an adequate private pension plan.

While waiting for such a system of voluntary social insurance to evolve, several short term reforms in the system should be made immediately. One, noted earlier is the removal of the earnings limit on Social Security recipients, thereby allowing them to keep pace with inflation. The other is similar: ending the loss of disability benefits for blind people who earn outside income. Neither group should be penalized for having the incentive to work, particularly if it is their own contributions that are being withheld.

Proponents of the status quo in Social Security will argue against these last two proposals on the grounds that they will increase the liabilities of the Social Security Trust Fund. However, it is these very proponents, by their refusal to acknowledge that the system must be made actuarily sound, who are responsible for the unfunded liabilities the system presently faces. Punishing those who have contributed all their lives in expectation of a decent retirement income is no answer; reform of the system to incorporate the private insurance principles of individual equity is a much better solution.

Foreign Affairs

Important as domestic policy may be, we cannot overlook foreign affairs, lest domestic reforms suddenly become academic. A quick survey of our foreign policy in recent years indicates that it, too, is in need of reform, not only from a fiscal but from an operational standpoint. While Communist designs have remained unchanged and Communist influence in the world has grown, the U.S. position vis-a-vis the Communist bloc, in particular the Soviet Union, has grown weaker from both diplomatic and military standpoints. Freedom is being challenged throughout the world by the force of totalitarianism; unless we alter our policies accordingly, we may find the torch of liberty extinguished, not just for others, but for ourselves.

To forestall such an eventuality two major readjustments in our foreign policy would seem appropriate. First, we should be more realistic and less utopian in our dealings with other non-Communist nations around the world. Inasmuch as they may share our concern about the Communist menace, which is above all *the number one threat* to our security, and given the fact that we cannot expect every nation to disregard its national experience and pattern its form of government after ours, there is no reason not to deal with these nations and take advantage of the assets they may have to offer. That does not mean we have to agree with, or support, all the policies such nations might adopt or that we should not encourage them to make certain policy changes; it does suggest that we should not cut off our nose to spite our face. There is a big difference between a country that is less than democratic in its domestic policies but, in foreign affairs, supports the free world, and the Communist powers which, by definition, are both totalitarian and expansionistic.

A case in point is South Africa. While apartheid is repugnant to the American belief in due process and equal opportunity, the fact remains that South Africans fought for the cause of freedom in World War II, have sided with the free world against the forces of Communism, and are located in a geographic position of great strategic value. It is ridiculous for us not to use the port facilities at Simonstown and not to work with the South Africans on problems of mutual concern. In fact, our willingness to do so may hasten the end of apartheid and prevent a bloodbath at the southern end of the African continent.

Similarly, Rhodesia should not be ostracized and left to the Communists. By placing an embargo on the importation of Rhodesian chrome, as has frequently been suggested, we would cut ourselves off from the only major source of that strategic metal outside of the Soviet Union. Vital as chrome is to our national security, we cannot afford to make that move. Moreover, when compared to the suffocating control exercised over the people in the Soviet Union (minority groups and political dissenters in particular), the hegemony of the present Rhodesian government over its native population may be viewed in a different perspective. Although the Rhodesian position is hardly laudable, neither is it unique. We face the necessity of choosing the lesser of two evils and by any objective analysis, the government of Rhodesia is a lesser evil than Communist control over the area. The experience in Angola proves that both the Cubans and the Soviets are eager to exploit the situation to the fullest; they should be given no encouragement.

Yet another example is South Korea. Despite the common bond forged by the 1950-53 struggle against Communist aggression and despite the willingness of the South Koreans to come to our assistance in South Vietnam, there are those who would have us discontinue military aid to that nation because of instances of alleged oppression and violation of civil rights. If we were to do that, we would not only increase the likelihood that oppression would become a living reality for all South Koreans, but we would put nearby allies—the Nationalist Chinese, the Japanese, and the Filipinos—in greater jeopardy. Moreover, such a cutoff of assistance would be viewed by our other allies as a further sign of weakness—a high price to pay for "idealism."

As for Latin America, where military dictatorship is the rule, it seems a bit incongruous to refuse to do business with an anti-Communist military government while negotiating with a pro-Communist military government in Panama for surrender of U.S. sovereignty over the Canal. Again, reality indicates that we should be taking tougher stands against those backing our enemies than those who will support us and our friends. More than a matter of principle, it is a matter of survival.

In a similar vein, we should reassess our policy towards the United Nations. That organization has in recent years been increasingly guilty of maintaining a hypocritical double standard at the expense of both the Western democracies and the UN Charter. Racism or aggression which we ignore when committed by Communist regimes such as the Soviet Union or North Vietnam is viewed as self-determination; self-determination, when practiced by non-Communist governments such as Israel, has been branded as racism and condemned. Contributing mightily to this trend is the fact that those nations who now have the political leverage in the United Nations have little responsibility for financing it. Thus they can be as hypocritical as they want without having to face the consequences.

At the very least, the best way to rectify this problem and to introduce a new element of reality into UN proceedings would be for the United States to reduce its financial contribution from its disproportionately high 25 percent plus level to a more realistic 5.6 percent. The latter figure is arrived at by shifting the contribution formula from one based largely on national income to one based on the population of member nations. If implemented by the UN, such a formula would mean that the so-called "third world" nations that, combined, contribute only 3.52 percent to the UN budget each year would contribute a more realistic 20.5 percent. India would have its contribution level raised from 1.2 percent to 16 percent and Red China, which has a Security Council seat largely paid for by the Republic of China, would have to pay 21.5 percent instead of 5.5 percent. The savings to American taxpayers would come to approximately $350 million a year.

Before leaving the subject of contributions, those to other nations in the form of foreign aid should also be reduced. Aside from the fact that we cannot afford it, foreign aid erodes the initiative of other nations in the same way welfare saps the incentive of people receiving it here in the United States. Thus, we need not only to reduce foreign aid but to change its thrust. In that regard, the adage, "Instead of giving people a fish a day, it is better to teach them how to fish," suggests a more realistic approach.

Greater realism should also be interjected into our relations with the Soviet Union. Pursuance of the policy of detente, for example, must not blind us to the realities of Soviet foreign policy. Regardless of what the Soviets may say or agree to, we must measure their intentions by what they do—and react accordingly. In short, Soviet military assistance to, and Cuban military involvement in, Angola is a far better barometer of the prospects for detente than a joint communique emanating out of some summit conference.

The ultimate test of detente, at least for the present, is the Strategic Arms Limitation Talks (SALT). Here, the United States agreed, in 1972, to numerical inferiority in strategic weapons in an effort to put a cap on the nuclear arms race. The quantitative disadvantage the U.S. agreed to was supposed to be offset by the qualitative advantage we enjoyed in weaponry. However, the Soviets did not guarantee our qualitative lead as we did their quantitative advantage, nor did they settle on precisely what constituted a heavy missile or illegal enlargement of missile silos. The upshot was that, within a year, we were to discover that much of our qualitative advantage had disappeared and by 1975 it was evident that the Soviets were violating the spirit if not the letter of the 1972 SALT agreements by swapping small missiles for bigger ones, enlarging their silos in more than one direction, jamming our legitimate attempts at monitoring their telemetry, developing "cold launch capability" for their missiles, and testing their radar in what appears to be an ABM mode. In short, it seems that, from the Soviet standpoint, SALT I was agreed to more because it suited their drive for military superiority than because of any real desire for a relaxation of tensions or a reduction of arms.

So far, the negotiations for a follow-up SALT II agreement

seem to be following the same pattern. If an agreement were to be accepted along the lines presently being discussed, the Soviets would have a guaranteed advantage in missile throw-weight of up to five to one by 1983 while the narrow qualitative lead still enjoyed by the United States would be left open to unrestricted challenge. The experience of SALT I and the ramifications of such a large Soviet lead in throw-weight should convince us that such an agreement is not in our national interest. Moreover, if those SALT II negotiations are indeed the barometer of detente, the the whole policy should be reevaluated.

But, while our foreign policy should be more pragmatic and more focused on the continuing nature of the communist threat, such a shift does not mean we should abandon our role as a leading force in behalf of individual liberty and democratic principles. In fact, the two thrusts—pragmatism and principle—can and should go hand in hand. Coupling them together can be achieved through the formation of an association of nations, committed to certain principles of individual liberty and due process of law and having as objectives the promotion of those principles and opposition to that which is antithetical to them, namely Communism.

While the idea is not new—both the League of Nations and the United Nations were born partially on the wings of such a concept—the *modus operandi* would be substantially different. First of all, instead of striving for universality or basing the organization on geographical proximity, the object would be to enlist nations that have a certain essential view of government's role in relation to the individual. And second, instead of peace being the prime objective, the ultimate goal would be to promote freedom —individual and national. The justification for these departures from previous practice is simple: peace without freedom is hardly worth achieving.

In line with that thinking, membership in an association of free and democratic nations would be strictly voluntary and would in no way involve the compromise of national sovereignty. However, nations that did not share certain common denominators such as adherence to the principles of freedom of speech, freedom of the press, trial by jury, equal opportunity, due process of law, freedom of association, the right of petition, and free elections would not be invited to join. Thus, such an association could include nations such as Japan, West Germany, France, Italy, and Sweden, as well as English-speaking nations such as Great Britain, Canada, Australia, and New Zealand. Excluded, at least for the time being, would be nations such as South Africa, Rhodesia, Chile, South Korea, India, many of the pro-western Latin American dictatorships and most of the so-called "third world" nations.

One could argue, as many will, that our support for, and participation in, such an association will alienate excluded allies and hurt our position in the world. In response, however, it should be noted that: 1) the very existence of such an association will act as an incentive for some non-Communist nations to become more democratic on their own and 2) the shift toward pragmatism suggested previously (which would go hand in hand with our support for the association) would give those excluded a basis for believing that, while we do not approve of all their policies and hope that they will change some of them, we will be willing to work with them on matters of common interest and national security as long as they do not go Communist.

As a practical matter, nations closely drawn together in such a manner could have considerable impact. Not only would they be able to exercise moral suasion in many instances but, by voluntarily acting in concert, they could exert considerable leverage in the areas of trade, energy, monetary policy, aid to developing nations and the like. Furthermore, this association would be able to act in behalf of freedom, where the UN cannot, as well as in instances covered by our treaty agreements. In short, this association would have the flexibility lacking in so many organizations plus the potential for successfully mastering the forces of freedom against the menace of Communism.

The famous Spanish Philosopher, Salvador de Madariaga, put his finger on the problem facing the forces of freedom when he said, "The trouble today is that the Communist World understands unity but not liberty, while the free world understands liberty but not unity. Eventual victory may be won by the first of two sides to achieve the synthesis of both liberty and unity."

Association, based on common adherence to the principles of freedom, might make it possible for the free world to achieve that synthesis first. Given what is at stake, it is worth the try.

A Last Word

Despite the massive tangle of entrenched, wrongheaded government policies in so many sectors, it is not too late to turn things around. On the contrary, the growing pressure for regulatory reform, the growing concern over ballooning welfare and food stamp rolls, the growing realization that cities, if not states and nations, can spend themselves into bankruptcy, and the growing disenchantment with big government emanating from Washington are all encouraging signs. Suspicion of government is a healthy thing; if nothing else it gets people to thinking about basic American values such as free enterprise and individual rights.

Once people start thinking and worrying about such concepts, programs like those just outlined will have a lot more meaning. Naturally, they are not all-inclusive, nor are they intended to be. However, they do provide a blueprint indicating a viable, positive alternative to the failures of welfare statism. Once people are willing to admit the possibility of alternatives, the battle is more than half won and the time for refinements of a "conservative reform platform" will be at hand.

Recommended Reading

CHAPTER ONE

Bastiat, Frédéric, *The Law* (Irvington-on-Hudson, N.Y.: Foundation for Economic Education, 1950).

Devine, Donald J., *The Political Culture of the United States; the Influence of Member Values on Regime Maintenance* (Boston: Little, Brown, 1972).

Dietze, Gottfried, *In Defense of Property* (Baltimore: John Hopkins Press, 1963).

Friedman, Milton, *Capitalism and Freedom* (Chicago: University of Chicago Press, 1962).

Hamilton, Alexander, James Madison and John Jay, *The Federalist Papers.*

Hayek, Friedrich A., *The Road to Serfdom* (Chicago: University of Chicago Press, 1944).

Locke, John, *The Second Treatise of Government.*

Rothbard, Murray N., *For a New Liberty* (New York: Macmillan, 1973).

Wood, Gordon, *The Creation of the American Republic, 1766-1787* (Chapel Hill: University of North Carolina Press, 1969).

CHAPTER TWO

Banfield, Edward, *The Unheavenly City; the Nature and Future of Our Urban Crisis* (Boston: Little, Brown, 1970).

Hazlitt, Henry, *Economics In One Lesson* (New York: Harper Brothers, 1946).

Shore, Warren, *Social Security: The Fraud in Your Future* (New York: Macmillan, 1975).

Silberman, Charles E., *Crisis in Black and White* (New York: Random House, 1964).

CHAPTER THREE

Hoffer, Eric, *The True Believer; Thoughts on the Nature of Mass Movements* (New York: Harper, 1951).

Roche, George, *The Balancing Act: Quota Hiring in Higher Education* (La Salle, Ill.: Open Court, 1974).

Sowell, Thomas, *Black Education: Myths and Tragedies* (New York: McKay, 1972).

Sowell, Thomas, *Affirmative Action Reconsidered: Was it Necessary in Academia?* (Washington: American Enterprise Institute for Public Policy Research (AEI), 1975).

CHAPTER FOUR

Buckley, William F., Jr., *United Nations Journal: A Delegate's Odyssey* (New York: Putnam, 1974).

Niemeyer, Gerhart, *Deceitful Peace* (New Rochelle, N.Y.: Arlington House, 1971).

Wetzel, John C., *The United Nations: Myth vs. Reality* (New Rochelle, N.Y.: America's Future).

CHAPTER FIVE

Edwards, Marvin H., *Hazardous to Your Health; a New Look at the "Health Care Crisis" in America* (New Rochelle: Arlington House, 1972).

Lindsay, Corton M. (ed.), *New Directions in Public Health Care: An Evaluation of Proposals for National Health Insurance* (San Francisco: Institute for Contemporary Studies, 1976).

Palyi, Melchoir, *Compulsory Medical Care and the Welfare State* (Chicago: National Institute of Professional Services, 1950).

Schwartz, Harry, *The Case for American Medicine; a Realistic Look at Our Health Care System* (New York: McKay, 1972).

Wardell, William M. and Louis Lasagna, *Regulation and Drug Development* (Washington: AEI, 1975).

CHAPTER SIX

Crane, Philip, *How to Cut the Federal Budget: A Proposal for Fiscal Reform* (Washington: American Conservative Union, 1975).

Fechter, Alan, *Public Employment Programs* (Washington: AEI, 1975).

Fulner, William, et. al., *Correcting Taxes for Inflation* (Washington: AEI, 1975).

Ott, David J., et. al., *Public Claims on U.S. Output: the Federal Budget Options in the Last Half of the Seventies* (Washington: AEI, 1973).

Reducing Unemployment: The Humphrey-Hawkins and Kemp-McClure Bills (Washington: AEI, 1976).

CHAPTER SEVEN

Chamberlain, John, *The Enterprising Americans; A Business History of the United States* (New York: Harper & Row, 1963).

Hazlitt, Henry, *Man vs. the Welfare State* (New Rochelle: Arlington House, 1969).

Röpke, Wilhelm, *A Humane Economy* (Indianapolis: Liberty Fund, 1971).

Röpke, Wilhelm, *Against the Tide; The Social Framework of the Free Market* (Chicago: H. Regnery Co., 1969).

CHAPTER EIGHT

Cohen, Manuel F. and George J. Stigler, *Can Regulatory Agencies Protect the Consumer?* (Washington: AEI, 1971).

Kolko, Gabriel, *The Triumph of Conservatism; a Re-Interpretation of American History, 1900-1916* (New York: Free Press of Glencoe, 1963).

Moore, W. S. (ed.), *Regulatory Reform* (Washington: AEI, 1976).

Weidenbaum, Murray L., *Government Mandated Price Increases: A Neglected Aspect of Inflation* (Washington: AEI, 1975).

CHAPTER NINE

Freeman, Roger A., *The Growth of American Government: A Morphology of the Welfare State* (Stanford: Hoover Institution Press, 1975).

Hyneman, Charles S., *Bureaucracy in a Democracy* (New York: Harper, 1950).

Mosher, Frederick C., *Democracy and the Public Service* (New York: Oxford University Press, 1968).

Seidman, Harold, *Politics, Position, and Power: The Dynamics of Federal Organization* (New York: Oxford University Press, 1970).

Von Mises, Ludwig, *Bureaucracy* (New Rochelle, N.Y.: Arlington House, 1970, c1944).

CHAPTER TEN

De Toledano, Ralph, *The Municipal Doomsday Machine* (Ottawa, Ill.: Green Hill Publishers, Inc., 1976).

Petro, Sylvester, "Sovereignity and Compulsory Public Sector Bargaining", *Wake Forest Law Review*, Vol. 10, No. 1, March, 1974)

Schmidt, Emerson P., *Union Power and the Public Interest* (Los Angeles: Nash Publishing, 1973).

Wellington, Harry H. and Ralph K. Winter, Jr., *The Unions and the Cities* (Washington: Brookings Institution, 1972, c1971).

CHAPTER ELEVEN

Burnham, James, *Suicide of the West; an Essay in the Meaning and Destiny of Liberalism* (New York: John Day Co., 1964).

Haldi, John and Joseph F. Johnston, Jr., *Postal Monopoly: An Assessment of the Private Express Statutes* (Washington: AEI, 1974).

Holt, Marjorie (ed.), *The Case Against the Reckless Congress* (Ottawa, Ill.: Green Hill Publishers, Inc., 1976).

Levine, Isaac D. (ed.), *Plain Talk* (New Rochelle: Arlington House, 1976).

Pfaltzgraff, Robert L., Jr. and Jacquelyn K. Davis, *Salt II: Promise or Precipice?* (Miami: Center for Advanced International Studies, 1976).

Schneider, William J. and Francis P. Hoeber *Arms, Men and Military Budgets: Issues for Fiscal Year 1977* (New York: 1976).

Thiebolt, Armand J., Jr., *The Davis-Bacon Act* (University of Pennsylvania, 1975).

U.S. Senate, *Postal Reorganization: Hearings Before the Committee on Post Office and Civil Service*, April 19-20, 1976).

A Free Book with every four books you order!

1. How to Start Your Own School, Robert Love. Everything a parent or principal needs to know, by someone who did it himself. "An important and readable book that tells you how to do it"—*Human Events.* $1.95

2. The Regulated Consumer, Mary B. Peterson. *The Wall Street Journal* contributor shows how seven Federal regulatory agencies have been captured by the businesses they were supposed to regulate! How this hurts consumers everywhere, and what can be done about it. "This thoughtful, challenging book can perform a great service"—*Fortune.* $2.95

3. The Defenseless Society, Frank Carrington and William Lambie. A scathing look at how the Courts and Congress have tilted the battle against crime in favor of the criminal and against society, with proposals for restoring the balance. Frank Carrington is the author of *The Victims,* executive director of Americans for Effective Law Enforcement. $1.95

4. The Case Against the Reckless Congress, Hon. Marjorie Holt, ed. Nineteen Republican congressmen contribute chapters on the major issues before Congress. All 435 Representatives' votes are recorded. "Not merely a naysayers political bible. The authors do offer alternative programs. Moreover, the book provides us with a chance to examine 'the conservative side' whether or not one agrees with it."—*CBS Radio.* $1.95

5. The Making of the New Majority Party, William Rusher. "If anyone can invigorate the ideological comradeship of economic and social conservatives, it is William Rusher. This is a well-written and thoughtful book."—*The Wall Street Journal.* $1.95

6. The Sum of Good Government. Hon. Philip M. Crane. The brilliant conservative Illinois congressman offers a positive program for solving the problems of American government in our country's 200th year. $1.95

7. The Gun Owner's Political Action Manual, Alan Gottlieb. Everything a gun owner needs to know to be politically effective in the firearms freedom fight. Includes voting records of all Congressmen on every pro-/anti-gun vote, how to use the media, and a large reference section on publications and organizations. $1.95

8. Sincerely, Ronald Reagan, Helene von Damm. The personal correspondence of Ronald Reagan as Governor of California. Covers his views on almost every national issue. "There is much in these letters that sheds new light on the man."—*Saturday Evening Post* $1.95

9. The Hundred Million Dollar Payoff: How Big Labor Buys Its Democrats, Douglas Caddy. "An extensively documented exposé of big labor's illegal largesse."—*Newsweek* $2.95

10. A New Dawn for America! The Libertarian Challenge, Roger Macbride. The Libertarian Party presidential candidate calls for a return to first principles. $ .95

11. The Municipal Doomsday Machine, Ralph de Toledano. "Forced unionization of public employees threatens American democracy. Toledano's book is must reading"—*Ronald Reagan.* $1.95

12. Jimmy Carter's Betrayal of the South, Jeffrey St. John. Reveals the *other* side of Carter, and shows how he may bring Labor Government and socialism to the U.S. $1.75

13. Why Government Grows, Allan H. Meltzer. How we got Big Government and strategies for rolling it back through constitutional tax limitation initiatives. (*Booklet*) $ .95

Green Hill Publishers, Inc.
Post Office Box 738
Ottawa, Illinois 61350

Please send me postpaid the following books:

(*Circle numbers*)   1   2   3   4   5   6   7   8   9   10   11   12   13

I understand that if I order four books, I get No._____ FREE.

I enclose $_____*, plus 50¢ for postage and handling.

_____

_____

_____

_____ Zip code _____

*Illinois residents please add 5% sales tax.

QUANTITY DISCOUNTS

The Sum
of Good
Government

by Hon. Philip M. Crane

Discount Schedule*

1 copy	$1.95	10 copies	$12.50	100 copies	$ 60.00
3 copies	$5.00	25 copies	$25.00	500 copies	$275.00
5 copies	$7.50	50 copies	$35.00	1000 copies	$500.00

*Illinois residents please add 5% sales tax

Good Government Book Fund
Post Office Box 214
Mount Prospect, Ill. 60056

Please send me postpaid_____copies of **THE SUM
OF GOOD GOVERNMENT** by Hon. Philip M. Crane. I en-
close_____plus 50 cents for postage and handling.

_____

_____

_____zip_____